PITTSBURGH THEOLOGICAL MONOGRAPHS

New Series

Dikran Y. Hadidian
General Editor

10

THE DIVINE DRAMA IN HISTORY AND LITURGY

Essays presented to Horton Davies
on his Retirement from Princeton University

Photograph by Philip M. Davies

THE DIVINE DRAMA IN HISTORY AND LITURGY

Essays presented to Horton Davies on his Retirement from Princeton University

Edited by
John E. Booty

PICKWICK PUBLICATIONS
An imprint of *Wipf and Stock Publishers*
199 West 8th Avenue • Eugene OR 97401

Pickwick Publications
An imprint of Wipf and Stock Publishers
199 West 8th Avenue, Suite 3
Eugene, Oregon 97401

The Divine Drama in History and Liturgy
Essays in honor of Horton Davies on his retirement from Princeton University
Edited by Booty, John E.

ISBN: 978-1-4982-2816-9
Publication date 1/1/1984

CONTENTS

Liturgy and Worship

The Ecumenical Movement

PREFACE

With this volume of essays we honor Horton Davies on the occasion of his retirement as Henry W. Putnam Professor of the History of Christianity at Princeton University. It is just and right that he be so honored. My own liveliest impressions of the man as I have come to know him over more than twenty-five years includes an appreciation of the scholar who first gained recognition through his widely acclaimed **The Worship of the English Puritans** (1948) and went on to write five substantial volumes on **Worship and Theology in England** from the Reformation to 1960 (1961-1975). His mastery of the voluminous literature, his insistence upon the interconnection of liturgy, theology, art and architecture, his ability to explain and describe complex ideas and events clearly and to synthesize fairly, along with his brilliant mastery of the English language, have put all of those concerned with the subject matter of his <u>magnum opus</u> in his debt. But I would also note here, and equally, the teacher presiding over a graduate seminar with firmness and charity, calling forth the best that his students had to offer, as well as lecturing on the Middle Ages to a class of undergraduates. He is a gifted teacher with unusual ability to make difficult, seemingly dull matters interesting and even entertaining. His treatment in that classroom of medieval thought from Augustine to Occam has stayed with me over the years and has helped to inform my own teaching. Then too, I recall that it was Horton Davies who opened my eyes to the relevance of art to the understanding of ecclesiastical history and of theology in general. It was through his eyes that I first saw Sir Jacob Epstein's Christ in Majesty, the great, controversial figure that looms over the interior of Llandaff Cathedral in Horton Davies' native Wales, and went on to be deeply moved and forever affected by Epstein's Lazarus at New College, Oxford. Horton Davies is a man of catholic interests, as those who know him readily attest. He possesses an ecumenical spirit, as deep and as genuine as any I have yet encountered. Under his tutelage many of us learned to respect widely differing traditions and to view our own more objectively and appreciatively. This I count as a great good. Finally, I would note that this eminent scholar--the greatest expert on Puritan worship--is a warm and kindly man.

To know him as teacher and adviser was for many of us to know him as colleague and friend, demanding when necessary, but always supportive.

This volume contains a few tokens of appreciation from amongst the great numbers of students, advisees, colleagues and friends who wish Horton Davies well at this turning point in his life. The essays represent some of the most prominent of his many interests, beginning with art. His son, Hugh M. Davies, of the La Jolla Museum of Contemporary Art in California, together with his daughter-in-law Sally Yard, discuss Robert Morris's depictions of nuclear holocaust as found in the artist's Fire Storm drawings and in his Jornada del Muerto, created for the Hirshhorn Museum. These works were influenced by Leonardo da Vinci's Deluge drawings and by the biblical themes of deluge and apocalypse. Morris makes clear, however, that the horror he depicts is the work of man, not God.

The selection of essays on historical subjects begins with a close examination of eight biographies whereby Dewey Wallace, of George Washington University, tests the hypothesis "that there emerged from 1650-1700 a Puritan hagiographical literature which drew on the old while it crystallized the new," imitating the traditional lives of the saints while highly regarding those virtues associated with Protestantism or modern sensibility. That such a literature evolved at all among those who decried traditional hagiography is remarkable and testifies to the necessity for "holy persons" to "concretize" the ideals of the Puritan religious community and to serve as signs of God in the midst of that community. Ellen Weaver, of The University of Notre Dame, recites with care the history of the histories and historians of the Jansenist monastery of Port-Royal and of Mere Angelique, from the seventeenth century to the twentieth. She shows that most of the historians were sympathetic to Port-Royal and that most were women, from the nun-historiographer of the movement, Angelique de Saint-Jean Arnauld d'Andilly, the niece of Mere Angelique, to Professor Weaver herself. It is of interest to this editor that several English women, including Hannah More, are involved in the story. Robert Monk, of McMurry College in Texas, explores the education of American lay ministers in the growing Methodist Church during the eighteenth and nineteenth centuries, in the light of John Wesley's insistence on well-educated lay persons and of the difficulties involved in obtaining an adequate education in early America. Monk describes how itinerating preachers struggled to find books and to read them. Emphasis falls chiefly upon Francis Asbury and the evidence found in Asbury's Journal and Letters concerning the books he read. William Seth Adams, of The Episcopal Theological School of the Southwest in Texas, presents a detailed description and analysis of William Palmer's **Narrative of Events** and in the process provides an interesting and different perspective on the Oxford Movement and the **Tracts for the Times.** The anti-Roman bias of Palmer is clearly indicated as well as his rather naive attitude toward John Henry Newman. John F. Wilson, of Princeton University, surveys writings on religion in America produced during the 1970's, from Sydney Ahlstrom's **A Religious History of the American People** (1972) to Catherine Albanese's **America, Religion and Religions** (1981). Professor Wilson is impressed by the variety and by an "increasing reliance upon a cultural framework for interpreting religion." In contrast to earlier writings, less attention was paid "to specifically intellectual history or to studies controlled by institutions." The essay provides a valuable bibliographical survey.

The section on liturgy and worship begins with a helpful essay by John Marsh, sometime Principal of Mansfield College, Oxford, on time in relation to biblical and liturgical understandings. His conclusions have to do with the suggestion "that human beings are able, within their inescapable confinement in time, actually to transcend time's passage as they hold communion with God who is infinite and eternal, holding in his timeless being the whole story of the universe." In my essay I explore the judicious Mr. Hooker's doctrine of Christ's presence in the Eucharist. Hooker was at odds with the Puritans on many things, and they with him, but he shared much with them, too. He was not altogether appreciative of Calvin, but I have concluded that his eucharistic doctrine was fundamentally in tune with Calvin's. Robert S. Paul, of Austin Presbyterian Theological Seminary in Texas, writes of Puritans--independents and presbyterians--in the Westminster Assembly severely divided on the issue of the exercise of discipline (coercive power) with or without the participation of the worshipping community. He concludes: "the Independents were trying to ensure that church discipline should never be removed from the context of a regularly worshipping community, and that mutual ministry to each other in the community committed to the gospel cannot be divorced from the Word and Sacraments through which the gospel is proclaimed." Howard Hageman, of the New Brunswick Theological Seminary in New Jersey, explores evidence indicating that some Reformed Churches in Europe and America used the lectionary contrary to the practice of Zwinglian and Calvinist Reformed Churches where the lectio continua prevailed. This leads him to conclude that there was a third type of Reformed Church, centered in Germany, sometimes called Melanchthonian, in which the lectionary was accepted and in use. Julius Melton, of Davidson College in North Carolina, reviews liturgical revision within American Presbyterianism in this century and in particular as found in the recent **Worshipbook** and the **Book of Common Worship,** "the two service books presently in use in the church," and the draft "Service for the Lord's Day," a trial use. One of the major issues discussed has to do with inclusive language, admittedly an important issue in liturgical reform in this last quarter of the twentieth century.

The final part of the book concerns the ecumenical movement. G. B. Caird, of The Queen's College, Oxford, contends that people continue to read the Bible "with the spectacles of their own tradition" in spite of their overt commitment to ecumenism. He discusses present difficulties "in the way of mutual understanding," points at which modern "New Testament scholarship had unwittingly provided escape routes for those who find travel on the main highway too heady for their comfort," and fallacies, pure and simple. L. A. Hewson, of Rhodes University College, Grahamtown, South Africa, tells of the gradual development of ecumenical theological education in South Africa, culminating in the arrival of Horton Davies who developed the first divinity program at Rhodes University College. The subject of this tribute is portrayed in this enlightening essay as one wholly committed to ecumenism, "not unduly perturbed by being termed an 'Ecumaniac.' " And thus we come to the end, quite suitably with praise for the one we honor concerning an episode in his life, long past but not to be forgotten.

We are indebted to Philip M. Davies for the photographic portrait of his father, reproduced here as the frontispiece, to Dr. Gordon Wiles for his portrait of Horton Davies, to Christine Wade for the chronology of her father, and to Marie-Hélène Davies for the Select Bibliography of her husband's writings. I wish to thank Russell Sherman, my research assistant, for his assistance and to salute, on behalf of all of the many friends of Horton Davies, Dikran Y. Hadidian, General Editor of Pickwick Publications, for taking the initiative in this project.

John Booty
The University of the South
Sewanee, Tennessee

ART

IMAGES OF DELUGE AND APOCALYPSE: THE RECENT WORK OF ROBERT MORRIS

Hugh M. Davies and Sally E. Yard

In our century artists have invoked religious themes as they have sought to express the human suffering of disaster and war. Picasso's Guernica of 1937, triggered by the bombing of the Basque town of that name during the Spanish Civil War, reads like a latter-day Massacre of the Innocents. The terror of Germany under Hitler was reflected in the raw turmoil of George Grosz's Rider of the Apocalypse (I was always present) of 1942, in the dissonance of Marc Chagall's White Crucifixion of 1938, and in the severity of Jacob Epstein's Ecce Homo of 1935. Kaethe Kollwitz in the late teens and late 1930's conceived as Pietas the mother and child imagery which preoccupied her throughout her career. During the years after World War II Francis Bacon, Salvador Dali, and Graham Sutherland produced substantial paintings of the Crucifixion tinged by the anguish of recent history. In the face of the Vietnam war, Nancy Spero created an extended series of drawings, including a Crucifixion entitled Christ and the Bomb of 1967.

More recently the possibility of cataclysmic nuclear war has prompted a range of images focusing on biblical subjects. The cross of Alex Gray's Nuclear Crucifixion of 1980, for example, is embedded in the looming form of a mushroom cloud. Like Picasso and Sutherland, Gray was powerfully affected by Matthias Grünewald's Isenheim altarpiece of c. 1510-15. As he had reflected, the Nuclear Crucifixion is perhaps unusual among contemporary works in containing the seeds of renewal. [1] Whereas such religious subject matter as the Crucifixion in the past generally was explored to convey internal conviction, it now functions more often as an iconographically void armature lending pathos by association to contemporary depictions of brutality and inhumanity. Peter Gourfain's Noah's Ark, designed as a banner for the anti-nuclear

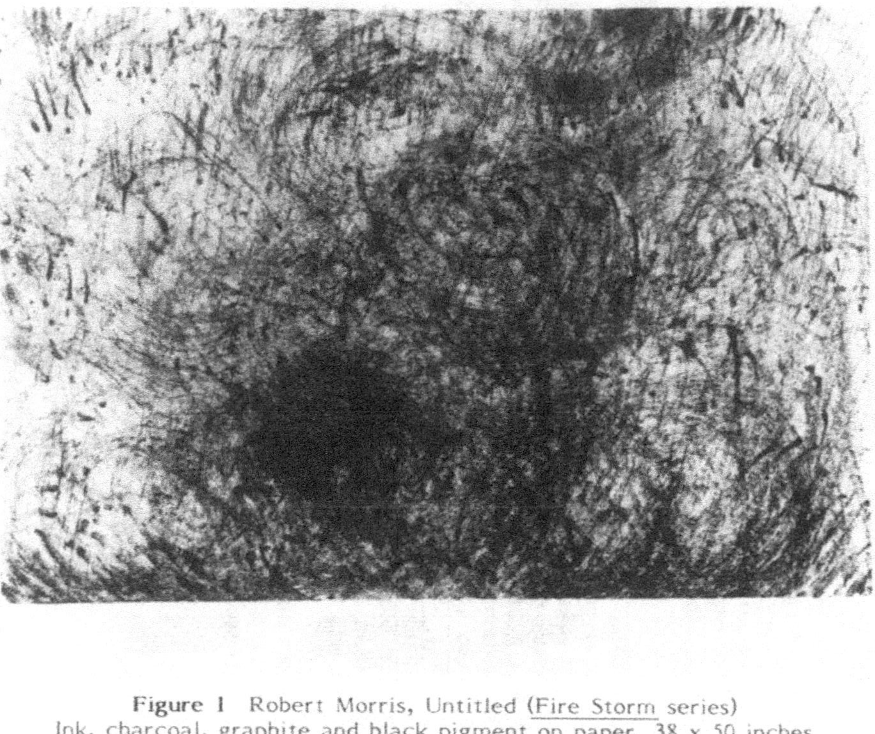

Figure 1 Robert Morris, Untitled (Fire Storm series)
Ink, charcoal, graphite and black pigment on paper, 38 x 50 inches

arms march held in New York in June of 1982, proclaims bluntly in large letters that "We're all in the same boat." A concentrated body of work made by Robert Morris during the past few years, including the Fire Storm series of 1982 and Jornada del Muerto (from "The Natural History of Los Alamos") of 1981, merges dark visions of the decimation of the earth by atomic bomb with the biblical imagery of Deluge and Apocalypse.

In the Untitled drawings of Morris' Fire Storm series a charred palette of black and white evokes the searing force of an atomic blast, while swirling patterns of line suggest the consuming onslaught of elements with a momentum beyond control. In the texts which are incorporated in the lower margins of several of these drawings Morris acknowledges their inspiration in the Deluge drawings done in the last years of Leonardo da Vinci's life, and links the Old Testament imagery of the Deluge to that of the devastation wrought by the Atomic bomb dropped on Hiroshima on August 6, 1945.

Essentially abstract, derived as they are from the similarly abstract images of Leonardo, the Fire Storm drawings are chilling in the absence of any intimation that a divine design underlies the strife and tumult of which they speak. Leonardo's images of the Deluge were decidedly more abstract than most that had preceded them. Departing from the depiction of mountains collapsing, overwhelmed by wind and water, Leonardo went on to focus on the essential forces of wind and water themselves. Compositionally related to the small studies of the Renaissance artist-scientist, Morris's works draw vehemence and gestural immediacy from their substantially larger scale. Morris's juxtaposition of texts is incisive, the matter-of-fact accounts of the fire storm which destroyed Hiroshima startlingly close to Leonardo's descriptions of Deluge.

One drawing (Figure 1) is inflected by the imprint of fingers pulled across its surface, literally revealing the hand of the artist and recalling Morris's Blind Time drawings of 1973. [2] Pencilled beneath these whirling marks are three texts, which in juxtaposition gather poignancy and force. The first voice is that of Leonardo, whose remarks are excerpted from a notebook passage dealing with "A Deluge and the Representation of it in Painting": [3]

> But it will perhaps seem to you that you have cause to censure me for having represented the different courses taken in the air by the movement of the wind, whereas the wind is not of itself visible in the air; to this I reply that it is not the movement of the wind itself but the movement of the things carried by it which alone is visible in the air.

The insights of Leonardo's notebooks assume a macabre pertinence beside the ghastly realities described in the text drawn from **Hiroshima and Nagasaki -- The Physical, Medical, and Social Effects of the Atomic Bombings** produced by The Committee for the Compilation of Materials on Damage Caused by the Atomic Bombs in Hiroshima and Nagasaki: [4]

> . . . conflagration broke out 50 minutes after the explosion and a fire storm started to blow. From 11 a.m. to 3 p.m. a violent whirlwind blew locally from the center toward the northern part of the city. In a conflagration the minute particles of carbon produced by fire are blown up with the cold air, where water vapor is formed. Between 9 a.m. and 4 p.m. "black rain" containing radioactivity poured down over a large area from north of the hypocenter to the west.

Here, confirming Leonardo's conclusions, the wind grows darkly visible "in the air," carrying the deadly ingredients of a poisonous rain. The dispassionate tone of the "narrator" who speaks of Hiroshima intensifies the horror of the facts. A third voice, that of the artist as he recalls his own detached vantage point in 1945, is introduced in this drawing: "Thirty seven years ago the hands that have traced spiralling currents of air and the nails that have here marked the path of a black rain turned the pages of a photo magazine to trace in idle curiosity the shape of a strange cloud over a distant city."

In another work of the series (Figure 2) Morris includes skeletal figures akin to those in a drawing of Destruction Rained from Heaven on Earth by Leonardo (Figure 3). But Morris's forms gain confrontational force by their virtually life-size scale, and evoke the burnt remains of those too close to ground zero when the atomic bomb known as "Little Boy" [5] was dropped from the B-29 Enola Gay. Whereas Leonardo's image contains the suggestion of a Last Judgment and redemption, [6] Morris's offers at best the hope of some sort of survival. So the first text beneath this image reads:

> There is no record of those who were instantly incinerated or of those buried under the ruins or of those who plunged into the rivers and were carried away or of those swept into the inferno of the tornado winds of the fire storm. Nor is there any record of those who crossed the Miyuki Bridge that morning, although Kinzo Nishida recalled the sight of a naked man standing by the river holding his eyeball in his hand.

The Miyuki Bridge, located 2500 yards from the hypocenter of the explosion, was one of the relief stations to which people "es-

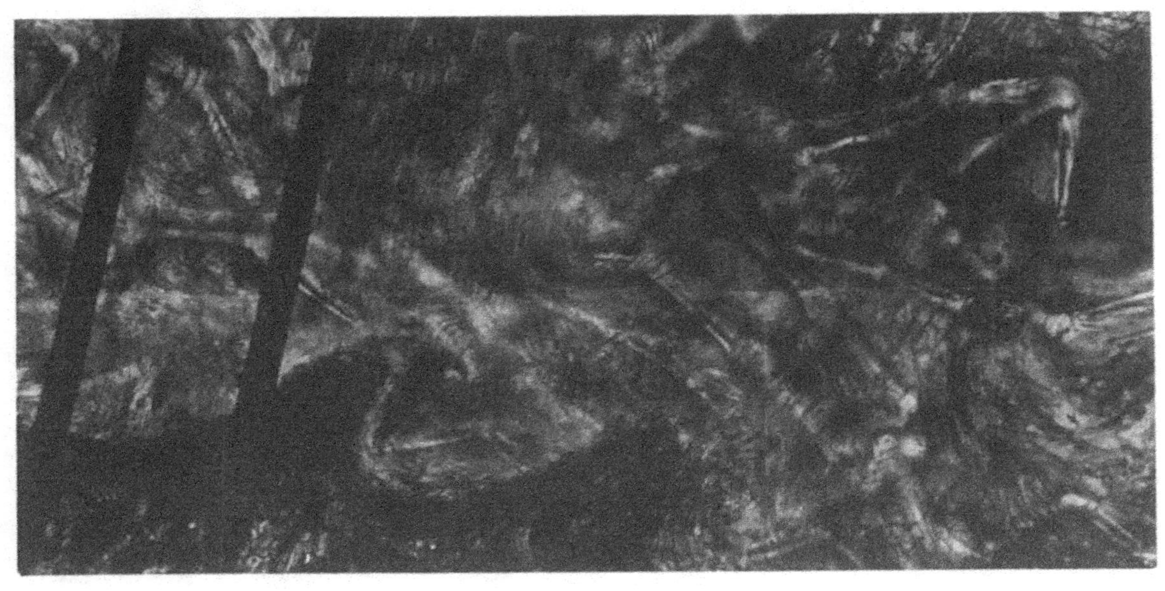

Figure 2 Robert Morris, Untitled (Fire Storm series)
Ink, charcoal, graphite and black pigment on paper, 76 x 150 inches

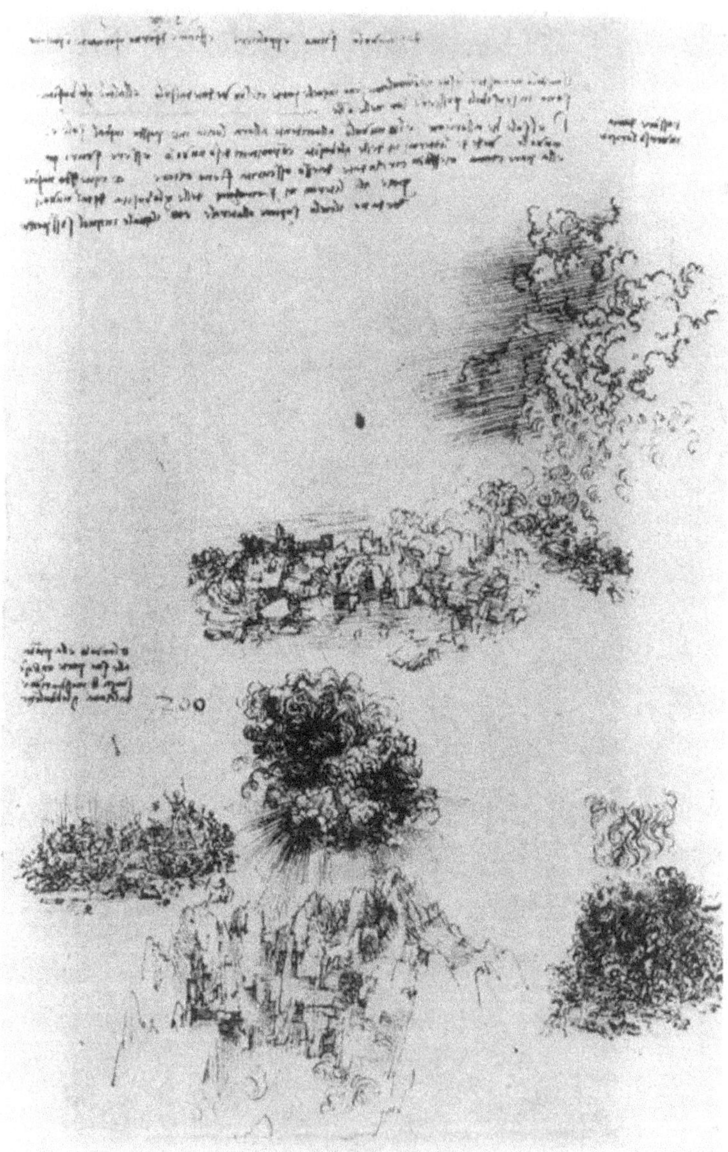

Figure 3 Leonardo da Vinci
Destruction Rained from Heaven on Earth, c. 1511-12
Pen over black chalk on paper, 11-13/16 x 8 inches
Royal Library, Windsor Castle

caped" on August 6. The eighty-two year old Kinzo Nishida's horrifying memory was recalled in 1974, thirty years after the bomb exploded in Hiroshima, and was included in the book **Unforgettable Fire: Pictures Drawn by Atomic Bomb Survivors.** [7]

In contrast to this first text, which speaks of obliteration and the absence of any record, the second text is a testament to survival:

> By 11 a.m. the ashes that had been swept upward into high black clouds began to fall as a sticky black rain. The clouds drifted toward the northwest and the rain continued until about 3 p.m. The rivers were black as Chinese ink. All that day survivors filed over the bridge toward the suburbs. Some burnt beyond recognition, sat on the pavement and begged for water. In the following days small paper signs appeared in the ruins. Each bore a name and the words, "I have survived."

The theme of survival is reiterated in a drawing with the pencil caption "The Miyuki Bridge" (Figure 4). Its curling, lively forms echo their source, acknowledged in a notation in the lower margin, "After a Deluge Drawing by Leonardo" (Figure 5), and share a dark buoyancy with the clouds photographed as they burst upward after the explosion of the atomic bomb (Figure 6). [8] The text records:

> In the first hours after the fire storm they gathered by the Miyuki Bridge. They begged for water. Many were burnt so badly that they could not bend their limbs. In the days that followed small boards appeared tied to the railings. Each bore a single name with the words, "I am alive." But the survivors at the Miyuki Bridge became outcasts in later years. No one wanted to remember their pain.

A dark center, echoing the frenzied vortices of the paintings of the Italian Futurists Boccioni and Balla, gapes as though to consume the light and line which surround it, in another drawing of the Fire Storm series (Figure 7). The prints of hands and fingers--details which identify the dead and the living--are visible in the lighter areas surrounding this ominous center and conjure visions of the clawing motion of a life-and-death struggle, as well as documenting the creative process of the artist. In the text beneath this the blunt facts presented by The Committee for the Compilation of Damage again gain resonance linked as they are to a more visionary passage by Leonardo. The Committee records:

> A conflagration broke out and then a fire storm began to blow. Between 11 a.m. and 3 p.m., when the fire

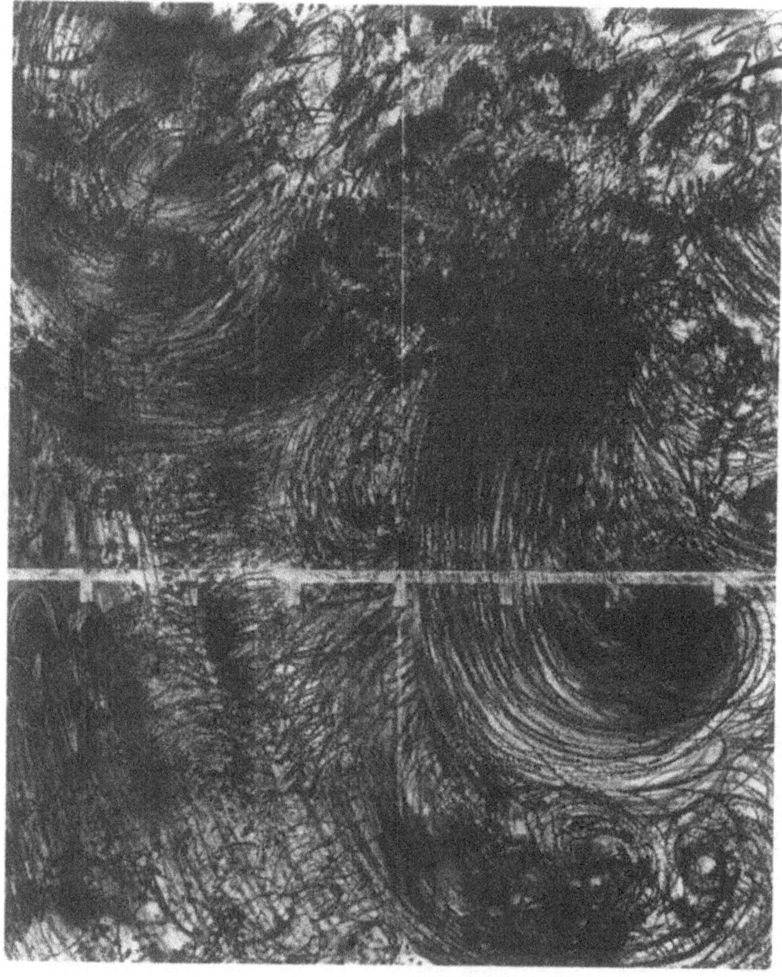

Figure 4 Robert Morris, Untitled (Fire Storm series)
Ink, charcoal, graphite and black pigment on paper, 76 x 83 inches

Figure 5 Leonardo da Vinci, Deluge,
Black chalk on paper, 6-3/16 x 8-1/4 inches Royal Library, Windsor Castle

Figure 6 Photograph of clouds bursting upward after the explosion of the atomic bomb in Hiroshima, August 6, 1945

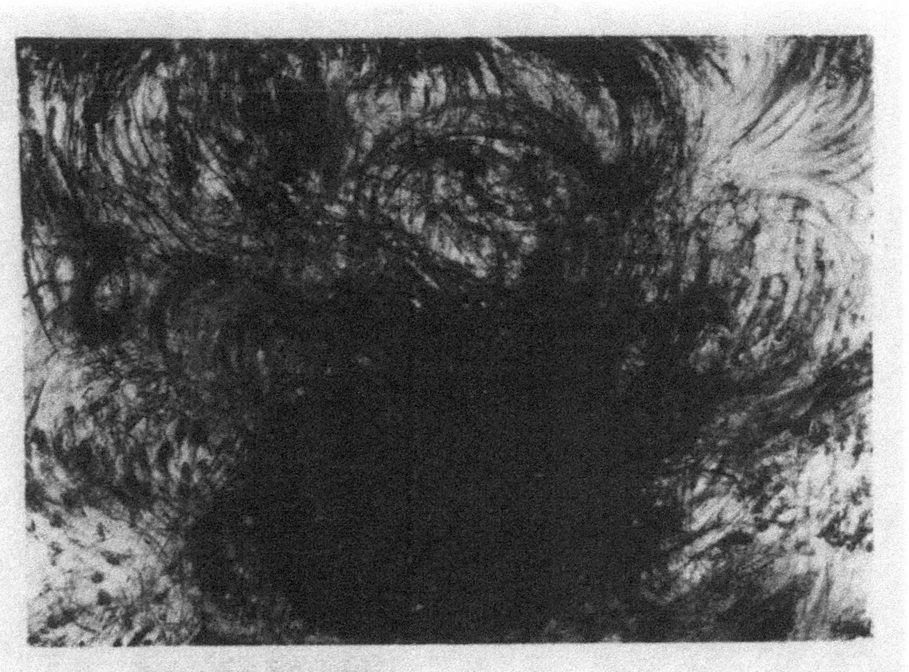

Figure 7 Robert Morris, Untitled (Fire Storm series)
Ink, charcoal, graphite and black pigment on paper, 38 x 50 inches

> reached its peak, a strong tornado developed locally in the central part toward the northern half of the city. The whirlwind developed near the front. Rumbling of thunder was heard between 10 and 11 a.m. Black clouds and smoke moved toward the northwest; and since there was a fall of "black rain," it was assumed that a southeast wind of 1 to 3 meters per second was blowing.

In contrast to the muted emotion of the Committee's reconstruction of the events, Leonardo observes, in a lively, dramatic discussion of the portrayal of Deluge:

> How many might you have seen stopping their ears with their hands in order to shut out the loud uproar caused through the darkened air by the fury of the winds mingled together with the rain, the thunder of the heavens and the raging of the thunderbolts. Others were not content to shut their eyes, but placing their hands over them, one above the other, would cover them more tightly in order not to see the pitiless slaughter . . .

As though to render this bleak scenario the work of man and not of God, Morris's ellipsis eliminates the final clause of Leonardo's description, which concludes "pitiless slaughter made of the human race by the wrath of God." [9]

The juxtaposition of Leonardo's Deluge drawings with images of atomic bomb blast had occurred before in Morris's work, in a major installation created in 1981 for the Hirshhorn Museum and entitled Jornada del Muerto (from "The Natural History of Los Alamos") (Figures 8, 9, 10). As Howard Fox has observed, Jornada del Muerto, "which means journey, or day's journey, or a day's work of death, is the traditional name of the parched desert valley south of Los Alamos where the bomb was first tested." [10] In Jornada del Muerto the apocalyptic references are amplified by the inclusion of Four Horsemen of the Apocalypse in modern guise, the horses of another era's battles replaced by the missiles of today's.

The installation is organized in "layers" which confront and surround the viewer. Presiding over the space, each astride an elongated bomblike form, are four skeletons. Painted black and attired only in military helmets, they recall the figure of Death in Ernst Barlach's Magdeburg Memorial. The conflation of imagery, of horseman and bomb, calls up the maniacal last ride of Slim Pickens in the movie Dr. Strangelove. [11] Behind the skeletal riders is an eerie backdrop: mimicking their ribs, white lines on a black ground describe the stylized mushroom cloud. The four macabre figures are seen in ghoulish distortion in the warped curving mirrors toward which they are aimed. Beyond

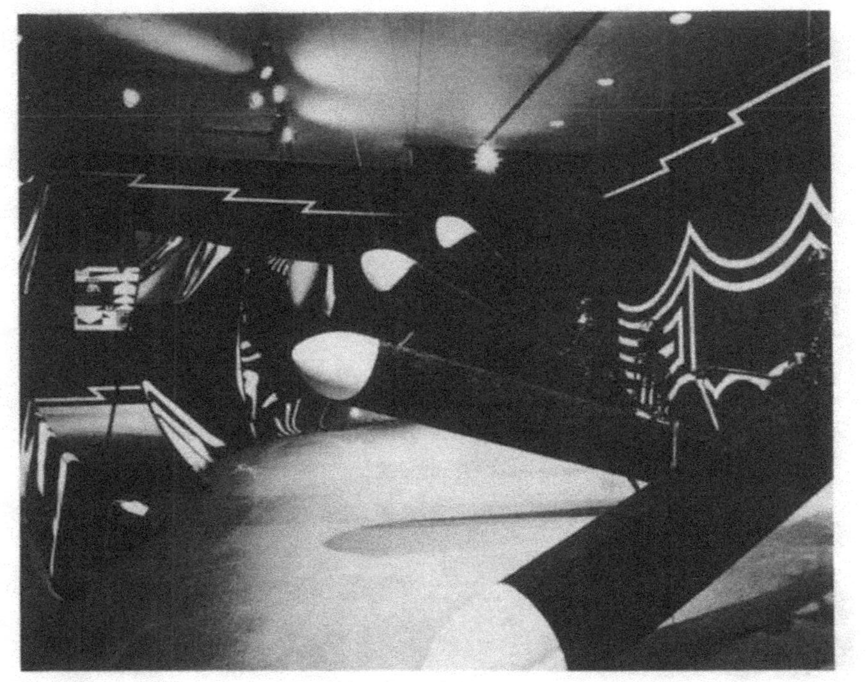

Figure 8 Robert Morris, Jornada del Muerto (from "The Natural History of Los Alamos"), 1981
Installation at Hirshhorn Museum and Sculpture Garden, 1982
Nylon, felt, paint, photomechanical reproduction, mirrors, steel, human skeletons
Overall dimensions of site approximately 28 x 35 feet

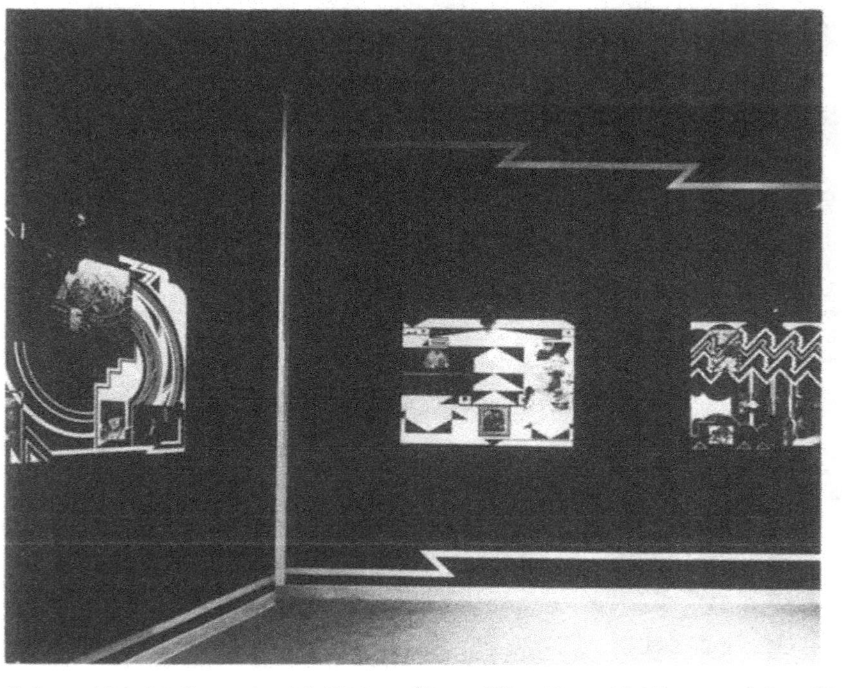

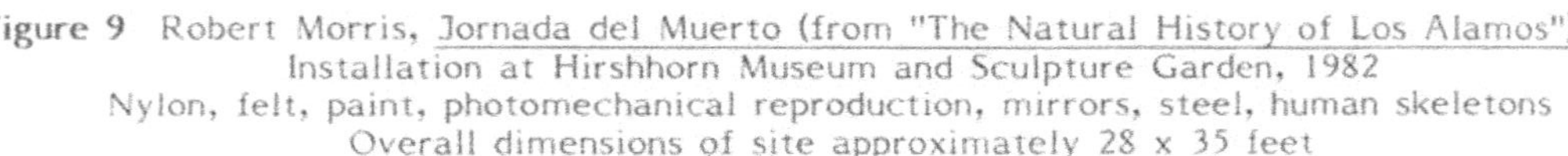

Figure 9 Robert Morris, Jornada del Muerto (from "The Natural History of Los Alamos"), 1981
Installation at Hirshhorn Museum and Sculpture Garden, 1982
Nylon, felt, paint, photomechanical reproduction, mirrors, steel, human skeletons
Overall dimensions of site approximately 28 x 35 feet

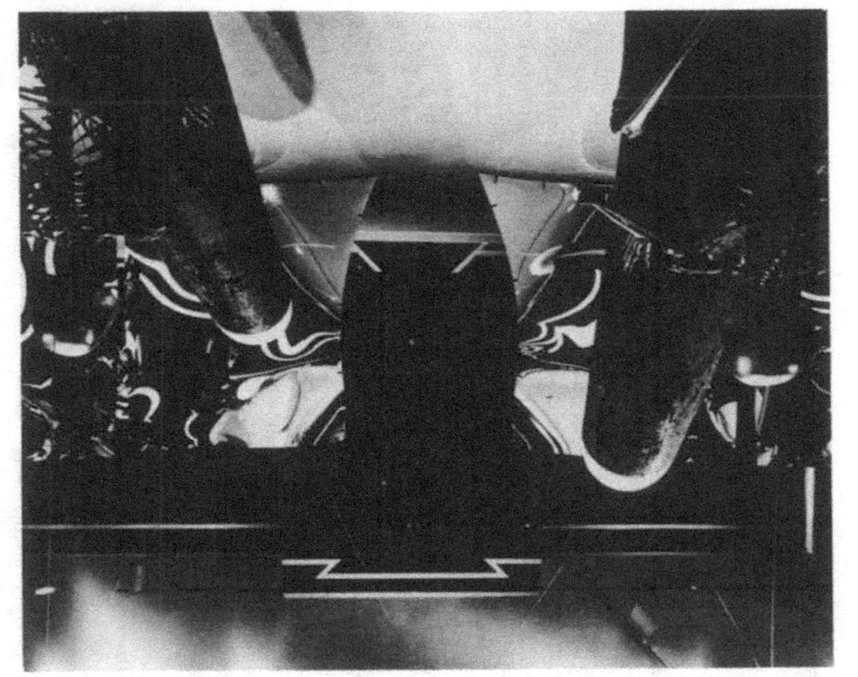

Figure 10 Robert Morris, Jornada del Muerto (from "The Natural History of Los Alamos"), 1981
Installation at Hirshhorn Museum and Sculpture Garden, 1982
Nylon, felt, paint, photomechanical reproduction, mirrors, steel, human skeletons
Overall dimensions of site approximately 28 x 35 feet

the mirrors the pattern of the American flag is visible in relief on two heavy, black felt rectangles. On the walls surrounding the grim foursome are six panels, each hung about a foot from the wall and structured with geometric patterns. These are overlaid with photographs dealing with the history of the bomb, from its development in the New Mexico desert to its demonic detonation in Japan. On the verso of these six panels, seen in reflection in mirrors fixed to the walls beyond them, are images of Leonardo's Deluge drawings.

In one of the six surrounding panels, each of which is surmounted by a blackened skull, a photograph of J. Robert Oppenheimer and Einstein is juxtaposed with the pitifully torn and burned back of a young boy, whose handsome profile and strong facial structure collide shockingly with the mutilation of his flesh. His brave face gazes toward the skull, its aggressive grimace proffering not solace but the certainty of the irrevocable erosion of his youthful form. One cannot help but here recall the doubts felt by Oppenheimer and Einstein when faced with the potentially devastating consequences of atomic fission. Linda McGreevy has called up the account of Oppenheimer watching the Trinity test and observing "the cloud soaring in brilliant greens and purple above him to the unexpected height of 41,000 feet in seconds. As the column leaned at an odd angle over the scattered spectators, its creator thought of a passage from the **Bhagavad Gita**, the sacred Hindu text, 'I am become Death, the Shatterer of Worlds.' " [12]

Morris's interest in Oppenheimer and in this theme of fearful destruction was evident in his 1981 article "American Quartet" which opened with Oppenheimer's musing: "But perhaps only a malignant end can follow the systematic belief that all communities are one community; that all truth is one truth; that all experience is compatible with all other; that total knowledge is possible; that all that is potential can exist as actual." [13] The essay closed with Morris's speculation:

> Have we become less concerned with absolutes, with our place in the Universe and with our own individual mortality? In some sense I believe we have . . . I would suggest that the shift has occurred with the growing awareness of the more global threats to the existence of life itself. Whether this takes the form of instant nuclear detonation or a more leisurely extinction from a combination of exhaustion of resources and the pervasive, industrially based trashing of the planet, that sense of doom has gathered on the horizon of our perceptions and grows larger every day. [14]

Morris's recent work speaks of the malevolent destruction

of life. In Jornada del Muerto the modern day Horsemen of the Apocalypse are themselves skeletal images of death, like the skulls which mark, tomblike, like Golgotha, each of the six panels. And in these panels the normalcy of such images as the laundry hung out to dry on the line in Los Alamos is disturbed by what we know now to be the outcome of those lives spent there, exploring the possibilities of fission: the flayed flesh that is documented in black and white photographs. Suggesting the optimism of the human race, Morris based one of the six panel's geometric patterns on a Hopi blanket motif of a rising phoenix. [15] This symbol of immortality and resurrection seems an especially pertinent one, reputed as this legendary bird is to burn upon a funeral pyre, only to rise from its ashes restored to youth. [16] But the allusion must surely be ironic, for a central element of the religion of the Hopi people, whose name translates as "good" and "peaceful", and who live in New Mexico where the bomb was perfected, is the propitiation of the deities of rain, needed to sustain life in an arid land. It is to the deities of a life-bringing, fertile rain, rather than a death-dealing, poisonous rain that they appeal. A Hopi thunderbird design appears just below the ceiling of Morris's installation, [17] reaching heavenward and invoking the mythical bird conceived by American Indians as the spirit of thunder and rain. Like the Fire Storm drawings, Jornada del Muerto parallels and differentiates these awesome natural forces and the man-made instruments of war. Morris seems, finally, to discover human culprits rather than divine plan behind these images of desolation and "pitiless slaughter," these visions of deluge.

NOTES

1. Letter from Alex Gray, November 15, 1983.

2. Morris produced the Blind Time drawings by rubbing graphite on paper directly with his hands, blindly--his eyes closed.

3. Leonardo's description "Of a Deluge and the Representation of it in Painting" was written in the period 1513-1515 and was intended for the **Treatise on Painting.** (Ludwig H. Heydenreich, **Leonardo da Vinci,** New York: Macmillan, 1954, p. 156.)

4. The Committee for the Compilation of Materials on Damage Caused by the Atomic Bombs in Hiroshima and Nagasaki, **Hiroshima and Nagasaki--The Physical, Medical, and Social Effects of the Atomic Bombings,** tr. Eisei Ishikawa and David L. Swain (New York: Basic Books, 1981).

5. The uranium bomb was called "Little Boy" in reference to Franklin D. Roosevelt by scientists in the United States, while the plutonium bomb was dubbed "Fat Man" for Winston Churchill. (Ibid., p. 31.)

6. Heydenreich, p. 155. For a discussion of the varied interpretations of this drawing, see Kenneth Clark, **The Drawings of Leonardo da Vinci in the Collection of Her Majesty the Queen at Windsor Castle,** second edition (London: Phaidon, 1968), p. 56.

7. This was edited by the Japanese Broadcasting Corporation (NHK) and published in New York by Pantheon Books, 1977.

8. Melissa Bryan, a member of the Museum Studies seminar taught by S. Y. at Mount Holyoke College in 1983, located this Leonardo image. The image of clouds after the bomb was dropped is taken from The Pacific War Research Society, **The Day Man Lost** (Palo Alto: Kodansha International, 1972), plate 34.

9. **The Notebooks of Leonard da Vinci,** ed. Edward MacCurdy (New York: Braziller, 1958), vol. 1, p. 915.

10. Howard N. Fox, **Metaphor: New Projects by Contemporary Sculptors** (Washington, D.C.: Hirshhorn Museum and Sculpture Garden, Smithsonian Institution, 1982), p. 62.

11. Linda F. McGreevy, "Robert Morris' Metaphorical Nightmare: The Journada del Muerto," Arts Magazine, Sept. 1983, p. 108.

12. Ibid.

13. Robert Morris, "American Quartet," Art in America, Dec. 1981, p. 93.

14. Ibid., p. 104.

15. McGreevy, p. 108.

16. E. S. Whittlesey, **Symbols and Legends in Western Art** (New York: Scribner's, 1972), p. 281.

17. Fox, p. 62.

HISTORY

THE IMAGE OF SAINTLINESS IN PURITAN HAGIOGRAPHY 1650 - 1700

Dewey D. Wallace, Jr.
George Washington University

In the five volumes of his **Worship and Theology in England,** Professor Horton Davies left the well-worn church historical ruts of doctrinal and institutional history in order to examine Christian worship, an aspect of religion that brings the investigator into touch with everyday religious attitudes and practices. To examine the cultus of a religion is to study an ingredient in popular religion, and however elusive the phenomenon to which that term refers may be, its importance in building a complete picture of any religious tradition is now widely acknowledged.

Something analogous can be said about the study of the lives of holy persons as an aspect of church history; this too can be a means of studying popular religious attitudes. For in any religion, the saintly life, especially as it becomes stereotyped, concretizes abstract ideals in a manner accessible to the humblest of the faithful. Whether of a Bodhisattva, a medieval Catholic miracle worker, or an heroic Protestant missionary, the stories of such lives both inform and crystallize the values of a religious community. Thus even though saints' lives, like liturgies, have usually been produced by religious elites, they can be studied as a means of understanding the popular religious mentality which they have so importantly shaped. Saints' lives, as Helen C. White has remarked, are "designed for popular consumption and popular influence." [1]

Several recent studies of medieval popular religion have focused on saints, their cults, relics, and shrines. [2] The saints have also been a means for the study of popular religion in Protestant countries, but usually in relation to the gradual disappearance of this element of religion so important to the common folk.

The Protestant Reformation rejected the medieval cult of the saints, the use of their images, and the doctrine of their intercession. The Reformers decried all this for obscuring the centrality of Christ, denounced medieval sermons for being little more than a retelling of the fabulous marvels of the saints, and restored the New Testament understanding of the saints as all those who believed in Christ. The political sponsors and popular followers of the Reformers emphasized all this by iconoclasm directed against shrines, relics, and images.

But that which is thrown out the front door has a way of returning by the back, and so it was with Protestantism and the saints. If holy persons are almost a necessity for the concretization of the ideals of a religious community, as well as theologically necessary as a "sign of God" [3] in a Christian community, then Protestantism could no more do without the saints than could medieval Catholicism. The question then becomes one of examining Protestantism for that within it which represented the transformation of the older saintly ideals. And it is remarkable how quickly Protestantism, notwithstanding its rejection of the veneration of relics or the intercession of the saints, constructed a rich hagiographical tradition of its own. In ancient Christianity the first special saints were those who had suffered for the faith, and similarly the Protestant world was quickly saturated with martyrologies. Protestantism was energized by the recognition of the heroic lives given in its behalf, and while these martyrs were not invoked in prayer, they were invoked in exhortations to the holy and sacrificial life. So while all the faithful were saints, some holy lives stood out as preeminent and were celebrated accordingly.

Protestant England had the monumental martyrological collection of John Foxe, which gave it a new band of heroic Christians. This work fit the vogue for biography in Renaissance and Reformation England. A large portion of the biographical output of the period memorialized the clergy. [4] Clerical worthies were celebrated in the compilations of Thomas Fuller and other energetic biographers, partly with the apologetical intention of proving that the Church of England was not behind the rest of Christendom (and certainly not Roman Catholicism) in the piety and learning of its clergy. "Stupor mundi clerus Britannicus," declared Bishop Joseph Hall. [5] With Izaak Walton English ecclesiastical biography gained literary stature. In Peter Heylyn's life of Archbishop Laud ecclesiastical biography became hagiography in the service of anti-Puritan polemic. [6]

But it was the Puritans Heylyn despised who made the greatest contribution towards a literature both distinctly hagiographical and distinctly Protestant. The emergence of this Puritan hagiography was recognized by William Haller, who described the Puritan penchant for teaching by example through the short biographies of notables which they appended to funeral sermons. Haller also called attention to the various biographical compilations of Samuel Clark. [7] The industrious Clark wrote some of these himself while borrowing and revising others; but in either case his lives have a formulaic character, emphasizing his subjects' conversion, learning, connections with earlier Puritan "greats," feats of prayer and fasting, diligence in preaching and pastoral labors, charity, and holy deaths. Of such lives the author of the standard history of English biography comments, "The authors have returned to the spirit of the saints' legends." [8]

By the second half of the seventeenth century the Puritan literature of this sort was becoming enormous. It included sermons that were little more than "improvements" upon the deaths of godly persons with eulogistic brief lives appended. Thus Simeon Ashe in a publication of 1655 attached a short biography of Ralph Robinson to a long sermon in which he developed the "doctrine" that "The death of godly ones should considerably be laid to heart." [9] In a similar production of the next year, Thomas Jacombe warned his auditors that they should put away those sins "which cause God to shorten the lives of painful Ministers." [10] Other sermons and appended lives went beyond the homiletic "uses" of the deaths of the godly to expatiate on the importance of such godly persons as examples: Robert Bragg declared in 1676 that "It is our duty to observe and take special notice of the good and godly man, both in his life and death." [11] Thirty years later the leading Puritan John Howe was called in his funeral sermon "an inviting example of Universal Goodness." [12] The most significant Puritan biographies, however, were separated from sermons, and began to explore many dimensions of personal holiness.

The Puritan literature after 1650 commemorating holy persons was not only extensive, but was also taking on a more distinct character. Building on the conventions of earlier clerical biography, Puritans in this period quite self-consciously attempted to develop and popularize a Puritan image of saintliness which drew on earlier Christian models at the same time that it crystallized newer Protestant ones. No doubt the persecution of Puritan dissenters which followed the restoration of the monarchy in 1660 abetted this process by reviving the mentality of the martyr and confessor.

To test the hypothesis that there emerged from 1650-1700 a Puritan hagiographical literature which drew on the old while it crystallized the new, I have chosen to analyze eight biographies of holy persons written by Puritans between 1650 and 1700, all of which treat subjects whose careers fell within the seventeenth century and who can be adjudged Nonconformist or Dissenter in outlook. Thus early English Protestant martyrs and conformist Anglican authors are excluded in the effort to see how Puritan authors depicted holy Puritans. The lives chosen also seem to have been written primarily for edification, not information, and the intended edification is not merely the homiletical improvement of their life, but their usefulness as examples. In several cases the authors or sponsors of the biography show considerable self-consciousness about the hagiographical art and tradition, making the choice of those works inevitable. In what follows, each biography will be introduced as an example of hagiography, and then the major themes running through all of them presented compositely. Needless to say, what is important in this analysis is not the determination of the facts of these lives, but the principal images of holiness found in them.

Some lives stand out during this period as classics of Puritan hagiographical art. Among them is the volume celebrating the holiness of Joseph Alleine, **The Life and Death of that Excellent Minister of Christ Mr. Joseph Allein**, first published in 1672 and reprinted seven more times until 1693. It brought together materials from many hands in its depiction of a leader of the dissenting Presbyterians who became well known as the author of the devotional classic **An Alarm to the Unconverted.** An introductory chapter was provided by Richard Baxter in which he declared that it was better to read the lives of "wise and holy men" than those of bloody conquerors, but that such saints' stories had for many centuries been corrupted "with so many impudent lies in the Popish Legends, as might render all such Narrative afterwards Contemptible and Incredible." However, he continued, since the gospel is not "system or law" but "the History of the Life and Death of Christ, and the wondrous works of Himself and his Spirit in his Servants," such stories of holiness must be told. "In the lives of Holy Men we see God's Image, and the Beauties of Holiness, not only in Precept, but in Reality and Practice." Such holiness incites further holiness, giving Christians "excellent Examples for their Imitation." Joseph Alleine in particular, he added, left behind an especially good example of "a right Minister of the Gospel." [13] This point was echoed by another contributor, who averred that Alleine, "this Holy Person," can be presented as an example of "the Portraiture of a compleat Gospel-Minister." [14]

The most important single part of this memorial volume, however, was the sketch of Alleine's life provided by his widow, Theodosia Alleine. Her narrative stressed his sufferings for the gospel, including his untimely death, which she understood to be the consequence of the impairment of his health by his long imprisonment for religious dissent. Thus Alleine is portrayed as a confessor, in the ancient sense of one who suffers persecution, and as a martyr, insofar as he died from the effects of persecution. And in the style of ancient martyrologies, Theodosia tells his story so as to parallel the sufferings of Christ: he was meek and composed before those who arrested him, mocked by his captors, and forgiving ("He pitied the condition of his Enemies, requesting for them, as the Martyr Stephen did for those that stoned him, that God would not lay this sin of theirs to their charge"). In all, like the ancient martyrs, "He rejoyced that he was accounted worthy to suffer for the works of Christ." Theodosia sums up her narrative by saying that "his whole life was a continual Sermon, holding forth evidently the Doctrines he Preached." [15]

One year after the publication of the volume commemorating Alleine, James Janeway, a dissenting minister known to posterity as the author of a book about the pious deaths of little children, [16] published a biography of his deceased brother entitled **Invisibles, Realities, Demonstrated in the Holy Life and Triumphant Death of Mr. John Janeway.** This book went through seven printings up to 1698. The subject of this biography was distinguished by no career in the ministry at all, but died at the age of twenty-four while still a student at Cambridge. This volume is also prefaced by Richard Baxter, who writes: "The Love of Christ in his holy ones, and the great usefulness of such History, command me to take it as a pleasing office to commend this real description of a Saint, to thy serious perusal and imitation. The good acceptance and success of the late published Life and Death of Mr. Joseph Alleine, the more encourageth me to serve thee in this." [17] There were two other prefaces to Janeway's life, both testifying to its accuracy, and one affirmed that "serious consideration of this narrative of his life and death, will (through God's blessing) beget a zealous imitation of this Saint." [18]

The third life to be examined is **The Life and Death of Mr. John Rowe of Crediton in Devon**, published in 1675. Rowe was a layman and magistrate, and his biographer was Theophilus Gale, a noted scholar among the Congregationalists who kept a dissenting academy and was the author of a huge investigation of natural theology and of an appreciative treatment of Jansenism. Gale knew Rowe through his father, Thomas Gale, with whom Rowe had lived for a while as a young man. Apparent in all of Gale's works, including this biography, was the author's conviction that grace and revelation alone were the sources of all truth, [19] and Gale repeatedly stressed that Rowe's life showed that grace can take a person beyond "the highest Attainments of the most Refined Morality." Of Rowe he says, "Grace seemed to have the whole command of him," for in him "Grace seemed to have made a perfect conquest of nature." Such emphasis on grace Gale considered necessary to "give check to the growing Atheisms of the age." [20] Gale was also a self-conscious hagiographer: "The Verity and Reality of Religion is Exemplified in the Lives of Holy Men," he argued, and added that in particular God had made Rowe "A Pattern as worthy of our Imitation as any this Latter Age hath produced." And just as a medieval saint's life might begin, Gale says "I shall give thee a little Image of this holy man," and thereafter he referred to him by such phrases as "this eminent saint," or "this now glorified saint." [21]

But perhaps it is the fourth of these lives, and the only one chosen from the literature of this sort written in New England, that is most self-conscious about continuity with earlier Christian hagiography. John Norton's **Abel being Dead yet Speaketh; or, the Life & Death of that deservedly Famous Man of God, Mr. John Cotton**, published in 1658, declared that the lives of holy persons demonstrated triumph over the world, sin, and Satan, and that "the greatest Object out of Heaven" is the earthly life of one of those "who now are in Heaven." Norton's description of Cotton's flight to the "desert" of New England echoes other saintly removals to the desert, and he also, quoting Cyprian to establish the point, regarded such flight in persecution as "a kinde of Confession of our faith, it being an open profession, that our faith is dearer to us than all that we flie from." Thus Cotton is enrolled among the saintly confessors, elsewhere being described by Norton as "Our Confessor (or Martyr, which you please)," and compared at his death to the early martyr Polycarp. [22]

The fifth example of Puritan hagiography chosen is **The Life and Death of Mr. Ignatius Jurdain, one of the Aldermen of the City of Exeter**, published in 1654. It was written by Ferdinand Nicholls, who declared that "this eminent Saint, this holy and just Man" should be "a Pattern of Piety and Charity" "to succeeding generations." [23] The slim volume was prefaced by the Presbyterian leader Thomas Manton, who remarked that God stirred up writers in every age to memorialize his faithful servants for the good of posterity. In the ancient church, Manton continued, such persons were listed in "Diptychs or publick Tables;" this worthy tradition of the memorialization of holy persons should be continued, in spite of the fact that the "Romanists" made canonization "ridiculous" through absurd legends, lest "true saints, God's Worthies, should be defrauded of their publick honour." [24]

The last three lives examined in order to build up a composite picture of the late seventeenth-century Puritan ideal of the saintly person come from Samuel Clark's 1683 compilation, one of his many publications which helped establish patterns of Puritan hagiography. One of these lives, that of Richard Blackerby, was not written by Clark, but, like others he borrowed, may have undergone his revisions and abbreviation. Blackerby himself was a relatively obscure Nonconformist who died in 1648. His anonymous biographer claims that "This holy Man was indeed an instance sent by God into the World" to demonstrate how holy a life can be, and the life includes many touches reminiscent of medieval hagiography. [25] The biography of Samuel Winter, a less obscure Nonconformist who died in 1666, was presumably written by Clark. His life was described as a "Pattern" to be imitated, and is noteworthy for the miraculous element within it. [26] The life of his wife Katherine, "this holy woman," was probably written by Clark. Her biography is a good example of many which depicted devout Puritan women. [27]

A number of themes and motifs stand out in these examples of Puritan hagiography and invite comparison not only with earlier and contemporary Christian hagiography--patristic, medieval, or Counter-Reformation Catholic--but also with the hagiographical art as it has been practiced in other cultures and religions. Still other themes in this material evince a distinctly Protestant and Puritan outlook, and represent a significant shift in the understanding of saintliness in Christian sensibility which occurred in the wake of the Reformation. The motifs and themes to be considered will be reviewed in an order that moves roughly from the most universally Christian to the more uniquely Puritan ones.

The earliest Christians to be especially distinguished as saints were those so set apart because of their sufferings for the faith, either as martyrs or confessors. This understanding of special Christian worthiness was revived by Protestants in the accounts of Reformation martyrs, and is prominent in Puritan lives of holy persons, many of whom suffered earlier in the seventeenth century as Nonconformists or later as dissenters under the Clarendon Code. Thus John Cotton was a confessor because he fled persecution, and Joseph Alleine "confessed" through the sufferings of several imprisonments, which may have brought on his early death, making him a martyr. Richard Blackerby, like many another in the pages of Clark, suffered harassment and suspension for his Nonconformity.

It is commonly maintained that the end of the persecutions in ancient Christianity gave impetus to the voluntary martyrdom of the ascetic life, and thereafter ascetic rigors became one of the distinguishing marks of the saintly person. Protestantism of course rejected asceticism as a path to God, but still allowed plenty of scope for self-denial as the devout response to the gift of God's grace, and though mechanical austerities rarely appeal in Protestant lives, austere self-denial frequently does. John Janeway's life can be considered a kind of martyrdom by asceticism, as his intense labors in study and prayer, with scant attention given to food or rest, were thought to have brought about his early death. Joseph Alleine allowed himself little sleep, often gave away his food, and when he ate never took as much as he desired. Only of Alleine are more mechanical measures recounted: having read of Catholic religious austerities, he set out to perform them, "though on better grounds," presumably not those of works-righteousness. [28] Baxter found it necessary to refute the charge that both Janeway and Alleine were culpably suicidal. [29]

Prayer has been for ascetics a discipline as well as a means of communion with the divine, and Puritan holy persons spent much time in prayer. Alleine, for example, "used to keep many dayes alone" in prayer; Rowe, though a layman, kept a monthly day of prayer and fasting. [30] Ancient and medieval holy persons kept prayer vigils late at night, but this is not mentioned of any of these Puritan saints; instead they rose early for prayer (arguably a more strenuous asceticism), Alleine habitually rising at 4 a.m. to "pray and watch," and Jurdain rising at 2 or 3 a.m. to pray until 6 a.m., and if he overslept, "he would much bemoan himself for that he had lost so much of sweet and comfortable communion with God." [31]

Having established holiness by suffering in persecution or through ascetic rigor, ancient Christian saints were thought to be fountains of spiritual wisdom and their sayings were treasured. Thus there grew up the lore of the "sayings of the fathers." The same phenomenon grew up around Puritan holy persons, the tradition going back at least to "holy Mr. Dod," as he was commonly known, who had been apt at an aphorism. [32] The laypersons in the present sample were less adept at this, but the others had some reputation for spiritual wisdom in this form. Portions of Janeway's letters of spiritual advice were reproduced in his biography, Blackerby was skilled in making "excellent, spiritual, short observations," and Winter was the source of such sayings as "his opportunities were his riches" and "Since our time is short, let us work the faster." But it was Alleine who excelled at this (His Phansie was as Aaron's Rod budding, ever producing fresh Blossoms of refined Divine Wit and Invention"), and a substantial portion of his commemorative volume consisted of the collecting of his aphorisms, such as "I delight in nothing in this World, further than I see God in it." [33]

The saint has been defined in the phenomenology of religion as a figure of power, both in person and through shrines and relics, [34] and miraculous power abounds in ancient and medieval saints' tales; accredited miracles became one of the credentials necessary for Roman Catholic canonization. The Protestant Reformers had decried such saints' tales as fraudulent, and both Baxter and Manton echoed that view in their prefaces to the lives of holy Puritans. Furthermore, Protestants characteristically argued that the age of miracles had ceased with the apostles, who had been given such special power in order to establish the faith. But in two forms the Puritan hagiographers allowed something akin to the miraculous: in those prodigies and divine interventions they called providences, and in answers to prayer. For example, divine retribution visited upon persecutors, a frequent motif in Foxe and Clark, [35] appeared in the story of Blackerby, where it was reported that those who had opposed his preaching were "blasted in their estates," all dying "miserably" but one. Similarly, a ruffian who menaced Rowe was "struck dumb." [36] Other providences were seen in the interpretation of striking events or in clairvoyant power. Rowe, for example, was "a curious observer of every passage of providence," who had premonitions: "When any great thing was approaching relating to himself, his family, or the Church, he had usually some warning and intimation from God beforehand concerning it." Skilled Rowe might well have been at interpreting providences, for his life had been preserved by providence at its beginning, Rowe thus being an example of those holy persons whose births were accompanied by the miraculous: given up for dead in his crib, "The Lord was pleased to restore him to life . . . intimating by this so Early and Signal a Providence that he had reserv'd him for some more than ordinary use." [37] If Rowe came into the world miraculously, Cotton left it attended by providential signs; Norton reported that a comet appeared shortly before that holy man died, warning of his coming death as well as of other calamities, and serving as a reminder that God often removes the righteous from evils soon to come. [38]

Blackerby also received communication from God through dreams, and exuded holy power: Daniel Rogers is represented in his biography as having said that he could not "come into the presence of Mr. Blackerby without some kind of trembling upon him; because of the Divine Majesty and Holiness which seemed to shine in him." Blackerby's holiness was also recognized by animals, for, when confronted with a raging bull "that used to do much mischief," he brought him under control by prayer, reminiscent of St. Francis and the wolf of Gubbio. And like St. Francis, Blackerby's sympathies reached to the animal kingdom, as he was "exceeding careful" about "God's Creatures;" "he would always have a Fowl or two allowed to come familiarly into his Eating Room, to pick up the lesser Crumbs that would fall from the Table." [39]

Answers to prayer were another kind of providential intervention, and stories of this kind abounded in Puritan lives. Janeway and Blackerby both received strange and immediate answers to prayer. But Samuel Winter was a kind of thaumaturge in his prayers, with many miracles of healing wrought by his prayers being recounted, illustrating the general phenomenon that the prayers of the devout have special power. [40]

Another aspect of the power of holy persons is power to control the demonic. This power was prized in early Christianity when the human problem was interpreted as subjection to evil forces. But in Protestant accounts this is usually demythologized: the assaulting demons might be persons fulfilling a demonic role (in ancient martyrologies demons and persecutors tend to blend into one another) or else the struggle with Satan is turned into an inward experience of temptation, there being nothing in them quite like the very physical assaults of demons which troubled St. Anthony or St. Martin. The first of these types appeared in the story of Blackerby, when demon-like, opponents "would sometimes rise up against his Preaching with Rage and Violence." [41] More common were inner, psychological attacks of the demonic, which usually took the form of an attempt to undermine the faith and assurance of the victim by suggesting bleak and hopeless thoughts. Thus immediately following her conversion Katherine Clark was assaulted by Satan in this way, "to stifle this new creature in its first conception." John Janeway had "gloomy days" of temptation when "The Devil shot his poisonous arrows at him," but he resisted, shooting arrows of faith and prayer back at Satan until he fled. John Cotton experienced times of dejection which Norton laid at Satan's door, especially when Cotton first entered his ministry. Alleine's main combat was at his death, when the tempter appeared, but he responded with a speech preserved by Theodosia: "Away thou foul Fiend, thou Enemy of all Man-kind, thou subtile Sophister . . . Trouble me not, for I am none of thine! I am the Lord's, Christ is mine, and I am his: His by Covenant . . . Therefore be gone." [42]

The authors of every one of these lives declared their subjects to be humble, and such humility insofar as it was submission to God, self-contempt, and self-abnegation was consonant with the saintly experience generally. Cotton was "clothed" with humility; Katherine Clark "had always a very low esteem of her self;" Rowe "was much in the acknowledgement of his own nothingness and vileness;" Alleine was "low in his own eyes, and despised the praise of men," admired "self-annihilation" and wanted to be "nothing, that God might be all." [43]

Humble saints were also obedient ones, but the obedience to religious superiors so much praised in medieval depictions of saintliness dropped out of the Protestant hagiographies. Instead obedience to God was emphasized, as when it was said of Rowe that he had "a broken will toward God." The only case where obedience to other persons was praised was in the life of Katherine Clark, who as a woman was said by her biographer and husband to have been "very exemplary in that reverence and obedience which she yielded to her Husband, both in Words, and Deeds . . . His word was a law unto her: she often denied herself to gratifie him." Deference to godly ministers was a highly regarded virtue in Puritan literature, but only in a few instances in the life of Rowe does it appear in these biographies, although John Norton left as his parting words at death his concern over the growing sin of "Korahism," or woeful disregard of the authority of ministers. [44]

Humility and obedience led to meekness, and this virtue was affirmed of most of the eight, and especially of Samuel Winter.

[45] But though humble and meek, these saintly persons were capable of spiritedness on God's behalf, several of them being notable for the seasonable rebukes they administered to others, both by way of the friendly correction of the godly and the upbraiding of the ungodly. Joseph Alleine was only angry when anger served God's glory, but then "He feared not the faces of Men, but where occasion was, he was bold in admonishing," although he managed this "ungrateful duty" with "such expressions of Love and compassion to Souls" as made his rebukes acceptable to the rebuked. When taking the waters at Bath for the recovery of his health he engaged in a ministry of reproof, "very close and plain," directed at prominent persons who were also there. His wife Theodosia testified that he did this so skillfully that his rebukes were accepted, and even "The vilest of those Persons . . . said of him, that he never spake with such a man in his life." Theodosia too received his reproofs, and took it in good part: "He was a faithful reprover of any thing he saw amiss in me, which I took as a great evidence of his real good will to my soul." [46]

John Janeway lacked Alleine's tact in reproof, for no sooner had he undergone his conversion than he set about correcting others. He began, at nineteen years of age, by writing a ministerial relative and advising him that he and his family lacked a deep experience of religion. And when one of his brothers fell asleep at family prayers, he showed him "What a high contempt it was of God." When he noticed godly persons grieving over the loss of goods or loved ones, he chided them for their unwillingness to abandon all earthly ties. [47]

The two magistrates, Jurdain and Rowe, did their rebuking through their official capacity. Jurdain's biographer says he was zealous against idolatry, displaying "an antilaodicean temper." Rowe, as high constable, was diligent in suppressing vice, so that his name "became a Dread and Terror to all the Prophane that were near to the place he lived." [48] Rebuking evil and correction of the erring has been a perennial activity of a certain sort of saint, and even the lore about St. Francis portrays that mild holy man as on occasion administering a stern rebuke. And yet this particular practice of the Puritan saints seems so close to the stereotype of the meddlesome Puritan, typified by Ben Jonson's "Zeal-of-the-Land Busy," that it should be pointed out that in half of the eight biographies there was no mention of this activity.

The humility, meekness, self-denial, and submission to God of these holy persons were the external characteristics of a spirituality of intense communion with the divine such as might be called mystical, and which has been characteristic of much saintliness everywhere. For this deeper kind of religious experience the favorite Puritan terms were "holiness" and "heavenly-mindedness," the latter being especially suggestive of their absorption in the divine realm. A large part of the biography of Katherine Clark consists of the reproduction of her private devotional papers which reveal her "heavenly-mindedness" as well as her "patience and holy submission" to God's will. Blackerby's absorption in God was evident in that he was "much in Closet Prayer" as well as "Walking Prayer," he being a "great Walker." John Cotton was "a man of much communion with God" who had "a deep sight into the Mystery of God's grace." Jurdain's "heart was so full of heaven" that he often spoke of heavenly things, and avoided all vain conversation. Alleine's conversation was "always mingled with Heavenly and Holy Discourses," and he often sang forth God's praises; He "lived much in delightful Communion with God," being especially cognizant of the "tenderness of the Divine Love." John Rowe was "very eminent for his Heavenly mindedness," and like "the ancient saints, he accounted himself but a Pilgrim and Stranger upon Earth." He had a deep acquaintance with "the great mystery of Faith and Godliness" that was not only "notional" but "affective." "His great desire was to be spiritual in all that he did." "Oh, how much did he depart from himself day by day, that so he might more intirely enter into and live in Christ? . . . Oh, what an amorous union with, and value for Christ did he gain by the Ruines of self-Love." Janeway too regarded himself as "but a Pilgrim that looked for a better country," for he lived like "a man that was quite weary of the world, and that looked upon himself as a stranger here, and that lived in the constant sight of a better world." Thus he had hours of prayer in which he had "sweet" and "holy familiarity" with God, with whom he conversed "as a friend." [49]

Charitableness is a quality almost universally attributed to the saintly life. Christian holy persons had practiced charity not only as an aspect of self-denial and unworldliness, but also as a means of serving God. This latter motive took on a somewhat different meaning in Protestantism, for Protestants regarded serving God through charity not as a way to earn merit but as an expression of gratitude to God. And this could mean (as it did to Luther) that charity was done with more attention to the recipient's need than to the giver's salvation. In the portraits of Puritan saints chosen for this study, Charity is highly valued (in Blackerby's case even charity to animals), and in the three portraits of lay saints as well as that of Alleine, it is a major element. There is some suggestion that charity was especially important to holy women, as it was characteristic of Katherine Clark, frequently mentioned in Theodosia's account of her husband's virtues, and mentioned of Samuel Winter's wife, who is joined with her husband in the recounting of charitable deeds. Only in the story of Janeway, whose youthful piety was of the hothouse variety, was charity not an important ingredient in the saintly picture.

Katherine Clark was charitable to the poor wherever

she lived, and "had a very melting Heart" towards those in need. William James has said that the saintly delight in helping the sick, and this was something at which Katherine was skillfull. Lay magistrates, as persons of wealth and responsibility, might be expected to show charity, and Rowe is pictured as hospitable, liberal towards needy university students, and "a constant relief to the poor of the place where he lived." Other godly persons gave him money to distribute to the destitute, and he was also adept at settling local quarrels. Jurdain was "open-handed" to the poor, and during the plague in Exeter fearless in helping others, as "his bowels yerned towards" those who in that extremity lacked food or medicine. His generosity was even accused of aggravating the beggary of the town. In his will he bequeathed one-third of his estate to the poor. He was also hospitable to strangers. Among the clergy, Winter was "eminent for his bounty" and gave large sums to "Pious and Charitable" uses. Alleine was also bountiful to the poor, and "did not think the little he had so much his own, as that his necessitous Brethren might not claim a part in it, and therefore gave them as if he had been paying Debts, and not bestowing Alms." At Taunton, he sought to relieve poor families, in prison he was charitable to "felons," and elsewhere he "gave alms daily." [50]

But there is a characteristic Puritan rationality in some aspects of this charitableness. Samuel Winter's wife kept a careful written account of amounts given to charity, unlike the indiscriminate approach of medieval saints. The same rationality appears in the attempt of Jurdain to give to the "honest poor," with Alleine who gave "especially" to godly persons, or in Rowe's life, where it is said that his hospitality was given particularly to the poor but godly. [51]

Sometimes Puritan hagiographers meant by charity concern for souls, especially the souls of the poor and unfortunate: thus Alleine, by preaching to prisoners, was said to be charitable to them. [52] This zeal for souls, which in the clerical saints was also diligence in the pastoral calling, was another highly praised theme among Puritan hagiographers, and it had been characteristic of many early medieval saints, such as St. Martin or St. Boniface. Less common among the often cloistered later medieval saints, though it reappears with St. Dominic, such concern for souls was also frequent with Counter-Reformation Roman Catholic holy persons. Zeal for souls was a major theme in Janeway's biography, even though he died before preaching more than two sermons. He was concerned that many ministers did not have sufficient care for the winning of souls, and labored for the souls of his relatives and fellow-students, "desiring to carry as many of them as possibly he could along with him to Heaven." But Alleine was the champion among these holy persons with respect to zeal for souls and diligence in the pastoral calling. To picture him as such was the principal motive behind the publication of materials about his life. "Insatiably greedy of the Conversion of Souls," he went from house to house to effect conversions, visiting even the "mean and low." "He was very urgent with those that were Unconverted, to look with more care after their salvation," weeping and praying for them, and "telling them how his heart did yearn for them." [53]

Many lives of Christian saints have been written as weapons in theological controversy. Thus Athanasius portrayed St. Anthony as a fierce opponent of the Arians. But of these eight Puritan lives only that by the doughty controversialist Gale is tendentiously theological. He tells Rowe's story to make a point about the absolute necessity of grace in a holy life, in order to refute all moralism and atheism. Rowe is said to have held no "private, particular, or novel opinion," but to have preferred the "old divinity" taught by "Orthodox Divines." Moreover, he prayed for those who fell into error. Cotton routed the Arminians who pestered him in his first pastorate. Janeway and Alleine, on the other hand, thought theological polemics often interfered with true godliness: the latter had a "healing spirit" while the former "groaned" over divisions among Christians. [54]

A life of holiness required completion in a holy death. All eight of the holy Puritans had such a death, which included patience under one's last sufferings, ardent longing to be with God, the overcoming of any last assaults of Satan, and the utterance of portentous spiritual wisdom. Katherine Clark died with great assurance of grace, enjoying serenity of soul in which Satan "had no power to molest her." "She earnestly desired to be dissolved, and breathed after a fuller enjoyment of Jesus Christ"--"Thus did this holy woman wear out," concludes her husband-hagiographer, appending to his account a list of the pious thoughts she wrote down in her final illness. The last illness of Jurdain was very painful, but his assurance remained unshaken. Samuel Winter's death takes up a large portion of his short life, for at the last his soul was "Wonderfully elevated," as "he died in very high Raptures, and great acclamations by way of Thankfulness unto God." John Cotton, "totally composed," prepared himself "for his dissolution, desiring that he might be permitted to improve the little remnant of his life without any considerable impediment to his private devotions, and divine soliloquies between God and his soul." John Rowe's peace at his death was undisturbed by Satanic assault, and "His whole carriage during his sickness, and at his death," was "suitable to his life, as he had lived exemplarily, so he died exemplarily." "He was not only willing to die, but he triumphed over death." Alleine suffered a long illness before his death, and during that time uttered no word of impatience; instead he was an unusually fruitful source of spiritual sayings. His assurance of a "saving interest in Christ" was complete, and while dying he had "frequent Ecstasies or Raptures of Spirit." [55]

However, it was in the account of the death of Janeway that a narrative of death became the point of life. The purpose of the whole story to provide an account of his final days. When his health failed so that he had little hope, "he received the sentence of death in himself with great joy," and was ashamed to pray for his life. He now received full "assurance," and never complained, speaking only of "his eager desire to be with Christ." When observers were horrified by his "Spitting of blood," he told them that it "was no ghastly thing to one that had his eye upon the blood of Jesus." thus "improving" even this circumstance. When his mother grieved, he told her to "cheerfully give me up to Christ." When a minister visited him, they fell together in such raptures of heavenly-mindedness that the visitor was loath to depart, fervently wishing that he too were dying. Janeway broke out into triumphant ecstasies "of praise and joy," crying out "Stand astonished ye Heavens, and wonder, O ye Angels, at this infinite grace!" On his last day he declared, "O he is come! He is come! O how sweet . . . and now I am sick of love, he hath ravished my soul with his beauty. I shall die, sick of love." As his body grew cold, he still had "fits of joy unspeakable." His brother-biographer concludes "Never was death more welcome to any mortal." Janeway fits William James' description of those "saints" who feed on "the thought of suffering and death--their souls growing in happiness just in proportion as their outward state grew more intolerable." [56]

Other characteristics of these eight works of hagiography seem to result from their Protestant origins. For example, the learning of most of these saintly persons is noted favorably. It is true that some earlier works of hagiography such as accounts of St. Augustine's life, praised learning, but more often the saintly (like St. Francis) achieve their sanctity without learning or if learned, are described as holy in spite of it. But several of the Puritan subjects were described as prodigies of learning, with this treated as an important attribute of a holy life. In none of them is learning mentioned with suspicion, and even the less learned Katherine Clark and Jurdain are praised for reading scripture or holy books. One factor which might account for this is that Protestantism was dependent upon literacy and the study of scripture, and wanted to claim the most profound learning for itself. Furthermore, in England there had been much scorn of unlearned "tub-preachers," and the depiction of holy Puritans as learned would belie such charges. Thus Rowe is described as having been proficient at Latin and Greek in his youth, and in later life an avid reader of Calvin's commentaries. Janeway is described as having been a prodigy of erudition. So learned was Samuel Winter that in his dying raptures he recited scripture in the original Greek and Hebrew. Of John Cotton's learning Norton says "The greater part of the Encyclopedia he excelled in . . . He was a good Hebrician, in Greek a Critick, and could with great facility both speak and write Latin in a pure and elegant Ciceronian Stile." Of Alleine it was said "Never had Learning a truer Drudge," as he pursued it day and night doing nothing when at school but "pray and study." Indeed, "his laborious Studiousness was as delightful and pleasant to him, as the highest Voluptuousness can be to the most sensual Sot." [57]

The engagement with the world of these holy persons is also characteristically Protestant. There had been lay saints before in Christian history, but usually as martyrs or ascetics who withdrew from the world. Thomas More, as a married man and magistrate, is a rara avis in the calendar of Roman Catholic saints, and he is from the era of the Reformation. But two of these eight Puritan saints were lay magistrates, and the pages of Clark record many more such persons. The one woman in the sample was married, and her holy life, like that of the magistrates, was lived by fulfilling in a Christian manner the ordinary tasks of civil and familial responsibility. All were married except for the young Janeway. Rowe was portrayed as careful in his selection of a godly wife. Alleine's saintliness included being a "Tenderly Affectionate Husband." Cotton was even praised for being made by God "a fruitful vine" through his many children. [58] Family prayer was one of the forms of devotion mentioned of many of these holy persons. The clergy were all praised for lives of active pastoral usefulness. Thus a Protestant model of sanctity was being forged in which the holy life was not a withdrawn life, but a realization of Christian ideals in family, congregation, occupation, and civic duty.

Several other aspects of the piety recounted of these holy Puritans further suggest the new style of Protestant piety. All eight of the saintly Puritans were Bible readers, and most were portrayed as being saturated with biblical idiom. Katherine Clark read both the Old and New Testaments daily. Janeway found the Bible "sweeter to him than his food." Preaching also played a prominent part in these lives, appropriate to a Protestant milieu where the preached word was essential. Katherine was diligent in attendance upon preaching, preferring "Plain, practical, and powerful Preachers." Rowe told his children and friends "that their first care should be to place themselves under a Godly and powerful Ministry." The clergy were all preachers, and Alleine and Cotton published many sermons, while Blackerby, who did not, was described as skilled in explaining scripture through his sermons. [59] Sabbath observance, an element of importance in Puritan piety by the latter seventeenth century, is mentioned in all but one of the lives. There are long descriptions of the exacting way in which Rowe and Cotton spent their sabbaths. Katherine Clark "carefully sanctified the day." [60] Finally, Protestant saints worried about wasting time: Blackerby seemed "never to lose one moment of time in idleness;" and Alleine "set a high value on his most precious Time," one of his spiritual sayings being "Value precious time, while time doth last." [61]

The motifs and themes present in the lives of these eight holy persons indicate the extent to which Puritan portrayals of saintliness both tapped universal roots of human religiosity and reproduced themes prominent in earlier Christian hagiography. Nor, as several of the prefaces point out, were these parallels to earlier saints' lives always unconscious, even though much in medieval hagiography was vehemently denounced by Protestants. Nonetheless, there is much in these lives which is new, and attributable to their Protestant provenance or to the more modern sensibility of the later seventeenth-century. The value placed, in an age of printing, on reading and preaching, and in an age when it was thought that the world could be shaped for the better by human effort, on pastoral, familial, occupational, or civic activities, suggests that these hagiographers were the heralds of a new ideal of Christian life. That this modern Christian ideal was related to Protestantism is obvious enough, but there were elements in Counter-Reformation Catholic piety which were analogous, for example, in Francis de Sales. Lawrence Cunningham, a recent Roman Catholic critic of traditional notions of sanctity, has advocated a fresh ideal of saintliness less dependent on the miraculous and more connected with the world of lay persons that has similarities to some of what appeared in the pages of these Puritan hagiographers. [62] Ernst Troeltsch spoke of the emergence of a Protestant, and especially Puritan "this-worldly asceticism;" that phrase is amply illustrated in these eight lives.

NOTES

* I wish to thank Elizabeth Fisher, my colleague at The George Washington University, for her helpful comments on an earlier draft of this essay.

1. Helen C. White, **Tudor Books of Saints and Martyrs** (Madison: Univ. of Wisconsin Press, 1963), 4.

2. Jonathan Sumption, **Pilgrimage: An Image of Mediaeval Religion** (Totowa, N.J.: Rowman and Littlefield, 1975); Patrick J. Geary, **Furta Sacra: Thefts of Relics in The Central Middle Ages** (Princeton: Princeton Univ. Press, 1978); Peter Brown, **The Cult of the Saints: Its Rise and Function in Latin Christianity** (Chicago: Univ. of Chicago Press, 1981).

3. The phrase is Thomas Merton's; quoted in Lawrence Cunningham, **The Meaning of Saints** (San Francisco: Harper & Row, 1980), 6.

4. Donald A. Stauffer, **English Biography Before 1700** (Cambridge: Harvard Univ. Press, 1930), 64-90.

5. Quoted in Patrick Collinson, **The Religion of Protestants: The Church in English Society 1559-1625** (Oxford: Clarendon Press, 1982), 92.

6. Peter Heylyn, **Cyprianus Anglicus: Or the History of the Life and Death of the Most Reverend and Renowned Prelate William by Divine Providence, Lord Archbishop of Canterbury** (London, 1671).

7. William Haller, **The Rise of Puritanism** (New York: Columbia Univ. Press, 1938), 100-108.

8. Stauffer, 89.

9. Simeon Ashe, **The Good Mans Death Lamented** (London, 1655), 5.

10. Thomas Jacombe, **Enochs Walk and Change, Opened in a Sermon . . . At the Funeral of the Reverend Richard Vines . . . with a short Account of his Life and Death** (London, 1656), 42.

11. Robert Bragg, **The Life and death of the Godly Man, Exemplified in a Sermon Preached . . . at the Funeral of . . . Mr. Thomas Wadsworth** (London, 1676), 2.

12. John Spademan, **A Sermon on the Ocassion** [sic] **of the justly lamented Death of the truly Reverend Mr. John Howe** (London, 1705), sig. A2^{r}.

13. [Theodosia Alleine et.al.], **The Life and Death of that Excellent Minister of Christ, Mr. Joseph Alleine** (London, 1677), 2-4, 28 (hereafter cited as **Life and Death of Alleine**).

14. Ibid., 112.

15. Ibid., 65-67, 73, 108.

16. James Janeway, **A Token for Children.**

17. James Janeway, **Invisibles, Realities, Demonstrated in the Holy Life and Triumphant Death of Mr. John Janeway** (London, 1674), sig. A3^{r}.

18. Ibid., sig. a5^{v}.

19. Dewey D. Wallace, Jr., **Puritans and Predestination: Grace in English Protestant Theology, 1525-1695** (Chapel Hill: Univ. of North Carolina Press, 1982), 178-180.

20. [Theophilus Gale], **The Life and Death of Mr. John Rowe of Crediton in Devon** (London, 1673), sigs A3^{v}, A6^{v}; pp. 82, 111-12.

21. Ibid., sigs. $A3^r$, $A6^v$, $A8^{r-v}$; p. 6.

22. John Norton, **Abel being Dead yet speaketh; or the Life & Death of that deservedly Famous Man of God, Mr. John Cotton** (London, 1658); rpt: Delmar, N.Y.: Scholar's Facsimiles and Reprints, 1978), 4-6, 19, 21, 43.

23. Ferdinand Nicholls, **The Life and Death of Mr. Ignatius Jurdain** (London, 1654), 1-2.

24. Ibid., sig. $a1^{r-v}$.

25. Samuel Clark, "Richard Blackerby," in **The Lives of Sundry Eminent Persons in this Later Age** (London, 1683), 65. (Hereafter cited as "Life of Blackerby".)

26. "The Life and Death of Dr. Samuel Winter," in Samuel Clark, **The Lives of Sundry Eminent Persons,** 95-109 (hereafter cited as "Life of Winter").

27. "The Life and Death of Mrs. Katherine Clark who Died, anno Domini 1671," in Samuel Clark, **The Lives of Sundry Eminent Persons,** Part II, 152-[167]. (Hereafter cited as "Life of Katherine Clark".)

28. **Life and Death of Alleine,** 32. 45, 49.

29. In Janeway, sig. $A5^{r-v}$.

30. **Life and Death of Alleine,** 43, Gale, 43.

31. **Life and Death of Alleine,** 49; Nicholls, 3.

32. Haller, 59-62.

33. "Life of Blackerby," 59; "Life of Winter," 102, 111; **Life and Death of Alleine,** 110, 114.

34. G. Van Der Leeuw, **Religion in Essence and Manifestation,** 2 vols. (1938; rpt. New York: Harper & Row, 1963), I, 236-239.

35. White, 165; Samuel Clark, **A General Martyrologie, Containing a Collection of All the Greatest Persecutions Which have Befallen the Church of Christ, From the Creation, to our Present Times** (London, 1677), 539-544.

36. "Life of Blackerby," 59; Gale, 22-23.

37. Gale, 1-2, 36, 66.

38. Norton, 47-48.

39. "Life of Blackerby," 63-65.

40. Janeway, 24; "Life of Blackerby," 63; "Life of Winter," 104-108.

41. "Life of Blackerby," 59.

42. "Life of Katherine Clark," 152; Janeway, 46; Norton, 15; **Life and Death of Alleine**, 100.

43. Norton, 26; "Life of Katherine Clark," 154-155; Gale, 88, 121; **Life and Death of Alleine**, 42, 45.

44. Gale, sig. A9^{v}, p. 55; "Life of Katherine Clark," 154; Norton quoted in Isaac Backus, **A History of New England**, 2 vols. (Newton, Mass.: Backus Historical Society, 1871), I, 308.

45. "Life of Winter," 96, 103.

46. **Life and Death of Alleine**, 40, 97, 104, 113.

47. Janeway, 8, 22, 30ff.

48. Nicholls, 5; Gale, 21-22.

49. "Life of Katherine Clark," 156; "Life of Blackerby," 58-59; Norton, 24; Nicholls, 4-5; **Life and Death of Alleine**, 39, 44-45, 131; Gale, sigs. A7^{r}-A8^{v}, pp. 70, 77, 112; Janeway, 21, [91].

50. "Life of Katherine Clark," 154-156; William James, **The Varieties of Religious Experience** (New York: Collier Books, 1961), 229; Gale, 100-103; Nicholls, 14-16; "Life of Winter," 103; **Life and Death of Alleine**, 37, 42, 72, 107.

51. "Life of Winter," 103; Nicholls, 14; **Life and Death of Alleine**, 107; Gale, 100.

52. **Life and Death of Alleine**, 38.

53. Janeway, 8, 16-17, 60-61; **Life and Death of Alleine**, 38, 48-49, 66.

54. Gale, 97-98; Norton, 16; Janeway 73; **Life and Death of Alleine**, 40.

55. "Life of Katherine Clark," 157; Nicholls, 21; "Life of Winter," 98-99; Norton, 45; Gale, 115-116, 119; **Life and Death of Alleine**, 134.

56. Janeway, 40, 92, 98-107, 119; James, **Varieties of Religious Experience**, 56.

57. "Life of Katherine Clark, 152-153; Nicholls, 5; "Life of Winter," 99; Gale, 2, 48; Janeway, 2-3; Norton, 24; **Life and Death of Alleine**, 31-33.

58. Gale, 17; **Life and Death of Alleine**, 104; Norton, 18.

59. "Life of Katherine Clark," 152, 154; Janeway, 60; Gale, 21; "Life of Blackerby," 59.

60. Nicholls, 6; "Life of Winter," 102; "Life of Blackerby," 62; "Life of Katherine Clark," 154; Gale, 53-54; Norton, 27.

61. "Life of Winter," 102; "Life of Blackerby," 58; **Life and Death of Alleine**, 110, 132.

62. Cunningham, 22ff., 50-53.

HISTORIES AND HISTORIANS OF PORT-ROYAL

F. Ellen Weaver

University of Notre Dame

When the Cistercian monastery of Port-Royal became involved with the Jansenist controversies of the seventeenth century its fate became a matter of passionate interest to followers of monasticism, reform, theology, and even politics in its own time and for generations to come. The stance taken by the nuns of Port-Royal against authority, royal and ecclesial, has been pointed to by one of the scholars of the movement, Louis Cognet, as a paradigm of the rise of the consciousness of personal rights and individual conscience which was to characterize modernity. [1] The nuns themselves have been hailed as heroines and damned as heretics, depending upon the point of view of the historian undertaking the task of telling their story. But whatever the point of view, all historians have had to return eventually to one major source: the letters, journals, and tracts of the members of the Port-Royal group. The only other major account based on first-hand experience and contemporary sources is the Jesuit history of Jansenism by René Rapin. [2] Thus Port-Royal can serve as another sort of paradigm: a case study of the manner in which the same materials are handled by historians of various periods and persuasions.

What is attempted here, in necessarily brief compass, is to sketch out the history of these histories of Port-Royal: first, the work of the nun who served as historiographer of the movement; next the manner in which the manuscripts were collected and edited in the eighteenth century; and then the succession of those who worked, sometimes from the manuscripts directly and sometimes from the eighteenth century editions, to retell and increasingly to analyze the story of Port-Royal.

Angélique de Saint-Jean Arnauld d'Andilly was the niece

of the reformer abbess, Mère Angélique, and the leader of the young nuns who led the opposition to the signature of the Formulary condemning the Five Propositions of Jansenius. Brought up by the nuns of Port-Royal, and especially her famous aunts Mère Angélique and Mère Agnes, to whom she was entrusted for education at the age of six, Angélique de Saint-Jean made her religious profession in 1644 at the age of twenty. By 1648 she had been given charge of the novices of Port-Royal des Champs. We know from her correspondence that she was close in affection to Mère Agnes but looked to Mère Angélique for guidance in important matters. [3] She was intelligent, well educated, ardently devoted to the community, and had a flair for letters. She was the obvious choice when the nephew of Mère Angélique, and first of the disciples of Saint-Cyran to enter the retreat at Port-Royal, [4] Antoine Le Maître, decided that the time had come to get into writing the story of the reform of Port-Royal. Mère Angélique was growing old, and so were the nuns who had aided her in the restoration at Port-Royal of the Rule of St. Benedict and the usages of the Order of Citeaux. Le Maître commissioned Angélique de Saint-Jean to begin to collect all the accounts possible of the nuns involved, as well as those who had known Mère Angélique in other capacities, and to set down whatever she herself remembered of the words and actions of her aunt.

In the preface to these accounts she tells us that she began in 1652 to work on these **Mémoires.** Around 1654 Le Maître and Angélique de Saint-Jean prevailed upon Singlin, the confessor of Mère Angélique, to order her under obedience to write her own account of the reform. This she did, reluctantly, but broke off after recounting only the early years of the reform. The work of Angélique de Saint-Jean was also interrupted several times, as she added duties as sub-prioress to those of novice mistress. After the death of Mère Angélique in 1661, however, it seemed more than ever imperative to write down all that could be remembered of her and her work, and Angélique de Saint-Jean was able to gather a large number of accounts of many nuns who had known the abbess. At this point Mère Agnes added her persuasion. After the death of Mère Agnes, Angélique de Saint-Jean tells us that she took time to review and order all the accounts and to finish her own up to the establishment of the new house in Paris. The balance she commends to posterity and she signs the preface, "Port-Royal des Champs, ce 26 fevrier 1673." [5]

A major reason for the interruptions in her work, of course, was that during the period 1664 to 1669 the nuns, and especially Angélique de Saint-Jean as a leader, were suffering various degrees of persecution because of their refusal to sign the Formulary. This period, however, produced two other important sources for historians of Port-Royal: the journals kept by the nuns during the period of persecution (and beyond--since the habit had been set), and a particularly fascinating genre, the so-called **Relations de la captivité**. The "captivity" referred to is the dispersion of the leaders of the opposition to various convents in the area where it was hoped that isolation, persuasion by the nun guardians who represented the pro-Formulary faction, and individual questionings by the archbishop and/or his envoy, would persuade the refractory nuns to sign. The **Relation** of Angélique de Saint-Jean is a classic of this genre. [6]

A final group of important sources includes the necrologies, letter collections, and personal notes and works of piety. [7] The remarkable thing about this material is that the large majority of it was directly written or edited by Angélique de Saint-Jean. Whenever the historian pushes back to the primary manuscript material he or she must ultimately trust that the person who wrote the letter or other account had an accurate perception of the event recorded. Usually it is safest to balance this version against another first-hand account. In this case other first-hand descriptions of what happened within the monastery simply are not available; and, although the accounts we have bear the names of many nuns, we must always be aware that one nun listened to them and wrote them down, or read them and corrected them, ordered and selected them. One of the historians of the eighteenth century, Dom Clemencet appended to his edition of the **Conférences de Mère Angélique de Saint-Jean** [8] a list of the writings of Angélique de Saint-Jean. [9] A comparison of this list with titles of the collections made of Port-Royal papers is revealing. There is, as indicated, very little that did not come under the eye and the pen of the niece of Mère Angélique. (A notable exception would be the **Mémoires** of the members of the hermit scholars, the "Messieurs de Port-Royal.")

In another place I have examined the implications of this. One is that the Port-Royal material allows us to examine the way in which chronicle- and myth-making coalesce. Louis Cognet has commented on the fact that the copious publications of **Mémoires, Histoires, Recueils** and so on by the Port-Royalists of the eighteenth century (mainly the appellants) cannot be said to give us a true knowledge of the profound aspects of the problem, but that it is a "Port-Royal mythique," reconstructed in the hearts and minds of this group who maintained a tradition connecting them with the messieurs and the nuns of the seventeenth century, their heros, heroines, and martyrs. [10] I would date this mythic Port-Royal earlier. I would suggest that the pressure of persecution inflated the work of the reformer abbess in the eyes of her niece even beyond the reverence for the founder or foundress which is usual in the second generation of a religious order recently founded or reformed. We know that Angélique de Saint-Jean burned the notes and letters of one of the abbesses of Port-Royal whose spirituality did not fit the model she had developed of the spirituality bequeathed by Mère Angélique. [11] How much more she did to mold the materials to her own perception of the reform and the ideal of Port-Royal one can only conjecture. Educated guesses may come very close, I believe, when all the facts that can be known are assembled. On the one hand we know that the Port-Royalists were lovers of history. Some of them, like Le Nain de Tillemont, were pioneers in historical criticism in an era when for most, as E. T. Dubois comments of Rapin, "history was . . . still largely considered as a literary genre" or, especially by the Jesuits, as a form of rhetoric. [12] We know something of the high ideals Angélique de Saint-Jean held for herself and for her community from the writings of her youth, and particularly from the **Relation de la Captivité**. We know that her final years were spent as abbess of the community as it entered into the last stage of persecution--it was she who presided at the profession of the last nun to take vows at Port-Royal, and that was an exception made because of legal obligation to carry out the stipulations of the will of a benefactress who had endowed a place for a choir nun. We know that she spent many of these last years struggling to obtain approbation from Rome for the new Constitutions, and to maintain other reform features of Port-Royal. There are legal and other records to document these events. I believe this allows one to say with a certain confidence that her accounts are historically accurate, although colored by a heroic, perhaps tragic, view of the mission of the Order and the movement.

In the history of reform movements it is ironic, but often true, that nothing succeeds like persecution. The stories of the founders, the necrologies and the pious writings of religious communities that lead uneventful lives moulder in attics, and the manuscripts of monasteries of unchallenged orthodoxy are used to wrap the pears for winter storage. Those of persecuted communities are sought, preserved, and reproduced with devotion. When, in 1709, the nuns of Port-Royal were dispersed one final time they managed to take some of their records with them. But nuns were old and few. Already in 1709 friends of the monastery, alerted to the delivery of the final blow, had begun to gather what they could of the precious relics--that is of the manuscripts--but most of the archives remained in the monastery. Before the monastery was razed in 1713 the policeman d'Argenson seized these archives. The next stage in the history of histories of Port-Royal is the story of the recovery and transmission of the manuscripts, and the formation of a society--in its inception only a fund--which supported their publication.

Symbolic of the personal nature of so much of this history is the fact that the best resumé of the story of the manuscript collections is a privately circulated pamphlet by a woman who stands in a direct line with the first friends of Port-Royal to rally to the cause of the preservation of its memory and whose account includes elements transmitted by oral history: Cécile Gazier. One of the important manuscript collections is conserved at the Bibliothèque de Port-Royal, where members of the Gazier family have been custodians since the turn of the twentieth century. Another significant feature of the history, which Cécile Gazier represents, is that the history of the manuscript collection is to a large extent women's history. But, let this be seen in the telling. [13]

Let us consider first the manuscript collection that owes its existence to Marie-Scholastique de Menilles de Themericourt. Mademoiselle Themericourt was one of the children who were sent home from the monastery in 1679 when the archbishop of Paris ordered that no more children could be accepted for education at Port-Royal, no more postulants received, no more professions made. Angélique de Saint-Jean was abbess. "La petite de Menilles" was eight years old. Like many others of these young women who had been in contact with Port-Royal at an early age, she never married and she kept in touch with the nuns. It is likely that she began her collection of documents before the dispersion of the nuns in 1709. What is sure is that she collected as many autographs of the members of Port-Royal as she could find, and copied many others. Mademoiselle Themericourt was the niece of abbé Jean Baptiste Le Sesne d'Etemare, who played an important role in the Church of Utrecht, which is sometimes referred to as the Jansenist Church of Utrecht because of the support it received from Pasquier Quesnel and other Jansenist theologians in exile there in the eighteenth century. [14] The abbé d'Etemare was too involved in the controversial issues concerning the appellants (of the papal Bull Unigenitus) and affairs of the Jansenists in exile in the Lowland to be much interested in the collection of the papers of the nuns, and gave them up easily to the canon lawyer and Jansenist polemicist, Adrien Le Paige. Le Paige treasured them along with the many other Port-Royal manuscripts and printed works which he collected throughout his life. When Le Paige died in 1801, impoverished by the Revolution and blind, his library, one of the richest of the time, passed to the Messieurs Roch and Amable Paris. The Messieurs Paris had bought it earlier to aid Le Paige at the end of his life, and it is surmised that they were acting for a society to which they belonged, the Société de Saint-Augustin (today the Société de Port-Royal) which administered a fund said to have originated with Pierre Nicole.

The Le Paige Library was moved to the residence of the Paris brothers, where it was frequented by Victor Cousin among others. By 1845 both brothers had died and the Society took possession of the library. By this time this Society had already become proprietor of the ruins of Port-Royal and of a house at 169 rue Saint-Jacques, where the Le Paige collection--including most of the Themericourt manuscripts--is housed today. [15] Others of the manuscripts collected by Mademoiselle Themericourt found their way to the Bibliothèques Nationale and Arsenal in Paris and the Bibliothèque Municipale in Troyes.

What is known as the St-Germain collection was preserved thanks to another woman, Françoise-Marguerite de Joncoux, a long-time friend of the monastery. At Port-Royal, as Mademoiselle Gazier has said, "on etait copiste par piètè." Letters of Saint-Cyran, Singlin, Mère Angélique, Mère Agnes, Mère Angélique de Saint-Jean, Antoine Arnauld, and so on, were copied upon reception or before being sent. The same is true of the **Relations**, the **Constitutions**, the **Conférences** and all the various papers of the nuns as well as the letters and **mémoires** of the Messieurs. When the end was approaching some of these were given to friends to take care of, and some were preserved in the archives of Port-Royal. When in 1709 the policeman d'Argenson seized the archives of Port-Royal, he was prompted by a scruple of conscience, which according to Gazier was in keeping with the judicial mores of the time. He did not destroy them. Instead he gave them to Mademoiselle Joncoux. In 1709 she had but six years to live. This time she used to transcribe and have transcribed the autographs given to her. At her death she willed them to a benedictine friend, Dom Duret, who deposited them in the library of Saint-Germain-des--Pres. This collection was one of the richest which at the Revolution went to the Bibliotheque Nationale, where it is known as the Fonds Saint-Germain. When Joncoux died in 1715 her work was continued by Themericourt. Louis Cognet, has noted that, oddly enough, there is no evidence to allow us to believe that these women worked together.

After the death of Mesdemoiselles Joncoux and Themericourt the copying continued. Themericourt died in 1745 having spent her life copying, perhaps having printed, all she could find of the Port-Royal manuscripts. Madeleine de Boullogne, a painter and Madeleine Hortemals, an engraver, added their talents to preserve the images of Port-Royal, copying all available seventeenth century works, including the paintings of Philippe de Champagne.

In the nineteenth century two sisters, whose brother was a member of the Société de Saint-Augustin, took up the task. Sophie and Rachel Gillet spent their life collecting books to add to the collection at 169 rue Saint-Jacques, as well as engravings and paintings and by 1906 had added some 10,000 volumes to the library. These two worked throughout their lives to collect and make copies of everything concerning Port-Royal held in libraries in France and abroad. They copied everything lacking to the Bibliothèque de Port-Royal or catalogued it. They also had printed many of the Themericourt manuscripts left by abbé d'Etemare. Rachel Gillet edited the letters of Mère Agnes for which Prosper Faugère wrote the preface and signed his name in 1858. They also prepared for publication the letters of Mère Angélique de Saint-Jean. This manuscript, carefully copied, annotated and indexed in the fine legible hand of Rachel Gillet, is one of the most valuable manuscripts at the Bibliothèque de Port-Royal.

Sophie Gillet was blind in her last years, but Rachel continued to work at the librarie on rue Saint-Jacques. It was she who accepted into the library Augustin Gazier, who became her successor as custodian of the library in 1872.

Augustin Gazier authored the important **Histoire Générale du Jansénisme** [16] and, with the collaboration of his niece Cécile Gazier, edited the **Mémoires de Godefroi Hermant.** [17] Mademoiselle Gazier became the archivist of the Bibliothèque de Port-Royal, and authored several books herself. Among them the most valuable is the **Histoire du Monastère de Port-Royal,** for which she used some of the unedited manuscripts of the library. [18] She left unpublished a critical edition of the **Mémoires de Fontaine,** a much needed correction of the flawed eighteenth century publication of this important work of one of the Messieurs. The Gazier custodianship of the Bibliothèque de Port-Royal was continued by the daughter of Augustin Gazier, Marie Gazier, and then the present custodian, André Gazier, brother of Augustin. [19]

This tracing out of the destiny of the manuscript collections has led into the twentieth century. But the history of histories must now return to the publications of the eighteenth. And first a word should be said about the funds which supported these printings, mostly on the Elzevier presses in Holland, sometimes on clandestine presses in France. The tradition is that the idea of a society (Amis de la Verité) was born in the heart of a servant of Nicole named Perette who economized from household funds to save up money in a box which she left to Nicole at her death, and which became the "boîte a Perette," a fund for the needy, eventually a fund for the society. There is no historical basis for this story, but elements of it can be found in fact. There did exist at Port-Royal a fund for the needy through which friends of the monastery when they were forced into exile were able to live, and by means of which Port-Royal material was published. Further, there is the fact that Nicole in his will organized a durable foundation. The three executors of his will were the first administrators of this fund of about 40,000 francs. They invested the fund wisely, and it was passed along by Port-Royalists. It was used, as Nicole had willed, to support the needy, to sustain the religious communities dedicated to the education of the poor (the Soeurs de Sainte-Marthe and the Frères des Écoles Saint-Antoine), to pay for the publications of the Society--and eventually--to purchase the ruins of Port-Royal and the building and collections at 169 rue de Saint-Jacques.

Whether paid for out of the "boîte à Perette" or other means, what is sure is that the Port-Royalist publications in the eighteenth century were abundant. First to appear were simple, non-critical editions of the manuscripts. Some such had been printed in the life-time of the monastery. The preface of an early edition of the **Relation** of Angélique de Saint-Jean in the **Histoire Abregée de Port-Royal** edited by Michel Tronchay [20] in 1710 is illuminating in this regard. He tells us that fifteen or twenty years earlier a copy of this **Relation,** "having falled into the hands of a printer, he began printing; and in fact there were five or six pages printed." [21] The nuns, he continues, were disturbed by this and paid the printer to recover the printing. Now, however, Tronchay points out, things are changed. The "holy place is no more." The time has come for the world to know the truth. [22]

Tronchay is a typical representative of the first group to rush into print. He was one of the messieurs de Port-Royal, a companion of the historian Le Nain de Tillemont, and had a sister who was a nun in the monastery. The conversations of Antoine Le Maître made up the greater part of a collection published in 1714: the rare **Mémoires et Relations sur ce qui c'est passé à Port-Royal des Champs depuis le commencement de la réforme du cette abbaye.** [23] Others of the messieurs set down their **Mémoires,** or kept journals, and these were published between 1736 and 1740. [24]

Most important for the history of Port-Royal, however, were the publications of the materials written and collected by Angélique de Saint-Jean, referred to above. In 1734 abbé Claude Goujet, one of the canons of the church of Sainte-Genevieve and the scholar responsible for the first **Vie de Nicole,** edited these papers under the title **Mémoires pour servir à l'histoire de Port-Royal.** [25] In 1742 the Le Maître collection and the material in Goujet (which had included some of Le Maître) together with many hitherto unedited manuscripts made up the three volume **Mémoires pour servir à l'histoire de Port-Royal et à la vie de la Reverende Mère Marie-Angélique de Sainte Magdelaine Arnauld, réformatrice de ce monastère** which was published in Utrecht. With this publication most of the Angélique de Saint-Jean materials on Mère Angélique and the reform of Port-Royal became available in printed form. Accounts of some of the lesser and later nuns became available when abbé Pierre LeClerc published the **Vies interessantes et édifiantes des religieuses de Port-Royal** in 1750-52. [26] The Necrologies had appeared beginning in 1723. [27]

Besides these editions of the Port-Royal papers, the eighteenth century produced significant histories by scholars working independently, in various manuscript collections, and often, unfortunately, at odds with one another. The one thing they agreed upon was their extreme devotion to the now mythic Port-Royal, and to the cause of Jansenism, even to the point of risking exile and imprisonment. The first to produce a **Histoire générale du Jansénisme** was the volatile defender of freedom of conscience, Dom Gabriel Gerberon. [28] (Racine had written a history of Port-Royal up to 1665 much earlier, probably around 1692, but it was not published until the end of the eighteenth century. [29]) Gerberon had transferred from the Oratory to the Benedictines of St. Maur, both communities sympathetic to Jansenism. His support of the Jansenists forced him into exile and he wrote his history in Holland. There in 1703 he was arrested with Quesnel and returned to Paris for imprisonment. Another benedictine of St. Maur, Dom Clemencet wrote a **Histoire générale de Port-Royal,** 10 volumes published in Amsterdam in 1755, [30] and a valuable **Histoire Littéraire de Port-Royal,** which is available only in manuscript form at the Bibliothèque Mazarine in Paris. [31] It is possible that Clemencet worked in the Themericourt manuscripts. Jerome Besoigne, a doctor of the Sorbonne who lost his position there and went into exile in the Lowlands because of his Jansenist sympathies, probably worked in the Joncoux collection at Saint-Germain-des-Pres to produce his six volume **Histoires de l'Abbaye de Port-Royal,** [32] published in 1752. In 1755-56 the seven volume **Mémoires historiques et chronologiques sur l'abbaye de Port-Royal des Champs (depuis la Paix de l'Eglise)** appeared from the presses of Utrecht. The author, Pierre Guilbert, a tonsured cleric, may have had access to the manuscripts of the Arnauld family at the chateau Pomponne. The quarrel among these three later historians is one of the less edifying episodes in the history of Port-Royal. [33] A handwritten note on the flyleaf of the copy of Guilbert in the Jesuit collection at Chantilly states:

> This work is without argument the best which the Jansenists have composed on Port-Royal. The author, abbé Pierre Guilbert, although fond of the Arnaulds, does not espouse the blind hatred of the Nouvelles Ecclesiastiques [the Jansensist journal and mouthpiece], of Besoigne, etc. [34]

In 1786, on the eve of the French Revolution, a pious laywoman, Mademoiselle Poulain, added a **Nouvelle Histoire abregée de l'abbaye de Port-Royal,** a four volume work which is more or less a resumé of Racine and Besoigne. [35]

As the years pass the amount of scholarship piles up, and it would be impossible to treat the nineteenth and twentieth century studies in the detail that was possible for the beginnings. The histories of Port-Royal, as all histories, reflect the age in which they were written. But in a particular way they also reflect the position of the writer on the issue of whether or not the Port-Royalists were heretical, and until the later twentieth century one senses a personal involvement of the writer with the subject.

Perhaps an analogy would be reformation studies. Four hundred years passed before scholars on both sides could raise critical questions in an unemotional way with regard to the material. After two hundred years of distance some scholars of French Jansenism are beginning to be able to do the same. To illustrate the various ways in which the story of Port-Royal has been told--working always from the same manuscript and early printed material--I have chosen some examples which I consider significant for a variety of reasons.

One significant feature of the histories of Port-Royal is the number of women involved. The role of women as copyists has been recounted. Following Mademoiselle Poulain a number of French women contributed to the growing volume of histories of Port-Royal, concentrating especially on Mere Angelique. **[36]** Among these the works of Cécile Gazier, mentioned above, stand out.

More unexpected, and interesting for that reason among others, is the number of British women who became quite fascinated with Port-Royal in the nineteenth and early twentieth centuries. As Ruth Clark has shown in her excellent study of the connections between England and Port-Royal, **[37]** much of the Jansenist literature was translated into English in the seventeenth and eighteenth centuries, and from the beginning there was a strong affinity between the Church of England and the Port-Royalists. The Angélique de Saint-Jean collection was, however, introduced into England by Hannah More (died 1833), the religious writer, philanthropist and friend of Dr. Samuel Johnson. In her enthusiasm for the reform of Port-Royal she sent a number of the books she had collected to a friend, Mrs. Mary Anne Schimmelpenninck. Mrs. Schimmelpenninck, a Quaker who was greatly attracted to the Roman Catholic Church, was completely charmed by what she found. She made a kind of pilgrimage to visit the ruins of Port-Royal, and met some of the circle of friends of the former monastery. Then she set to work translating selections of the material, published as **Select Mémoires of Port-Royal** in 1829. **[38]** Charles Beard credits Mrs. Schimmelpenninck with "having rescued this subject from the neglect of almost a Century." **[39]**

Mrs. Schimmelpenninck in the Introduction to her **Select Mémoires** presents the "celebrated Institution of Port-Royal" as "that brilliant but brief light of Catholic Christendom," a "learned and religious society, who distinctly taught justification by faith, and who were assiduously occupied in the universal dissemination of the Scriptures." She expresses the hope that "the truly enlightened Protestant will rejoice at being presented with examples of eminent holiness in a church where his education may least have taught him to expect it." **[40]**

Frances Martin in 1873 wrote in novel form the story of **Angélique Arnauld, Abbess of Port-Royal**, "a Roman Catholic Abbess who lived more than 200 years ago, at a time when Pope and priest stood between the people and a God whom they feared but did not love." [41] Despite the fact, however, that Angélique "differs . . . in creed, ritual, and observance," the author clearly admires the abbess of Port-Royal, and urges the reader to "emulate the virtues which make Angélique Arnauld so noble and so great." [42]

The next two British women to write histories of Port-Royal come out of the Anglo-Catholic, or "High Church," tradition of the late nineteenth century. For them Port-Royal gathers up what I suspect are their own ambivalent attitudes toward Rome. Ella King Sanders writes in her 1905 **Angélique of Port-Royal:**

> To minds that are specially alive to the errors of Rome, Port-Royal seems to represent an oasis of Protestantism in a wilderness of bigotry and priestcraft, but such an impression is fatal to comprehension of the real spirit and intention of the Arnaulds and of the community of which that extraordinary family was the nucleus. Their work was crushed out of existence by the authority of the Church, it is true, but none the less, they have a part with her, and though sentence is passed upon them in her name, it was zeal for her honour that had led them to depart from the well-trodden paths that offered safety. [43]

Ethel Romanes in **The Story of Port-Royal** (1907) puts it this way:

> In writing this book, my purpose has been to show what kind of people, what sort of Christians, were the Port-Royalists. It seems strange on reading what the true Port-Royalists . . . write on the things which pertain to the Kingdom of God--that anyone should have ever charged them with, or credited them with, tendencies to unsacramental religion, Calvinism, or any heresy which the Church has condemned. Catholics they were; Ultra-montanists they were not. [44]

Two years later, in 1909, Mary E. Lowndes presented her book based on, and including, long excerpts from the narratives of the nuns, **The Nuns of Port Royal.** [45] Lowndes notes that she intends to counter the bias of Mrs. Schimmelpenninck toward insisting on the protestant elements in Port Royal, as well as the attempts of Sanders and Romanes to make the nuns and <u>messieurs</u> appear as faithful children of the Roman Catholic Church. "The present account," she contends, "insofar as it may claim to strike an individual note, would do so by complete impartiality, even indifference, on this point . . . and would gladly rouse a purely human interest in these nuns." [46]

This group is rounded off by the most ambitious attempt to offer a full history of Port-Royal in English, **The Enthusiasts of Port-Royal** by Lilian Rea. [47] Rea's use of enthusiasm (from the Greek entheos, "full of the god") to interpret the movement represents a move away from simple chronicle toward a more interpretive mode.

One more thing to note about this group of histories of Port-Royal, other than their authorship by women, is that all for one reason or another are sympathetic to the movement. This may simply be because they all write out of some degree of protestant affiliation. It might be worthwhile, though, to raise the question of whether or not this interest had anything to do with the rising feminist consciousness in nineteenth and early twentieth century England. Pursuit of this question is beyond the scope of this essay--and the present research of the author--but let it be raised.

As a matter of fact many of those sympathetic to Port-Royal are not so motivated by religious connections. The great Sainte-Beuve--and how could one write a history of histories of Port-Royal without mentioning its historian par exellence!--never committed himself to any Church, protestant or Catholic. He was drawn first by his appreciation of the literature of the Port-Royalists. One feels that he stayed out of fascinated attachment to Port-Royal. [48]

On the other hand, those whose histories of Port-Royal categorize the movement as heresy and the nuns as heretics are Catholic. The most virulent of these is by another woman, Margaret Trouncer. Her use of the materials is a striking example of how the same manuscript can be read to say opposite things. [49]

The works of Louis Cognet and Jean Orcibal turned the studies of Port-Royal in another direction; toward critical editions of the manuscripts, and critical, scholarly studies of various aspects of the movement. [50] Lucien Goldmann's marxist interpretation of the Port-Royal movement opened up new questions. [51] Recent studies by American scholars indicate that the work on the material to bring this important episode in the religious history of modern France before the English reading public is only beginning. [52]

Year after year scholars wend their way back to the libraries and archives of Paris, Utrecht, Troyes, and wherever a new collection of Port-Royal papers is discovered. Mostly they leaf through the much turned pages of the manuscripts of Angelique de Saint-Jean, the messieurs, and the early "friends of the truth." Their work is a vivid illustration of what every serious historian knows: "What actually happened" is an elusive quarry; but with patience, the right questions, and some good analytic tools the scent becomes stronger, and sometimes one is almost certain of having laid hold of a fleeting hoof.

NOTES

1. **Le Jansénisme** (Paris, 1968) 134-35, and in others of his works. This small book in the **Que sais-je?** series of the Presses Universitaires de France and Cognet's article in the **New Catholic Encyclopedia**, vol. VII, 820-24, are recommended as brief and accurate resumés of the movement. For the spirituality of Port-Royal see Cognet, **La Spiritualité Moderne** (Paris, 1966) "Le premier Port-Royal," 453-95.

2. **Histoire du Jansénisme,** published (very badly) by abbé Domenech in 1861 and **Mémoires de P. René Rapin** published by Leon Aubineau, 3 volumes (Paris, 1860-65). See the article "A Jesuit History of Jansenism," **Modern Language Review,** vol. 64 (1969) no. 4, 764-73 by E. T. Dubois for a good commentary on the value of Rapin's work.

3. See early letters of Angélique de Saint-Jean in the unpublished manuscript, "Lettres de la Mère Angélique de Saint-Jean copie par Rachel Gillet," Bibliothèque de la Société de Port-Royal (Paris), Mss Let. 358-61. Also the unpublished thesis of Brigitte Sibertin-Blanc, **Angélique de Saint-Jean Arnauld d'Andilly d'après sa correspondance de 1624 à 1669** (École des Chartes, Paris, 1962) 34-35, 52.

4. A group of these disciples, known as the "messieurs de Port-Royal" lived at the monastery from 1638 until 1648 during a period when Mère Angélique had moved the community to larger quarters in a new monastery, Port-Royal de Paris. In 1648 when part of the community returned to Port-Royal des Champs the messieurs moved to a nearby farm house, Les Granges, maintained today as a museum by the Société de Port-Royal.

5. [Goujet] **Relations sur la vie de la reverende Mère Angélique de Sainte Magdelaine Arnauld, ou Receuil de la Mère Angélique de Saint-Jean Arnauld d'Andilly sur la Vie de sa Tante la Mère-Angélique de Sainte Magdelaine Arnauld, & sur la réforme des Abbayes de Port-Royal, Maubuisson & Autres, faite par cette Sainte Abbess,** 3 volumes (S. 1., 1737), III:iii-vii. For more detailed analysis of this work see F. Ellen Weaver, **The Evolution of the Reform of Port-Royal. From the Rule of Citeaux to Jansenism** (Paris, 1978) 125-27.

6. The critical edition is Cognet, **Relation de Captivité d'Angélique de Saint-John Arnauld d'Andilly** (Paris, 1954).

7. See comments in Weaver, 128-29.

8. 3 volumes (Utrecht, 1760).

9. Ibid., III:329-47.

10. **Le Jansénisme,** 121. See also Weaver, 130-131.

11. [Goujet] **Mémoires pour servir à l'histoire de Port-Royal,** 3 volumes (S. 1., 1734), II:308. (Note this is the work of which volume three bears another title, **Relations sur la vie . . .** as given in note 5 above.) The nun was Mère Geneviève le Tardiff. See comments in Weaver, 135.

12. "A Jesuit History of Jansenism," 764. See Bruno Neveu's fine study of a major historian of Port-Royal, **Un Historien à l'école de Port-Royal. Sebastien Le Nain de Tillemont,** 1637-1698 (La Haye, 1966).

13. **Histoire de la Société et de la Bibliothèque de Port-Royal. Avant-propos de Louis Cognet** (Paris, 1966). I owe to this pamphlet in the main the following account of the manuscript collections and the society.

14. For a full account of this Church of Utrecht see E. Preclin, **Les Janséninstes du XVIIIe siècle et la Constitution civile du clergé: La Développement du richerisme, sa propagation dans le bas clergé, 1713-1791** (Paris, 1929), especially 197ff; Augustin Gazier, **Histoire Générale du Mouvement Janséniste. Dupuis ses origines jusqu'a nos jours,** 2 volumes (Paris, 1924) II:30-33 and elsewhere; and M. G. Spiertz, **L'Église Catholique des Provinces-Unies et le Saint-Siege Pendent la Deuxieme Moitié du XVIIe Siècle** (Louvain, 1975).

15. For a brief but illuminating account of the Bibliothèque de Port-Royal see Richard M. Golden, "The Bibliothèque de la Société de Port-Royal," **French Historical Studies,** vol. XII, No. 2 (Fall 1979) 278-80.

16. 2 volumes (Paris, 1924).

17. (Paris, 1905) Godfroi Hermant a canon of Beauvais & doctor of the Sorbonne, was a friend of Antoine Arnauld. Sainte-Beuve categorizes him as contentious (see Ste-Beaux **Port Royal,** ed. of 1953, I:519).

18. (Paris, 1929), **Les Belles Amies de Port-Royal** (Paris, 1930) is less scholarly, but useful.

19. Monsieur André Gazier was still presiding when I visited the Bibliothèque de Port-Royal in 1979, but I always fear I will not find him on my next visit. He is very old and frail.

20. (Paris, 1710).

21. Ibid., 95.

22. Ibid.

23. (S. 1.)

24. Nicolas Fontaine (1625-1709), **Mémoires pour servir à l'histoire de Port-Royal,** 2 volumes (Utrecht, 1736); Thomas du Fosse (1634-1698) **Mémoires pour servir à l'histoire de Port-Royal** (Utrecht, 1739); Claude Lancelot (1634-1698) **Mémoires touchant la vie de M. de Saint-Cyran,** 2 vols. (Cologne, 1738). These are reissued with added material as **Recueil de Plusieurs Pieces pour servir à l'histoire de Port-Royal. Ou supplement aux Mémoires de Messieurs Fontaine, Lancelot et Du Fosse** (Utrecht, 1740).

25. 3 volumes (S. 1.) see Note 11 above.

26. 4 volumes (S. 1.)

27. [Dom Rivet de la Grange] **Nécrologe de l'Abbaye de Nostre Dame de Port-Royal** (Amsterdam, 1723); [Hughes Le Febvre de St-Marc] **Supplément au Nécrologe de l'Abbaie de Nostre Dame de Port-Roial des Champs** (S. 1., 1735); [René Cerveau] **Nécrologe des plus célèbres défenseurs et confesseurs de la verité & Supplément au Nécrologe,** 7 volumes (S. 1., 1760-78).

28. 3 volumes (Amsterdam, 1700). On Gerberon's position see Alexander Sedgwick, **Jansenism in Seventeenth Century France. Voices from the Wilderness** (Charlottesville, VA, 1977) 178-80, 189.

29. See notes in Jean Racine, **Abrégé de l'Histoire de Port-Royal,** edited by Augustin Gazier (Paris, 1908) vii-xiii.

30. 10 volumes (Amsterdam, 1755).

31. Max. Mss 4533-4539.

32. (Cologne, 1752).

33. For details see Cognet in the preface to C. Gazier, **Histoire de la Société de Port-Royal,** 3; also A. Gazier, **Histoire générale du Jansénisme,** II:127-8.

34. Translation mine.

35. (Paris).

36. Guillaume Dall [pseudonym of Madame Lebaudy], **La Mère Angélique, abbess de Port-Royal, d'après sa correspondance** (Paris, 1898) is a small book written from a very sympathetic viewpoint, but with little scholarly, critical depth; M. R. Monlaur [pseudonym of Madame Reynes], **Angélique Arnauld** (Paris, 1901) is a polemical pamphlet and is full of inaccuracies; Jane Pannier, **La Mère Angélique** (Paris, 1931) is a brief account written for the "Je sers" series by a protestant with a good comprehension of the material.

37. **Strangers and Sojourners at Port-Royal** (Cambridge, 1932; rpt. New York, 1972).

38. 3 volumes (London, 1829). Ms Schimmelpenninck later became a Moravian, and perhaps Methodist--moves in the direction of Rome.

39. **Port-Royal. A Contribution to the History of Religion and Literature in France,** 2 volumes (London, 1861) I:vi-vii.

40. Schimmelpenninck, xix.

41. (London, 1873) v.

42. Ibid., vi.

43. [First edition gives author as A. K. H.] **Angélique of Port-Royal** (London, 1905) xxvi.

44. (London, 1907), vii.

45. (London) 1.

46. Ibid., viii.

47. (London, 1912).

48. **Port-Royal,** edited with notes by Maxime Leroy, 3 volumes (Paris, 1953).

49. **The Reluctant Abess** (New York, 1957). An example of using a manuscript to reflect your own point of view is the famous characterization of the nuns by Archbishop Perefixe as "pure as angels and proud as devils." Trouncer presents this as a quite literal description of the heretics. Actually the quotation appears in the nuns' own journal of 1661 and they report it to illustrate the extent to which the archbishop lost his temper in the course of the interrogations of the nuns.

50. To the works of Louis Cognet already mentioned should be added: **La réforme de Port-Royal** (Paris, 1950), **Mère Angélique et St François de Sales** (Paris, 1951), **Les Petites écoles de Port-Royal** (Paris, 1953), and numerous articles. Jean Orcibal's major works are the **Les Origines du Jansénism: I. Correspondance de Janseius** (Paris, 1947); **II. Jean Duvergier de Hauranne, abbé de Saint-Cyran et son temps, 1581-1638** (Paris, 1947); **III. Saint-Cyran et son temps, appendices, bibliographie et tables** (Paris, 1948); **IV. La Spiritualité de Saint-Cyran avec ses écrits de piété inédits** (Paris, 1962) and more directly connected with the history of Port-Royal: **Port-Royal entre le miracle et l'obéissance. Flavie Passart et Angélique de Saint-Jean** (Paris, 1957).

51. **Le Dieu Caché, étude sur la vision tragique dans les Pensées de Pascal et dans le théâtre de Racine** (Paris, 1955).

52. In addition to the works of Weaver and Sedgwick mentioned above (notes 5, 28) there is the important work of Dale Van Kley who worked in unedited materials in the Le Paige collection: **The Jansenists and the Expulsion of the Jesuits from France, 1757-1765** (New Haven and London, 1975); and one of the first to take the episode of the convulsionaries seriously: B. Robert Dreiser, **Miracles, Convulsions, and Ecclesiastical Politics in Early Eighteenth-Century Paris** (Princeton, 1978).

EARLY AMERICAN METHODIST MINISTERIAL EDUCATION

Robert C. Monk

McMurry College

The religious societies which gathered around the preaching of John and Charles Wesley from their beginning depended on laypersons to exhort, examine, encourage, and supervise each other. John Wesley's decision to allow laymen to preach has traditionally been understood to have been a reluctant one influenced by his mother after she urged him to hear one of his laymen, Thomas Maxfield, preach. Frank Baker suggests that perhaps this incident, so often cited as the beginning of the use of lay assistants and preachers, really began with Wesley's use of Charles Delamotte as a lay assistant in America when he was a missionary here. [1] In any case, Wesley early came to the realization that laymen could effectively preach as well as serve as class leaders and exhorters. Therefore, when the movement grew too rapidly for the Wesleys and their relatively few sympathetic clergy colleagues to minister adequately to the societies, it was not surprising that they turned to laypersons to serve as itinerant pastors.

To use laymen in this capacity meant, however, that these pastors would need training for their expanded tasks. How was Wesley to train them? In time a two-fold pattern emerged. First, Wesley adopted the most convenient and perhaps the most effective pattern in a form of ministerial apprenticeship. Local society participation produced class leaders, exhorters, and ultimately local preachers who were natural assistants to the itinerating clergy. These persons, if they proved to be dedicated and effective in the local society tasks, were logical choices as persons who would itinerate and assist the clergy in their rounds. Learning by precept and example they then became independent itinerants themselves. This apprenticeship method proved very effective, giving the Wesleys a continuing supply of assistants.

The second element in the training came from Wesley's own dedication to education. As an Oxford Don he had spent much of his life teaching others and that training was adapted for his Methodist followers, particulary his preachers. Although drawn from the lower social classes where formal education was not stressed, Methodist laypreachers were expected to educate themselves under Wesley's tutorage. In the 1744 Minutes of the Methodist Annual Conference the preachers are instructed to "read the most useful books, and that regularly and constantly." When one of the preachers evidently commented, "But I have no taste for reading," Wesley responded, "Contract a taste for it by use, or return to your trade." [2]

If they had no books Wesley promised to supply them as fast as they could read them. A series of letters he exchanged with Joseph Benson in 1768 suggests that Wesley also intended that his preachers read only those books he thought profitable and in their proper order. [3] To assure that the preachers and other Methodists might be instructed, Wesley set out early in his career to provide them with what he considered to be appropriate reading material, which, if consistently used, would "educate" and assist them in their Christian life. Next to the scriptures, his own numerous works, particularly his **Sermons** and **Explanatory Notes on the New Testament**, became primary texts. To supplement these, he entered a life-long practice of publishing the works of other Christian leaders he felt would be instructive to the Methodist people. Most of these were abridged, sometimes extensively, and provided to his people in inexpensive binding for widespread dissemination. [4] Original and abridged publications ultimately amounted to more than 400 works in his lifetime. The most extensive and consistent abridgment project was published in the 1750's as **The Christian Library**, a fifty volume set of what Wesley termed the "choicest Pieces of Practical Divinity." Suggestions for other readings, beyond those he produced, were also numerous. Education denied the Methodists in their normal circumstances could and should, according to Wesley, be provided through this method of self-education. For the preachers it was a second but nonetheless vital aspect of their ministerial training.

Apprenticeship to an experienced preacher, albeit often rather brief, and a life-long pattern of reading became the corner stones of Methodist ministerial education for Wesley's "connection." The effectiveness of this two-fold method of ministerial training was repeatedly attested to by the success of the Methodist preachers. Although education among Methodists did not take on formal characteristics until Wesley began to support schools for the children of Methodist preachers, it was nevertheless one of the emphases of early Methodism in England.

American Methodist Ministry

Irish Methodist immigrants organized the first societies in this country in early 1766. Led by laymen, some of whom had been local preachers in Ireland, the societies appealed to Wesley for missionaries in 1769. Wesley responded by sending eight missionaries over a period of several years. As the movement expanded local ministers were enlisted for service in the societies. Their training followed the pattern Wesley had established in England. Jesse Lee, an American native, began to attend Methodist services when he was sixteen and recounts how he, over a period of years, took more and more responsibility moving from an exhorter to classleader to local preacher and ultimately to the traveling ministry. He began by agreeing rather reluctantly to travel in the company of Edward Drumgoole as he was laying out a new circuit in North Carolina. The success of the effort convinced him to continue. [5] Freeborn Garrettson recounts a similar process by which he entered into the ministry ultimately traveling with Thomas Rankin, one of Wesley's missionaries. [6] The experience of these men and many like them indicate that Wesley's pattern of apprenticeship was the principal means by which they were trained.

What of the second element of the British pattern? Lee in his history of American Methodism extensively quotes Wesley's regulations concerning education for ministers and recounts how Methodists in America early began to reproduce Wesley's works for ease of distribution in this country. [7] The few books mentioned by Garrettson relate to his early Christian experience before he became a Methodist. [8] Neither Lee nor Garrettson provide an extensive catalogue of their own readings, but they make it clear that reading was expected and pursued where possible. However, one is not left without insight into this important part of ministerial training in early America. The **Journals and Letters of Francis Asbury,** provide a graphic picture of one who took seriously Wesley's instructions that pastors continually educate themselves through reading. In doing so he set an example for other American pastors.

Francis Asbury and Education

Francis Asbury came to America in 1771 as one of the missionaries sent by Wesley. He was the only one of those missionaries to stay in this country through the revolution. By the end of the War, he was clearly the leader of American Methodism, exerting influence and authority matched by no other, and becoming so involved in the work in America that he never returned to

England. His contributions to American Methodists over his forty-five year ministry in this country earned him the title of the "father of American Methodism."

Asbury had dropped out of formalized education at the age of thirteen and entered into two successive apprenticeships to local craftsmen. While formal education was cut short, he appears to have been an able student as may be seen in his reading patterns throughout the rest of his career. [9] Asbury began his association with the Methodists at fourteen years of age and by the time he embarked for America was thoroughly established in their doctrinal emphases and disciplinary patterns. His entry into the Methodist itinerant ministry made him a "helper" to James Glassbrook. When Asbury set sail for America in 1771 he had been an itinerant Methodist preacher in John Wesley's English "connection" of religious societies for four years. [10]

Wesley's reluctant decision in 1784 to allow the establishment of an independent American Methodist church included a decision to ordain ministers in this new church. Asbury was the first to receive ordination and was appointed, along with Thomas Coke, another English missionary and ordained presbyter of the Church of England, to the joint "superintendency" of Methodism in America. Asbury, acutely sensitive to the American social and political scene, insisted on election to the office by vote of his fellow American preachers, rather than simply accepting Wesley's appointment. The office was quickly transformed into that of a Bishop, with Asbury later wielding the autocratic control over American Methodism which Wesley enjoyed, without the title, in England. By insisting on election, and at the same time taking the office of Bishop, Asbury effectively established two basic elements of American Methodist polity: a modified episcopacy supplemented by a representative policy making body.

His mature attitudes toward formal education were, at best, ambivalent. His one venture, along with Thomas Coke and the Methodist conference, in establishing a degree granting college, Cokesbury College in Maryland, ultimately failed and Asbury expressed as much relief as remorse at its demise. [11] As his **Journal and Letters** repeatedly suggest, he had a lively suspicion of a "learned" ministry--that is, one college or university trained. In his words, "Every candid inquirer after truth will acknowledge, upon reading church history, that it was a great and serious evil introduced, when philosophy and human learning were taught as a preparation for Gospel ministry." (II, 488). Or a similar statement quoted by William Duren: "It is said that there is a special call for learned men to the ministry; some may think so, but I presume a simple man can speak and write for simple, plain people, upon simple, plain truths." [12] While such sentiments certainly reflect a disdain for formalized ministerial education, they were intended to reflect that the preaching of the gospel did not require such education. In an address to Bishop McKendree late in Asbury's life, he comments, "I have not spoken against learning. I only said that it cannot be said to be an essential qualification to preach the gospel." (III, 481) These sentiments must be seen in the cultural context in which Asbury's ministry took place. In the America of his day, education was rudimentary; and formalized education tended to separate one from the common man--the section of society where Methodism was most effective and appreciated.

Indeed, Asbury was certainly not against general education. As a true Wesleyan, he was convinced that it was the Methodists "duty and privilege . . . to give the key of knowledge in a general way" to all persons willing to learn. It is from this concern that he could urge the establishment by every large society of a school house for Methodist children and others. His interest here was that the Methodists enjoy the rudiments of education in order to, at least, be able to read and improve themselves.

The clue to Asbury's attitude toward learning lies in his address to Bishop McKendree:

> Further, it may be asked, Is it proper to have no learned men among us? Answer: Men who are well read I call learned men; and we have men of learning among us, both traveling and local. Where are our young men who were bred to the law? and some are doctors; and many others who are very studious and making great progress in Latin and Greek; and many have competent knowledge of the English language. (III, 491)

The key for Asbury lay in his understanding that men who were well read were learned and educated men. Learning did not have to be formalized to take place; the patient and constant task of reading could provide it as well. Asbury certainly followed this precept in his own education, and the **Journals and Letters** often recommend this course to others. His attitude toward formalized education might be negative or at best ambivalent, but his attitude toward learning was equally as clear and positive.

Wesley's Writings as Asbury's Spiritual Guide

Asbury's own method of constant reading is well documented in the **Journal** beginning with his comments about his trip to this country. He recounts, "When I came to Bristol I had not one penney of money; but the Lord soon opened the hearts of friends, who supplied me with clothes, and ten pounds." (I, 4) If he had no money, he evidently carried with him a packet of books. Some three weeks later, while at sea, a journal entry records:

> I spent my time chiefly in retirement, in prayer, and in reading the Appeals, Mr. de Renty's Life, part of Mr. Norris Works, Mr. Edwards on the Work of God in New England, the Pilgrim's Progress, the Bible, and Mr. Wesley's Sermons. (1, 5)

This is a most interesting list for, with the exception of the Bible, they are all works of Wesley himself or works that he abridged. The Appeals no doubt refer to Wesley's **An Earnest Appeal to Men of Reason and Religion** and **A Farther Appeal to Men of Reason and Religion.** These works were Wesley's apology, defense, and explication of Methodist doctrine and practice. Wesley abridged **The Holy Life of Monr. de Renty, a late Nobleman of France**, a popular seventeenth century ascetic biography. Cambridge Platonist, John Norris' work, **A Treatise Concerning Christian Prudence,** was one of the first items abridged and published by Wesley. Wesley had also published Jonathan Edwards' **A Narrative of the late Work of God, at and near Northampton** and **Some Thoughts Concerning the Present Revival of Religion in New England.** Perhaps it is the latter of these to which Asbury refers. Asbury could have also had John Bunyan's **Pilgrim's Progress** in an abbreviated version published by Wesley. Wesley's **Sermons on Several Occasions** were printed in a variety of editions over a number of years and formed the standard body of sermons required of all Methodist preachers. With the exception of Wesley's **Appeals** and **Sermons,** each of these works dealt with the Christian life and practical piety; topics foremost in Asbury's readings throughout his ministry.

This list of works indicates that Asbury was certainly dependent, at least on this occasion, on Wesley and his publications. The fact that Asbury carried these works to America with him suggests the importance attached to reading and Wesley's directions for that reading in this early stage of American Methodism.

That Asbury should be appreciative of John Wesley and his spiritual guidance, particularly in his early years, is not surprising. The extent of this could hardly be more eloquently stated than this note written in March, 1798:

> I have also received much instruction and great blessings of late in reading Mr. Wesley's works. There is a certain spirituality in his works, which I can find in no other human compositions. And a man who has any taste for true piety, can scarce read a few pages in the writings of that great divine, without imbibing a greater relish for the pure and simple religion of Jesus Christ, which

> is therein so Scripturally and rationally explained and defended. (I, 263)

In Asbury's last address to the General Conference of the American Methodist church (which met in the year he died), he indicates that in those early years he had "almost laid aside all other books but the Bible, and applied himself exceeding closely in reading every book that Mr. Wesley had written." (III, 533) Events in the life of the nation, the church, and between the two men were to bring Asbury to a position of independence in later years and certainly his readings broadened, but the appreciation for Wesley's spiritual guidance in his writings and abridgments continued.

References in Asbury's **Journal** to specific Wesley works are most often to the **Sermons** and **The Explanatory Notes on the New Testament**, which would be most appropriate since these were the standard materials every Methodist preacher was to use as his guide to doctrine. Next to these stands Wesley's **Journal**, which Asbury found particularly inspiring. Wesley's **Works**, mentioned regularly, incorporated a number of different items, perhaps indicating a rather broad spectrum of Wesleyan materials. In addition to these, other specific references include **The Explanatory Notes on the Old Testament, A Calm Address to our American Colonies, A Calm Address to the Inhabitants of England** (works in opposition to the American Revolution), **A Plain Account of the People Called Methodists, Primitive Physic** (Wesley's practical guide to health cures and remedies), and **Hymns and Sacred Poems.** Asbury also notes reading extensively in **The Christian Library**, the multi-volume work of abridgment.

In addition to these specifically noted works by Wesley, Asbury refers to some twenty-three other works which he probably read in abridgments by Wesley. Obviously, whether he read them in full editions or as part of Wesley's publications is a matter of speculation since he most often mentions only titles. However, it would seem logical that he read them in editions published by Wesley as these were more likely to be available to him.

Although the specific list of Wesley writings is rather small, it would also seem appropriate to assume that Asbury read more widely in Wesley's materials than the list indicates. We are dependent on a journal record that cannot be assumed to be a complete summary of all his readings.

For Asbury, Wesley certainly held central place in his reading and contributed greatly to the molding of his thought and practice. Sometimes the dependence had become so great that even Asbury could not be sure of what was his thought and that of Wesley: "Some of his sentiments I have adopted, and thought them my own; perhaps they are not, for I may have taken them first from him." (I, 339) Yet, Asbury, as one might expect, certainly did not accept Wesley's teachings and interpretations without careful and judicious examination and occasional disagreement: "I have lately been reading Mr. W. on the ruin and recovery of man: he is a judicious writer, in the main, and generally illustrates his subjects well; but some of his sentiments relative to infants, I think are very exceptionable." (I, 94) [13]

Asbury's Other Readings

Asbury's **Journals and Letters** record comments or notations on some 194 different pieces of literature--most of them books. Of these, 164 are credited to 125 different authors. The others are uncredited and simple list titles. [14] By modern standards, such a list may appear slim, but it should be remembered that Asbury's situation was much different than our own and even from many pastors of his own day. He maintained no home throughout his ministry; therefore, he had no permanent library. He, like other Methodists, was dependent for books on what he might use from the libraries of others or those he might purchase in his travels. There also seems to have been a broad scale exchange of works among Methodists. As they came on useful books, they shared them; and obviously, Asbury gained many works this way. "Oh what a prize! Baxter's **Reformed Pastor** fell into my hands this morning." (II, 647) His greatest lament about the loss of Cokesbury College was that the college's library had been lost in the fire. (II, 75)

Dependence on the libraries of others is illustrated by Asbury's extensive catalogue of readings. During the revolution he could not travel freely between the colonies because some of them required oaths of allegiance and rejection of allegiance to England. Asbury, attempting to maintain neutrality in the war and a pacifist by religious conviction, could not accept such an oath and retired to the home of Judge Thomas White in Delaware. Judge White's well stocked library provided Asbury with an unusual opportunity for a wide range of reading during the several months when he could only itinerate in the local area.

Asbury clearly used every opportunity he was afforded to read. Using representative titles from the works which he notes throughout his journals and letters one is able to see the variety and extent of his study habits.

Scripture

Central to all of Asbury's reading was the scripture.

Hardly a day is recorded in the **Journal** without reference to Biblical readings or preaching from certain Biblical texts. He supplemented this Bible study with rather extensive consultation of the commentaries available to him. Wesley's **Notes** were an "especial blessing to my soul" during the revolutionary years when Asbury found himself confined to Delaware and unable to travel. (I, 266) He consulted J. A. Bengelius', **Gnomon Novi Testamenti,** on which Wesley had based a major portion of his **Notes.** John Guyse's **The Practical Expositor: An Exposition of the New Testament in the Form of a Paraphrase** and Phillip Doddridge's **The Family Expositor**, referred to by Asbury, had also been extensively used by Wesley. (II, 695; I, 100, 284) Asbury has particularly high praise for Doddridge's exposition "well calculated for forming of the minds of young preachers," although he disagreed with its suggestions on "the unconditional perseverance of saints." (I, 284) Henry Hammond's critical **Notes on the New Testament** was consulted. (I, 19) Readings in Martin Luther's **Commentary on Galatians** is noted without comment! (I, 261) Thomas Newton's **Dissertation on the Prophecies** afforded a "good key for many passages, but [he] confines himself too much to the literal meaning of the Revelation." (I, 127, 300) Asbury's fellow Methodist, Adam Clarke, began to publish a **Commentary with Critical Notes** during Asbury's lifetime. Asbury comments that he was well instructed by the work and yet amused for "He [Clarke] indirectly unchristianizes all old bachelors. Woe is me!" (II, 675)

Clearly, Asbury was well grounded in the scripture and much of the commentary upon it in his own day. He did not hesitate to accept that which he thought accurate and question that with which he could not agree. It should also be noted that he often studied the scriptures in Greek and Hebrew and evidently knew Latin. (I, 735; II, 144)

Doctrine

Asbury's basic doctrinal formulations were those given to him by Wesley; and while there was no emphasis in his **Journal** on other readings in "Divinity," this area was not neglected. Supplementing Wesley's doctrinal instructions, for Asbury, was John Fletcher's **Checks on Antinomianism** and **Further Checks.** Fletcher, an Anglican vicar and strong supporter of Wesley, substantiated Wesley's opposition to his Calvinistic critics. Asbury was especially complimentary of Fletcher's work, "the style and spirit in which Mr. Fletcher writes, at once bespeak the scholar, the logician, and the divine." (I, 128-9, 300, 330) He also has high praise for Fletcher's **Portrait of St. Paul.** (II, 400)

A work of an American contemporary, J. F. Ostervald, entitled **A Compendium of Christian Theology** was consulted by

Asbury and found "simple, plain, and interesting." (I, 745; II, 290) References to D's **Study of Divinity** leave one wondering what work this is, but Asbury found it of little value, except for the list of works on divinity it provided. (I, 568)

Jonathan Edwards' **Treatise Concerning the Religious Affections** (perhaps read in Wesley's abridged version) found Asbury praising it as a "very good treatise," particularly for young professors, except for the "small vein of Calvinism which runs through it." (I, 300-1) The sharpest theological differences between American Methodists and their fellow Christians were over Calvinistic tenets, particularly predestination. It is not surprising then that Asbury, during his retirement in Delaware, undertook a review of foundational documents of English Calvinism: **The Westminster Confession of Faith, The Assembly's Catechism, The Directory of Church Government**, and **The Form for Public Worship.** While he found these pieces were "calculated to convert the judgment, and make the people systematical Christians," he also commented "now I understand it [the **Confession**] better than I like it." (I, 322-23) Nevertheless, if one with these opinions had some insight to offer, Asbury was not hesitant to accept and to compliment its author: a Mr. Knox, of the West Indies, is much praised for providing a "sublime and spiritual" defense of "revealed religion" so that Asbury can "esteem him as one of the best writers amongest the Presbyterians I have yet met with." (I, 455)

Interest in broader theological issues includes notations on Uzal Ogden's **On Revealed Religion**, an answer to the "deistical, atheistical oracle of the day, Thomas Paine." (II, 54) Deism was also the interest in his notation of John Claget's comments on Thomas Chubb, an English Deist. (I, 363) Other interests are noted in his recommendation of Devereux Jarrett's answer to the Baptists and a similar work by Joseph Moore. (II, 795; I, 353)

To these may be added continual references to the doctrinal materials included in the **Form of Discipline** of the Methodist Episcopal Church. This **Discipline** became, in Asbury's lifetime, the basic manual of polity for the American Methodist church. It contained the **Articles of Religion** (Wesley's reduction of the Anglican **Thirty Nine Articles**), the doctinal passages of Wesley's **Larger Minutes,** and until 1808 a number of other theological tracts. In 1798 Asbury and Thomas Coke produced a series of **Notes on the Discipline** supplementing and explaining its distinctive Methodist theological emphases. (II, 117, 135)

Asbury was clearly familiar with doctrinal treatises and used them when appropriate as he emphasized and explained Methodist doctrine and argued against theological positions he opposed. Nevertheless, his central concern in the writings of divinity lay far more in those works which gave practical instruction in Christian living.

Practical Divinity

John Wesley's concern in the **Christian Library** to provide works of "Practical Divinity" actually reflects a broad interest in seventeenth and eighteenth century theology. Instruction in a dynamically active life modeled after the life of Christ was central to Christian writings of the day. It was this "practical" aspect of the application of the gospel to everyday living that captured the interest and attention of the age.

Among Asbury's choices in this area were some of Wesley's favorites. Thomas à Kempis' **Imitation of Christ** seems to have been Asbury's constant companion, being read and often referred to from 1775 to 1803. (I, 158; III, 263) Asbury also notes à Kempis' **Valley of Lilies** and wonders why Wesley never abridged it. (I, 383) William Law's **Serious Call to a Devout and Holy Life** and Jeremy Taylor's **The Rule and Exercise of Holy Living** were also important sources for him. (I, 248, 334, 152)

Puritans and Nonconformists wrote extensively in these areas and Asbury selects many works from these writers. Joseph Alleine's **An Alarm to Unconverted Sinners** and his **Letters** were consulted. (I, 771, 266) For Richard Baxter, Asbury had a special love and appreciation. Five of Baxter's works are noted with highest appreciation being expressed for his **Call to the Unconverted** which Asbury said was "one of the best pieces of human composition in the world, to awaken the lethargic souls of poor sinners." (I, 248) Baxter's **Saints' Everlasting Rest** along with Isaac Watt's **Treatise on the Rest of Separate Sinners** were called books in which we "find the marrow of Methodism; that is, pure religion, and sound doctrine which cannot be condemned." (I, 242) Asbury traditionally comments that he would like to read the **Saints' Rest** once each quarter. (I, 408) A less well known work of Baxter's **Poor Man's Family Book,** also finds commendation. (I, 711) John Bunyan's familiar works **Pilgrim's Progress** and **Holy War** were read with appreciation early in Asbury's American career. (I, 5, 268-69) His general opinion of some of these classical works and their usefulness is seen in this September 1793 comment:

> Our Americans are not fools; no books sell like those on plain, practical subjects; as the **Saints' Rest,** Baxter's **Call,** Alleine's **Alarm,** and Thomas à Kempis. (II, 771)

Works of a later time but concerned with the same practical divinity which Asbury read over the years included Phillip Doddridge's **Rise and Progress of Religion in the Soul** about which Asbury comments "I think an abridgment of this work would be a great service to our societies." (I, 268, 324; II, 302) An additional Nonconformist work, Thomas Watson's **A Body of Practical Divinity,** did not "comport" with Asbury's general sentiments, but two of the sermons on temptation were worthy of abridgment. (I, 297) Young's **Poems** (perhaps Edward Young's **The Complaint, or Night Thoughts on Life, Death, and Immortality**) along with John Mason's **Self-Knowledge** receive attention with complimentary comments. (I, 330, 158) These latter two were eighteenth century English writers. From the same period came one of the few works written by women noted by Asbury, Elizabeth Rowe's **Devout Exercises of the Heart.** (I, 668) This list of works of practical divinity might continue as these are only representative titles but it is obvious that this area attracted Asbury's repeated and constant attention.

Sermons

Supplementing the interest in practical divinity and perhaps a part of it was Asbury's regular reading of and attention to sermons. Asbury found John Wesley's **Sermons** a "particular blessing to my soul" throughout his ministry and as late as September, 1809, calls them "my study in divinity." (II, 615) To these many others were added through the years. He recounts how, when he was "awakened" to religion at about the age of fourteen before he joined the Methodists, he had begun to read the sermons of George Whitefield and John Cennick, early leaders of the evangelical revival. (I, 721) John Brandon, a seventeenth century divine, through his meditations greatly "melted" Asbury's heart. (I, 109) [15] Phillip Doddridge's **Sermons to Young People** receives high praise. (II, 33, 154) Jeremy Taylor's **Sermons** provide "many instructing glosses on the Scripture." (I, 668) "A collection of sermons delivered at Berry Street, London, 1733, by Watts, Guyse, Jennings, Neal, Hubbard, and Prince" was read and appreciated. (II, 60) Obviously, sermons were an important source for Asbury's thought and preaching.

Religious Biography

Religious biography supplemented the concern for practical divinity during the period and Asbury is certainly no exception to the pattern. References to such works are numerous. The works most often mentioned were Jonathan Edwards' **Account of the Life of the Rev. Mr. David Brainerd** and **The Holy Life of Monr. de Renty.** (I, 195, 287, 427; II, 5, 193, 304) Martyrologies such as Samuel Clarke's **General Martyrology** and Richard Burnham's **Select Martyrology** are joined with Daniel Neal's **History of the Puritans** to form a general picture of the trials of Christians through the centuries. (I, 748, 296, 141) George Fox's **Journal** is called "truly wonderful." (II, 647) Calvin's predestinarian views brought negative comment from Asbury as he read a **Life of Calvin.** (I, 121) Numerous other "lives" are cited, usually with the notations of their inspiration for the reader: Bernard Gilpin, Hugh Latimer,

John Bruen, John Langston, and Halleburton to note only a few. (I, 193, 287, 427)

The lives of Asbury's contemporaries and colleagues also drew his attention. In 1812 he comments "If I recommend you to read any book but the Bible it will be **Fletcher's Life** by Joseph Benson which I have read during this camp meeting."(III, 465, 548) He was understandably distressed, however, by John Whitehead's publication of a **Life of John Wesley** which was highly critical of Wesley's ordinations. For Asbury, Whitehead had "vilified" Mr. Wesley (and perhaps Asbury himself). (III, 548-49; II, 723)

Religious biography was most important for Asbury in the example that it set, particularly during times of stress or criticism, and as a pattern for ministers. It formed, therefore, a significant portion of his reading and recommendations to others.

Pastoral Care

Instruction in the duties of a pastor were included for Methodists in the **Minutes, Discipline**, and various **Rules.** To supplement these Asbury found particular help in Richard Baxter's **Gildas Salvianus, or the Reformed Pastor** as it comments on the spiritual health of pastors, methods of overseeing one's congregation, visitation, teaching, etc. Asbury finds it a "most excellent book for a Gospel preacher" and comments "Baxter is excellent, superexcellent, and excels the whole." (I, 250; II, 647; III, 436-7) Wesley used portions of this work for instruction of his ministers in the **Minutes** and Asbury comments that Wesley had intended to abridge it. Perhaps it is this work that Asbury, in 1813, notes marking to "reprint." (II, 722)

Church History and Ecclesiastical Polity

Works on church history occupied much attention in the eighteenth century and Asbury seems to have shared this interest. In Echard (probably Lawrence Echard's **A General Ecclesiastical History**) Asbury found much "of the Jews and the Romans, and very little of the pure church." (II, 772) Johann Mosheim's **An Ecclesiastical History** is judged to be "dry and speculative." (I, 148, 578) However, Thomas Prince's **The Christian History** is found to be "Methodist in all its parts" and Asbury had "great desire to reprint an abridgment of it, to show the apostolic children what their fathers were." (II, 4) Martyrology also had historical interest, for Asbury could wish to pattern his life after that of Origen after reading Clarke's account of this ancient church father. (I, 121)

While Asbury himself could be critical of those he disagreed with, he saw Johnson's **Apostolical Canons** as revealing a violent Churchman "who had little charity for the Presbyterians upon whom he is unmercifully severe." (I, 555-56) [**16**] Asbury's own biases are evident in his agreement with David Simpson's condemnation of the Church of England in **A Plea for Religion and the Sacred Writings.** According to Asbury, if Simpson was correct, the Church of England "has the mark of the Beast in her hands at least," and is "antichristian" because of the abuses of the episcopacy and the corruption of morals and manners. (II, 600, 514)

Reading in church history had other attractions for Asbury than simple interest in previous movements or ages. He was under rather intense criticism at several points in his career for the establishment of an episcopacy in America and particularly for his handling of the office. To support his opinion that he had reestablished an apostolic episcopacy, we find him, in 1799, selecting passages from William Cave's **Lives of the Fathers,** a seventeenth century history of the fourth century which had also influenced Wesley's decision to ordain for America. (II, 184, 290; I, 599) [**17**] Thomas Comber's **A Discourse upon the Form and Manner of Making, Ordaining, and Consecrating Bishops, Priests, and Deacons** is credited as adding to Asbury's knowledge of the episcopacy. (I, 312) John Potter's **Discourse on Church Government** and Comber's comment reinforce Asbury's conviction that the episcopal mode of church government was superior to that of the Presbyterians. (I, 351) However, it is a work by Thomas Haweis printed in 1800 and entitled **An Impartial . . . History of the Rise, Declension, and Revival of the Church of Christ, etc.** that becomes Asbury's principle source of support for his position. Asbury notes that Haweis was a moderate Episcopalian, judicious and impartial in his opinions. Asbury was not too pleased with Haweis' Calvinism, but when he writes to Bishop McKendree in 1813, he quotes pages of the book to defend the modified episcopacy found in Methodism. (II, 421-22, 488; III, 479ff.)

Methodist history is, as one would expect, of particular interest to Asbury, who reports having read a thousand pages of Charles Atmore's **The Methodist Memorial: Being an Impartial Sketch of the Lives and Characters of the Preachers . . . and a Concise History of Methodism.** (I, 486, 556) Controversy among the Methodists received careful attention and comment in a variety of references. Some of the publications which arose out of these are listed. James O'Kelly's **Apology for Protesting Against the Methodist Episcopal Church** as well as Nicholas Snethen's **Reply to Mr. O'Kelly's Apology** are noted. (II, 204, 246-47) Also, Asbury responds to an unidentified book by B. J. Smith against "our doctrine, discipline, and administration." (II, 757) The work of a British novelist, T. B. Smollett, **The History of England,** is chided for its lack of understanding of the Methodists. (I, 94)

Two works which emerged out of the seventeenth century Puritan conflicts with the Church of England provided Asbury with solace and arguments against James O'Kelly and others who separated from the Methodist community: **Heart Divisions, the Evil of our Times** by Jeremiah Burroughs and **The Cure of Church Divisions** by Richard Baxter. (I, 434, 388) Asbury thought them significant enough to abridge and conflate the two and publish them under the title **The Causes, Evils and Cure of Heart and Church Divisions.** (III, 45-46) Obviously, history was not only informative to Asbury but its lessons were also used to Asbury's advantage wherever possible.

Items of General Interest

Theology and ecclesiastical interests without question dominate Asbury's readings, but a brief look at some of his more general interests reveal broader interests as well. There is little note of classical philosophers except an appeal to John Locke and Jean Jacques Rousseau for support of the Methodist admonition against idleness and play. (III, 56) John Milton's **Treatise on Education** is recommended without further comment. (III, 55)

Asbury's interest in history, shared by many in the eighteenth century, carries him into several areas. Josephus' **The Jewish Antiquities**, edited by William Whiston, indicates a curiosity about the Jewish community, although he found Josephus to be a "dry, chronological work." (II, 494; I, 254, 260) Charles Rollin's **Ancient History of the Egyptians, Carthaginians, etc.** provides commendation of the Persians and acquaintance with the life of Socrates. (I, 400-01) The activities of the Romans and Goths as well as accounts of the early church are appreciatively gleaned from **An Universal History from the Earliest Account of Time** printed for T. Osborn. (I, 245) Asbury says he had read sixteen volumes of the work that contained sixty-four volumes! He was sympathetically drawn to the Waldensians and Albigenses in an uncredited work and impressed by an extensive **History of the French Revolution** (I, 121; II, 41) To these were added curiosity about other lands in works such as Mungo Park's **Travels in Africa,** which Asbury found to be so extraordinary that the descriptions appeared to be like a romance. (II, 494-95)

American history seems to have been of particular interest to Asbury. William Gordon's **The History of the Rise, Progress, and Establishment, of the Independence of the United States of America** is praised for its general view but especially for its picture of Washington's farewell to his troops. (I, 709, 748; II, 4) John Marshall's **Life of Washington** gains praise for "There is nothing in the work beneath the man of honour; there are no malevolent sentiments, or bitter expressions, derogatory to the character of a Christian." Only perhaps Jeremy Belknap's **American Biography** could exceed Marshall. (II, 484) **An Historical . . . View of the United States** by William Winterbotham reminds Asbury that by 1797 George Washington was being criticized for being partial to aristocrats and continental officers. Asbury suggests that since it was the officers who fought for liberty they deserved any commendation they received. He adds, "As to myself the longer I live, and the more I investigate, the more I applaud the uniform conduct of President Washington in all the important stations he filled." (II, 76, 115) Obviously Washington was one of Asbury's favorites. Other matters of American history also receive attention. Asbury's reference to Ramsey's **History** as he itinerated in South Carolina perhaps refers to David Ramsey's **The History of the Revolution in South Carolina** although Ramsey also published a number of other historical works. (II, 622) Thomas Jefferson's **Notes** are read in their "most essential parts." If this is a reference to Jefferson's **Notes on the State of Virginia**, perhaps Asbury read the work for theological purposes since it contained passages which brought charges of infidelity against Jefferson. (I, 732)

Asbury, like Wesley, shared a concern for the physical well-being of his people, wanting to help their bodies as well as their souls. The Englishman Richard Brooke's **The General Practices of Physic** is mentioned and Asbury himself seems to have been instrumental in encouraging Henry Wilkins, M.D., to publish an American equivalent to Wesley's **Primitive Physic.** (III, 500-01) The full title of the work is curious and shows Asbury's conviction that only Americans could deal with their peculiar diseases: **Family Adviser, or a Plain and Modern Practice of Physic: Calculated for the Use of Families Who Have Not the Advantages of a Physician and Acquainted to the Diseases of America, to Which is Annexed Mr. Wesley's Primitive Physic.**

Retrospect

From this catalogue of readings by American Methodism's most influential and well known early Bishop it can be seen that the second element in Wesley's method of training laypastors was taken seriously and, applied over a life-time, provided an impressive education. Several items stand out in a review of these readings.

It was possible during the American Revolution and the years following for a man who incessantly traveled the length and breadth of the country to continue to educate himself. While such an education could not compare with that of the Wesleys or formally trained American ministers, it was extensive for a person in Asbury's circumstances. This education might not be classical but it was fairly broad, including languages. Finally, Asbury's failure to publish sermons or other books in which we might have direct insight into his theology does not leave us totally devoid of information about his theological interest, beliefs, and ideas. The **Journal and Letters** and the lists of books they contain provide us with insights into these areas.

Wesley's conviction that laypersons could and would train themselves for ministry certainly proved to be a valid one in America. Asbury's example is followed by many and Methodist ministerial education continued to contain a large element of informal education into the present century. Expanding on Wesley's basic principle, the American church in 1816 began to develop a specific "Course of Study" for its ministers, essentially a specified reading list, which still depended on the individual pastor to educate himself as he served his congregation. Formal college education among Methodists would slowly become available with seminary education only developing late in the nineteenth century, but Methodists were not left untrained. Wesley's instructions that one must read and develop a taste for it were continually repeated throughout the American Methodist conferences which were ultimately responsible for a persons ministerial qualifications.

NOTES

1. Frank Baker, **From Wesley to Asbury: Studies in Early American Methodism**, (Durham, N.C.: Duke University Press, 1976), 29.

2. John Wesley, **The Works of the Reverend John Wesley**, ed. Thomas Jackson, 14 vols. (Grand Rapids, Zondervan Publishing House, n.d.) VIII, 315.

3. **Works**, XII, 409.

4. For an analysis of Wesley's method of abridgment see Thomas W. Herbert, **John Wesley As Editor and Author** (Princeton: Princeton University Press, 1940).

5. Minton Thrift, **Memoir of the Rev. Jesse Lee with Extracts from His Journals** (New York: N. Bangs and T. Mason, 1823), 12, 20, 42-3.

6. Freeborn Garrettson, **The Experiences and Travels of Mr. Freeborn Garrettson** (Philadelphia: Printed by Barry Hall, 1791), 24-49.

7. Jesse Lee, **A Short History of the Methodists in the United States of America** (Baltimore: Printed by Magill and Clime, 1810), 99, 126.

8. Garrettson, 15-17.

9. Baker, 106-112; L. C. Rudolph, **Francis Asbury** (Nashville: Abingdon Press, 1966), 15.

10. Baker, 112-13.

11. Francis Asbury, **The Journal and Letters of Francis Asbury**, eds. Elmer T. Clark et al. (Nashville: Abingdon Press, 1958), II, 75. Hereafter cited in the text by volume and page numbers only.

12. William S. Duren, **Francis Asbury: Founder of American Methodism and Unofficial Minister of State** (New York: The Macmillan Co., 1928), 70.

13. See also I, 181 and III, 533.

14. Edward M. Lang, Jr. has helpfully identified many of these and offers interesting suggestions concerning others. Edward M. Lang, Jr., **Francis Asbury's Reading of Theology: A Bibliographical Study**, Garrett Bibliographical Lectures, No. 8, Garrett Theological Seminary Library, Evanston, Ill., 1972.

15. The editors of Asbury's **Journal and Letters** suggest that perhaps this was Brandon's **Happiness at Hand** but that appears to be a treatise rather than meditations or sermons.

16. Perhaps John Johnson's **The Clergy-Man's Vade-mecum: containing the Canonical Codes of the Primitive and Universal Church** (London: Printed for R. Knaplock, 1714).

17. Cave's full title was **Ecclesiastici, or a History of the Lives, Acts, Deaths, and Writings of the most eminent fathers of the Church in the Fourth Century.**

WILLIAM PALMER'S NARRATIVE OF EVENTS: THE FIRST HISTORY OF THE "TRACTS FOR THE TIMES"

William Seth Adams

The Episcopal Theological Seminary of the Southwest

For historians of the Oxford Movement, William Palmer's **Narrative of Events** is a standard source. Written in 1843, the **Narrative of Events connected with the Publication of the Tracts for the Times** enjoyed immediate popularity (among those who thought well of it) and went through several editions and reprintings in the first year of issue. [2] It received considerable critical reaction in the religious press, favorable and otherwise, and at least one notable book was written in direct reaction to its claims, i.e., **The Ideal of a Christian Church** by William George Ward, 1844. Interestingly enough, its circulation in the U.S. reportedly exceeded that in England. [3] On the fiftieth anniversary of the beginning of the Oxford Movement, Rivington's, the London publisher, invited the author to re-issue the **Narrative**. Palmer accepted the invitation and with the re-issue published a new introduction and supplement. The 1883 edition marked the end of the volume's publishing history.

As a history of the earliest years of the Oxford Movement, 1833-1834 the **Narrative** serves as a primary document for the reconstruction and interpretation of those times. At the same time and more to the point, Palmer's book was offered as a strong defense against the increasingly numerous charges of Romanism being leveled at the Oxford High Churchmen. In many ways, the **Narrative** was Palmer's apologia. As such, it grew out of the turmoil which Palmer and others experienced in the late 1830's and early 1840's.

We intend to explore the setting, content and importance of Palmer's book, hoping that doing so will illuminate yet another dimension of the larger history of the Oxford Movement. (Given the nature of most of the contemporary writing about the Movement, our's is an uncommon point of view, i.e., that of the "Z's"--the derogatory term Froude and Newman were sometimes wont to use for people like Palmer. [4] The conservative High Churchmen were generally unsuitable candidates for memberhsip among the "Apostolicals.")

As students of the Oxford Movement will know, William Palmer (1803-1855) was one of the five men who met at Hugh James Rose's Rectory in Hadleigh, Suffolk, in July, 1833, to discuss the dangers facing the Church of England in the person of Latitudinarianism. From that embryonic meeting, the Movement itself grew. Palmer was educated at Trinity College, Dublin, in his native Ireland and came to Oxford in 1828, at the age of 25. Though he received his M.A. from Magdalen in 1829, he began an association with Worcester College in 1831 from which his typical sobriquet "of Worcester College" derives. His connection with Newman, Keble, Froude and the other Oxford men was prompted by their approbation of his important liturgical work, **Origines Liturgicae** (1832). In this work and his equally important **Treatise on the Church of Christ** (1838), Palmer established himself as a capable and agressive advocate for the catholicity and apostolicity of the Church of England. In both these major works, the Church of Rome stood as the agency against which the Church of England needed to be defended. The **Narrative of Events** is properly placed in this lineage of apologetical works.

If we are to gain a rightful perspective on this "history," then, we must take seriously a series of events and confrontations which brought Palmer, in the summer of 1843, to the task of writing his **Narrative,** in which writing Palmer moves from the principled and aggressive defense of a much-loved but nonetheless abstract notion--the catholicity of the Church of England--to the defense of himself and his own personal reputation. Aspects of this rather complex story are three: Nicholas Wiseman's literary "attack" on the English Church, Palmer's defense of Newman following Tract 90, and the Romanizing tendencies of the British Critic after Newman gave over the editorship to Thomas Mozley. [5]

* * * * *

Wiseman (1802-1865) was the son of Irish Roman Catholic parents. [6] In 1850, he was to become the Archbishop of Westminster at the restoration of the Roman hierarchy in England. The battle with Wiseman which engaged Palmer's attention had two dimensions, one related to a pair of articles published in Wiseman's **Dublin Review** in 1838 and 1839, and the other a set of letters Palmer wrote to Wiseman following the appearance of Tract 90.

In 1838, while he was the Rector of the English College in Rome, Wiseman began the publication of the Dublin Review. Whatever else might have been the journal's intention, from its inception, the anonymous writers were particularly apt at following and encouraging the development of the Oxford Movement. It seems to have been Wiseman's assumption, if not his hope, that the Oxford men would eventually lead the Movement to Rome.

The tactics of the Review were subtle and probably effective. A good example of the approach can be found in the review of John Keble's sermon, "Primitive Tradition recognized in Holy Scripture." [7] In the discussion of Keble's views, the anonymous reviewer observed, "Strike out a few sentences, in which he tacks his theory to the Thirty-Nine Articles, and the sermon might have been preached in St. Peter's at Rome." [8] Such praise could hardly do Keble and the Movement any good within their own territory. Likewise, in an article on the Tracts, the writer praised the general thrust of the view contained therein, which was said to be rooting-out Protestantism. [9]

In addition, however, to the applause given the Movement, there were also strong and specific criticisms of the English Church. It is at this point that Wiseman and the Review caught Palmer's attention.

Wiseman wrote two articles on "Anglican Claims to Apostolical Succession." The first one appeared in October, 1838, and dealt almost exclusively with Tract 15, the only Tract with which Palmer had any contact. [10] The second article was published in August, 1839, and contained Wiseman's treatment of the Donatist Schism. The interpretation he gave to the fourth century schismatics was completely to unsettle John Henry Newman. [11] These two articles elicited from Palmer a book-length response, **The Apostolic Jurisdiction and Succession of the Episcopacy in the British Churches Vindicated Against the Objections of Dr. Wiseman in the Dublin Review.**

Tract 15, entitled "On the Apostolic Succession in the English Church," presented an argument that Palmer later extended into a major part of his **Treatise on the Church of Christ.** He argued that the succession of the English bishops had not been broken at the Reformation and that the English Church, therefore, was not schismatical. "There was no new Church founded among us, but the right and the true doctrines of the Ancient existing Church were asserted and established." [12] The suppression of papal authority constituted no more than the discontinuance of usurped and therefore illegal powers, not inherent in the office.

The differences in assumptions and application between Wiseman and Palmer were sharp and clear. This can best be illustrated by looking briefly at Wiseman's conclusions and then comparing his reasonings with Palmer's. That they could not and did not agree was the nature of the case.

In his article on Tract 15, Wiseman concluded,

> First, the Church has, from the beginning, held that a bishop however validly consecrated, if placed in possession of a see contrary to the canons actually in force in the Church, or by means contrary to those regulations which it considered essential to legitimate nomination, acquired no jurisdiction in or over it, and did not enjoy a part in that apostolic succession, which can only be transmitted through legitimate occupation. Secondly, that the canons appointing the forms of such legitimate occupation, or the bars thereto, were not particularly those of Nicaea, but generally such as the Church agreed in at a given time. Thirdly, that patriarchal jurisdiction is legitimated and determined by usage, and that this sanctions it with the force equal to that of canons. [13]

On the first point, after conceding the possibility that an Anglican bishop might have been validly consecrated (Matthew Parker, for example), Wiseman argued against that bishop's being in possession of the succession of the Apostles because his jurisdiction was not valid. That is, Wiseman argued that the bishops consecrated under Elizabeth I took already occupied sees. Therefore, the new bishops were usurpers, without valid jurisdiction. In addition, these bishops were nominated without consent from Rome. Thus, their elections were without proper sanction.

Palmer, on the other hand, argued that the Elizabethan bishops were simply restored to previously usurped sees, and that papal sanction was never essential to episcopal election. Both Palmer and Wiseman argued from historical precedent, choosing sources carefully and in full knowledge of the necessary bias. Consequently, the citations, for the most part, either cancelled each other or completely missed the opponent's point. There was no persuasion of the opponent expected or really desired.

Quite significant issues arose on Wiseman's second and third points--that the canons of Nicaea were not determinative for the problem at hand and that patriarchal jurisdiction was determined by usage. The specific matters of concern were the question of the fixity of conciliar decrees, and the manner in which papal authority was acquired.

What distinguished Wiseman's approach most significantly from Palmer's was his willingness to accept and validate the process of development, a notion virtually abhorent to Palmer. When arguing against the immutability of conciliar decrees, Wiseman spoke of that on which "generally . . . the Church agreed in at a given time." [14] The mind of the Church at a certain time constituted the authority for that certain time.

It was by the fact of development that Wiseman wanted to legitimate papal jurisdiction in England. Seemingly willing to grant Palmer that the Pope had not always had jurisdiction there, the fact that he had gained it at a later time, even by usurpation, gave it "a force equal to that of canons." [15] Validation, then, consisted in the existence and acceptance of that fact. Whereas Palmer argued that a return to the primitive canons superceded anything that happened in the meantime, Wiseman wanted to require acceptance of what had come to pass. Wiseman stated "that possession and ancient usage constituted a right to patriarchal jurisdiction." [16] To the contrary, Palmer asserted "that patriarchal jurisdiction acquired by usurpation, and in violation of the canons, was schismatical and null." [17] No accord could possibly have been reached between these two antagonists until this breach was closed. It never was.

In Wiseman's second article, published in the Dublin Review in August, 1839, the author drew a parallel between the Catholic Church of the fourth century and the Roman Church of his own time, on the one hand, and the Donatists and Anglican on the other. Quite straightforwardly he suggested that it was undeniably true that the world at large did not consider the Church of England to be part of the Catholic Church, just as the Donatists, regardless of their claims, were held schismatics by the whole Church of the fourth century. As his ally, Wiseman took Augustine, whom he quoted, "For the whole world judges with assurance (securus judicat orbis terrarum) that they are not good who separate themselves in any part of the world from all the world." [18]

This claim Palmer took on in the second part of his **Apostolic jurisdiction** and dispensed with it in short order. Whatever claims Augustine might have made about the orbis terrarum, Palmer was able to "prove" that it was, after all, the Roman Church in England that was schismatical and not the English Church. [19] In effect, Palmer was able to turn the tables on Wiseman. "The question is not," Palmer said,

> whether the whole eastern and western church united in one communion, or the English Church, is the church of Christ. It is, whether the western church [meaning the Roman Church], separated from the communion of the eastern as well as of the British, is the whole Catholic church or not, and therefore whether the mere fact of not being in communion with it, is any proof of schism. [20]

That body which separated was not the English Church but the Roman! How useful, then, Palmer would ask, was an analogy which equated the Donatists with the Anglicans?

If the English Church was catholic and its ministry valid--clearly Palmer's conviction--then the same could not be said for the Roman Church in England and its ministry. There could be only one catholic church in England, and that was the Church of England. With this conviction, Palmer satisfied himself that he had dispensed with Wiseman. Probably to his surprise, such was not to be the case.

Following the publication of Tract 90 and the public outcry that it set in motion, Wiseman wrote publically to Newman in response to the tract. [21] Newman made no reply. Palmer did.

Between April, 1841, and March, 1842, Palmer wrote eight letters to Wiseman. [22] Wiseman responded with only one letter, written after Palmer's first, and treated by Palmer in his fifth letter. The content of Palmer's letters is, in large measure, a repetition of both his **Treatise** and the **Apostolic Jurisdiction.** What distinguishes the Letters, however, is a change of emphasis.

In his earlier work, Palmer's aim was the validation of the English Church, authenticating it as a true and catholic Church of Christ. In the **Letters to Wiseman,** especially letters two through eight, Palmer's stress was on the errors of Romanism rather than the strengths of the English Church. This is a significant difference, a difference which was instrumental in the later appearance of the **Narrative of Events.**

The apparent reason for Palmer's change of emphasis was his fear that faithful Churchmen would be lured into the Roman net. He was eager to curtail conversions. Since he viewed Wiseman's approbation of Newman's theology as a subtle device intended to persuade the unwary of the similarities between Tractarian theology and Rome, Palmer was forthright in his disclaimer. "You have vainly imagined," he wrote to Wiseman in the second letter,

> that because the study of Catholic Antiquity has recently acquired a new importance . . . that this movement was destined to promote your objects, and to bring converts to you. You have buoyed yourselves up with this hope . . . You have indeed been compelled to assure your people, that men who studied Christian Antiquity, with a disposition to submit to its doctrines, could not fail to become Romanists. [23]

Although he nowhere said so himself, it is nonetheless clear that his attack on Romanism was undertaken in order to expose Rome as an altogether unworthy alternative, not only theoretically but practically. Hence, he concluded Letter IV in this way,

> how extreme would be the insanity, how desperate the wickedness, of that man, who should plunge his soul into eternal perdition, by forsaking the Communion of the Catholic Church in England, to unite himself to your corrupt and schismatical community? [24]

* * * * *

By tracing the outline of Palmer's dealings with Dr. Wiseman, we are able to identify the various aspects of Palmer's anti-Roman feelings. These are basic to our understanding of the **Narrative.** Yet another fundamental dimension to that same understanding is Palmer's defense of John Henry Newman following the publication of Tract 90.

Newman's aim seemed simple enough--to show that the Thirty-Nine Articles were capable of a catholic reading. The reaction, however, to such claims was quite extraordinary. Twenty-five hundred copies were sold in the first two weeks. By the end of May, 1841, over 10,000 copies were in circulation. [25] Newman was cheered by a few, castigated by many. He was publicly condemned by four tutors at Oxford; he was asked to terminate the Tracts at the request of Richard Bagot, Bishop of Oxford (the Tracts stopped publication on March 26, 1841); and correspondence from the Archbishop of Canterbury (Howley) on the matter crossed Bagot's desk more than once.

Palmer's role in all of this is most interesting. Although he had argued vigorously the high Anglican (and anti-Roman) position against Dr. Wiseman in print, Palmer had, as Liddon put it, "held aloof from the Tract-writers" since about 1838, the time of the publication of Froude's **Remains** and his own **Treatise.** It is for this reason that his activities on the occasion of Tract 90 are of such note.

Among the modest number of letters in the known Palmer corpus, there are no more significant letters than the two he sent Newman in the aftermath of Number 90. The first letter, unfortunately not dated, must have been written in either late February or very early March, 1841. Its importance requires reproducing in full.

St. Giles, Tuesday

My dear Newman,

Though I have taken no part in the discussion relative to the Tracts, I yet feel it a duty to express to you, under present circumstances, the gratification which I have derived from No. 90 just published.

While I would hesitate to commit myself to every statement contained in it, I have no hesitation in expressing an opinion, that it is the most valuable of the series of the Tracts that has come under my observation. It will tend to take people out of their implicit reception of traditionary [sic] interpretations which impose human opinions as little less than articles of faith. It will lead to a very critical system of interpreting the Articles, and will ultimately produce more union on the articles of the Catholic faith and more toleration of opinions, which have been at all times tolerated in the Universal Church.

I may perhaps have seen a few expressions that I could have wished otherwise, but on the whole I most cordially thank you for this excellent Tract, and if my opinion can be of any use to you, I do not wish to conceal it.

Ever yours,

W. Palmer

Palmer's approbation should come as no surprise. Though it has typically gone unnoticed by later observers, the basic interpretation Newman used in his effort to claim that the Thirty-Nine Articles were "to say the least, not uncatholic," [27] was very like the view Palmer expounded in his **Treatise on the Church of Christ.** [28] When Newman said, for example, "The Romish doctrine concerning purgatory . . . [is] repugnant to the Word of God . . . [but that] the Primitive doctrine is not condemned in it, unless, the Primitive doctrine be the Romish, which must not be supposed," [29] he spoke in harmony with Palmer. Both were convinced that claims for the continuity of the English Church had to be founded on this kind of view, the primitive doctrine needed to be seen residing below, or within, the actual formulations of the Church. When Palmer attempted to reconcile Henry VIII's **King's Book** with the Articles, he was acting on the same set of necessary assumptions on which Newman's Tract 90 rested. [30]

Newman apparently took Palmer's offer of aid and made the letter available to those working in his defence. A letter of March 13, 1841, from J. B. Mozley to his sister, Anne, indicates that Palmer's letter was going to be presented to the members of the Hebdomadal Board at Oxford "in the hope that Palmer's known character as a theologian and a moderate man would have some effect on them." It was finally decided that such a move would accomplish nothing, given the "commotion" of things. [31] Regardless of the final results, which of course went against Newman, Palmer's respected place in the Oxford scene and his view of Newman are, at least, suggested by these events.

It appears that Newman responded to Palmer's letter by asking him for more specific remarks on Tract 90. Why he did so and what he actually requested are questions to which there are no answers. Palmer's letter in compliance with the request provides one of the very few places in which Palmer expressed his views on Newman's work in any detail. Rather than being critical, Palmer's notes were corroborative. Palmer virtually reiterated Newman's assumption that it was Roman not catholic doctrine and practice which were condemned by the Articles. [32] Palmer concluded his letter with a piece of advice.

> I would add that it would seem to be advisable in a second edition to be as explicit as is consistent with taste, in disapprobation of Romish abuses and error. It might be of most material importance--The object of the Tract was not in the first instance to explain your actual views, but to show that they [the Articles] ought to be interpreted liberally as well as accurately. [33]

Palmer was not a close friend of Newman nor was he privy to his most intimate secrets. He did not know that Newman was in the process of receding from the center of Tractarian life, nor was he at all aware of Newman's changing view toward Rome. Palmer did not, in fact, know what Newman's "actual views" were. It is in this regard that one begins to suspect that Palmer may have had a real inability to know, or an unwillingness to admit knowing, what Newman was actually doing. It was not until after the **Narrative** had been written, and Palmer was involved in the editorship of the English Review, that any substantial hint emerged in his writing to suggest that he was aware of Newman's shift. Others knew long before.

Although there were other expressions of Palmer's interest in defending Newman, one of which was his **Letters to Wiseman**, enough has been said here to illustrate the point, viz., that even in the midst of his increasingly strong anti-Roman sentiments and fears, Palmer was nonetheless a vigorous supporter of John Henry Newman. Palmer's handling of Newman in his **Narrative of Events** will be an extension of this disposition.

* * * * *

A third piece of contextualization remains. It is both the most immediate to Palmer's **Narrative** and the most briefly recounted.

Palmer's disenchantment with the British Critic began as early as July, 1841. Until that time, this journal had been edited by Newman and served as the organ of the Movement. Under Newman, the journal's articles had espoused the Oxford High Church view with care to disavow Rome as a model, a posture most acceptable to Palmer. The July, 1841, issue was the first offering from Newman's successor, Thomas Mozley. The change in editor marked a change in tone, signalled by Frederick Oakeley's article on the life of Bishop Jewel. [34]

Oakeley was a second generation Tractarian, joining the Movement well after its inception. From 1839 until his conversion to Rome, he was the vicar of Margaret Chapel, London, where his liturgical and ceremonial activities produced no small interest. It was Oakeley as much as anyone else who sparked interest in Roman practice. [35] Like others, he began to deprecate the supposed "reforming" activities of the Reformers, an attitude which appeared in more than one article from his pen. The Jewel article was of such a quality.

Upon reading the article, Palmer wrote immediately to Newman.

> The whole article is written in a spirit of hostility to the Reformation generally and is anything but a friendly spirit towards the Church of England . . . I do not think that I have ever seen anything like this before . . . and I fear that it will not tend to render Church principles more acceptable to the Church. [36]

Newman could or would do nothing. Palmer's distress could only grow.

Shortly thereafter, Palmer wrote to Pusey. It is in this letter more than anywhere else that one confronts the extent of Palmer's personal distress. No longer is he concerned about Church principles in some academic and presumably "objective" way. Now he sees himself in jeopardy.

St. Giles--Oxford
August 2, 1843

My dear Pusey,

. . . .

For myself, I have often thought that all my power of usefulness to the Church was at an end--I have even regretted sometimes that I had ever written on Church subjects. No one knows the mingled pain and pleasure with which I have seen the progress of Church-principles,--I do not allude to the opposition experienced, when I speak of pain, but to the mixture of evil with which this great work has been gradually tinged--the unfortunate tendency to Romanism against which I long endeavored to close my eyes, but which becomes every day more evident. I am sure that you feel very much in the same manner, though not in the same degree perhaps; and if I am satisfied of anything, it is that you have most sincerely endeavored to resist this tendency. I examine myself and inquire whether I have been instrumental in assisting the tendency, and could I clearly see that any sentiments of mine have been so, I would, in the face of the world, acknowledge my fault, and retract any errors which I have committed. Yet, having written in maintenance of Church-principles, I feel myself in some degree mixed up with evil--though not in intention. I feel as if I had assisted in laying the foundation; as if I was still supporting myself however feebly the superstructure which has been erected on Church principles by men with whom I am unacquainted. I feel, too, that notwithstanding the disapprobation which is generally felt by Churchmen at Romanizing tendencies of certain men and of the British Critic--notwithstanding the disavowals which are made in private society--notwithstanding all the moderation of tone which individuals may exercise--the cause of Church principles is inextricably involved in the public mind with ultra and Romanizing views. It is in vain that we endeavor to be free from those views, to disciminate between them and Church-principles. It seems to me that while matters continue thus, there is absolutely no hope before us. It is true that Church principles may be spreading, but are they not accompanied by a wide-spread tendency to Romanism?

. . . .

I think therefore that it has at last become necessary, if we would save Church principles within the English

> Church from destruction--to speak on the subject of ultra views--to let our sentiments be publicly known--to sever ourselves from those views with a firm and convincing hand. [37]

Within one month, from "a firm and convincing hand," Palmer's pamphlet, **A Narrative of Events connected with the Publication of the Tracts for the Times, with Reflections on Existing Tendencies to Romanism, and on the Present Duties and Prospects of Members of the Church**, appeared.

* * * * *

In form, the **Narrative** is just what its extended title claimed. It is a narrative history of the first few years of the Movement; a collection of reflections on the Romanizing tendency apparent, especially in the British Critic; and a presentation of duties and prospects for the Church. In addition, however, to these obvious ingredients there was yet another. The **Narrative** provided Palmer with a means of defending himself.

"At the beginning of the summer of 1833, the Church in England and Ireland seemed destined to immediate desolation and ruin." [38] With this as his starting point, Palmer presented his own "eye-witness" recounting of the events of that year and the next. [39] His reason for doing so he stated in the Preface, "to clear those who uphold Church principles from the imputation of approving certain recent tendencies to Romanism." Further, he "hoped that a plain statement of facts, avoiding controversy altogether, might conduce to the removal of mistakes on a point of much importance." [40]

The first two chapters are actually the servants of the third. That is, Palmer's exposition on the Association of Friends of the Church (Chapter I) and on the "Tracts for the Times" (Chapter II) find their real rationale and justification in Chapter III, entitled "Party Spirit--Tendency to Romanism." In these two initial chapters, Palmer tells us that there were two early expressions of the spirit of the Oxford men, both of which grew out of the meeting--at the Hadleigh Rectory in July, 1833. The first, and his own personal interest, was the Association, designed,

> 1. To maintain pure and inviolate the doctrines, the services and the discipline of the Church; that is, to withstand all change, which involves the denial and suppression of doctrines, the departure from primitive practice in religious offices, or innovation upon the Apostolical prerogatives, order, and commission of bishops, priests, and deacons.

> 2. To afford Churchmen an opportunity of exchanging their sentiments, and co-operating together on a large scale. [41]

Intended to be planted "throughout all England," [42] Palmer saw the Association's method of operation as largely a matter of making public statements of support for the Church of England, in the form, for example, of an Address to the Archbishop of Canterbury. [43]

It was Palmer's conviction, in retrospect, that the Association had been successful

> in awakening the slumbering spirit of religion and of patriotism, a spirit which mere political Conservatism might not have found it easy to evoke.

Obviously, then, the members of the Association could not be accused of any tendency away from Church principles toward Romanism.

Whereas the Association, by Palmer's recounting, was the first expression of the Oxford sentiments, the Tracts followed closely thereafter. While Palmer was promoting the cause of the Association, Newman was setting the first "Tracts for the Times" before the public. Palmer tells us very carefully that although his "respect and regard" for the authors made him "anxious to place the most favourable construction on everything which they wrote, he nonetheless felt that not enough "caution was exercised in avoiding language calculated to give needless offense." [44] For this reason, he proposed to Newman the formation of a committee of revision. He assured Newman "that in proposing a system of revision by some Committee, there was not the least wish to lower the tone of doctrine, or to conceal any part of Catholic truth." [45]

The prudence and political sensitivity evidenced by Palmer's proposal was lost on the Tract-writers. Palmer's primary concern was effectiveness, that the movement might actually succeed; Newman's was rather more interested in action. This was an important difference. Methodologically, Palmer felt "it [was] necessary <u>as much as possible</u> to gild the pill, and adapt it to delicate stomachs." He wanted to achieve, thereby, "the greatest possible advantage." [46] This attitude Palmer translated into prudence as a tactical necessity. The review committee he so strongly advocated was an example of his caution. On the one hand, he did not trust private, uncensored personal opinion, while, on the other hand, he wanted to insure the fact that the Association would be kept quite free from the threat of harm posed by these same opinions. He was willing to allow Newman free expression, but not the others. [47]

By early 1834, with the failure of the proposal for the revision committee and the continued publication of the Tracts without it, Palmer was "led to the conviction that any further direct co-operation with [the Tract-writers] was impossible. I accordingly ceased to take any active part in their proceedings . . . " [48] However, having begun to sever his ties with the Tracts, and even though greatly concerned about errors they might contain or disillusionment they might cause, Palmer remained convinced that the Tracts "only result would be, to establish great Ecclesiastical principles, and a firmer attachment to the English Church, in the public mind." [49]

The major thrust of the **Narrative** began in Chapter III, in which Palmer set about his real delineation between Church principles and the new deviations. What Palmer does is a most natural extension of his earlier anti-Roman writings.

He began his exposition in a most important way. He requested the attention of the reader on the basis of his [Palmer's] qualification to speak. As he identifies these qualifications, one comes to understand more fully how Palmer saw even his earlier apologetic writings.

> I would . . . address myself most respectfully to that large and important portion of the Church, which is, in various degrees, favourable to the principles advocated by the 'Tracts for the Times.' If warm personal affection and esteem for the principal authors of those Tracts, cemented by the most sacred associations, and never in thought, or word, or deed, diminished; if community of suffering beneath undeserved imputations; if anxiety for the welfare of the Church; if a life devoted, to the utmost extent of limited powers and attainments, to the inculcation of sound and Catholic principles; if some experience, as one who at the very beginning took part in that movement which has exercised so deep an influence; if these constitute any claim on attention, I trust, in humility, that I may be heard. [50]

The message which Palmer most urgently wanted to communicate to the reader was that it was <u>not</u> the old guard, Keble, Pusey and Newman, about whom he was alarmed. It was rather "a new School," [51] those stressing a party spirit leading toward Romanism. To the members of this school, in fact, "the spirit of Newman, Pusey, and Keble [had] not been transmitted." [52]

In order to set before the reader the plainest evidence, Palmer made repeated citations from the Tracts themselves, hoping to show that the authors were not advocating Romanism. The truth was quite the contrary--the Tract-writers were opposed to Romanism. His defence of the Tracts at this level was simply unremitting.

In contrast, recent articles from the British Critic were cited to show the direction being taken and advocated by certain extravagant young men who were left unnamed. "There is," Palmer charged, "a decided leaning on the whole to Romanism, and there is nothing in opposition to this tendency [in the British Critic]." [53]

Of the unnamed young men who contributed to the Romeward lean, one has been mentioned, Frederick Oakeley. The other person was William George Ward. These two "runaway horses," as Tom Mozley called them, wrote most of the offending material. Ward, for example, in his article on Athanasius in the October, 1842 Critic, asked the imprudent question, ". . . is the English Establishment the Church?" [54] He dealt with the question in such a way as to put the English Church in irredeemable doubt.

Along with doubt, however, Palmer cited examples of uncertain allegiance to the Church, denigration of the Reformation, the equation of Romanism with catholicism, and blatant approbation of Roman doctrine and practice. All of these Palmer disavowed and condemned.

Of particular importance in Palmer's delineation were four principles which he felt were most destructive of the good of the English Church. Of the four, the most crucial principle was the emergent acceptance of the doctrine of development in matters of doctrine. The other three were an unwillingness to condemn "Roman corruptions," the acceptance of the (then) contemporary Roman Church as a sufficient model, and the suggestion that Roman Catholics might accept the Thirty-Nine Articles if they felt the Pope's authority was not de jure. [55]

In his Preface, Palmer had clearly stated that his criticism of development was not aimed at the view "of an eminent and much respected writer" whom he then did not name. The writer in question, of course, was John Henry Newman. Newman's view, Palmer felt, gave no offence "when rightly understood." [56] **The Essay on the Development of Christian Doctrine** was not published until late 1845, but Newman delivered and published a sermon called "The Theory of Developments in Religious Doctrines," dated February 2 (Purification), 1843. [57] It was on the basis of this sermon that Palmer expressed himself.

What Palmer criticized in the British Critic essayists was their assumption that

> it is the nature of Christianity to develop itself gradually in the course of ages, and under change of circumstance;

> so that Christianity in the middle ages, was more perfectly developed than in primitive times; it was the expansion of a system which existed at first, merely in germ; and probably, on the same principle, the existing system of the Roman Catholic Church may be still more perfect than that of the middle ages, and be itself less perfect than that which is to be hereafter. [58]

Whereas he understood the British Critic to assert that it was the nature of Christian theology to develop, Palmer wanted to read Newman as accepting only the possibility of development as a function of the applicaion of reason and language to faith. This is the understanding Palmer applied to Newman's observation that the "controversy between our own Church and the Church of Rome lies, it is presumed, in the matter of fact, whether such and such developments are true (e.g., Purgatory a true development of the doctrine of sin after baptism,) not in the principle of development itself." [59]

In order to make his own position clear, Palmer fell back on a distinction he had made earlier, in the Treatise, although he spoke of it in different language. What was important at the highest level was that time could not displace "the faith once delivered to the Saints." "The principle of the church has always been, to hand down and bear witness to the Catholic verities which she received from the Apostles, and not to argue, to develop, to invent." [60] There were, however, developments "which are inferences from Revelation" and developments "which are mere expressions of Revelation." The former need not be articles of faith; the latter "have been at all times held substantially by the Church." [61] These latter can only be developments in a certain way. As he put it, "they can only be novel in form." [62]

The distinction Palmer made is of a piece with the opinion in the **Treatise** that there was a difference between doctrines of the Church and mere religious opinions. Opinions might be subject to alteration or even abandonment. The fixity of essential truth was axiomatic.

It appears that in his discussion of development, Palmer wanted to accomplish three ends, to deny any change in essential doctrine, to admit development only in matters of opinion, and to defend Newman. His attempt to do all three at once necessitated (again) that he smooth over what appear to be obvious differences of opinion between himself and his disenchanted friend. It was only after Newman presented his Essay on Development that Palmer was able to criticize pointedly and specifically the views of his Oxford friend, then a new convert.

By assertion and evidence, Palmer made it abundantly

clear that the errors of the British Critic were quite distinguishable from the main thrust and intention of the original leaders of the Movement. The approbation of things Roman was not truly to be associated with the men at Hadleigh in 1833 or the Tract-writers.

> The doctrine and practice of Rome are not our model or our standard; and we are resolved, with God's aid, to "stand fast in the liberty wherewith Christ has made us free, and to be in bondage to no man." Such I am persuaded, are the principles of the body of Churchmen; such seem to me to have been the principles even of the "Tracts for the Times" in general; and those who now admit the Papal supremacy, the worship of saints and angels, purgatory, and certain theories of development, really hold views as inconsistent with those Tracts, as with the sentiments of the great body of Churchmen. [63]

Having made his point so clearly, what remained to be said he called "a warning." [64] The warning formed the final chapter in the **Narrative**.

One of the things Palmer observed about the Critic essayists was that their views tended to minimize the role of the Bible in the life and doctrine of the Church. Consequently, his first piece of advice was to say that "the orthodox Christian . . . disapproves any tendency to undervalue Scripture." [65] But, he went on to say, "Scripture is the inestimable, but not the only gift of God." [66] In so saying, he struck an essential balance between Scripture and the other gifts, the sacraments and the Church.

The frankness and realism with which Palmer treated these other gifts provides an important dimension to the understanding of the **Narrative** as a whole. This is especially true when he spoke of the Church.

> It is evident from the Bible and the annals of Christianity, that the Church is symbolized by its vital manners; that infirmities, sins, and corruptions, are found in it--that it is at one time more pure than at another; at one time more animated by faith and charity than at another; and yet that God is still directing and guiding it amidst many infirmities and backslidings, and sometimes, notwithstanding grievous sins; still urging it onwards, and accomplishing his promise, that "the gates of hell shall not prevail against it." [67]

The remainder of Palmer's warnings dealt with the avoidance of controversy and the exercise of the Victorian virtues--propriety, moderation and prudence. In regard to this last, Palmer could not pass the chance to reiterate the admonition to prudence he had given his fellows in 1833, at the outset of the Tract-writing. [68] His caution about controversy was put in most interesting terms. He warned against it because religious matters were becoming too familiar to the wrong sorts of people. [69]

In spite of the personal discomfort which Palmer withstood during the period from the mid-1830's to the time of writing the **Narrative**, he ended his book full of confidence that he had discharged his appointed task and thereby vindicated Church principles (and himself) from any Romanizing stigma. Sure that his advice would bear adequate fruit, Palmer offered an effusive evaluation of the past and prospects for the future.

> A Theology deepened and invigorated; a Church daily awakened more and more to a sense of her privileges and responsibilities; a Clergy more zealous, more self-denying, more holy; a laity more interested in the great concerns of time and eternity; Churches more fully attended; sacraments and divine offices more frequently and fervently partaken; unexampled efforts to evangelize the multitudinous population of our land, and to carry the word of God into the dark recesses of Heathenism. In all this there is very much to awaken our hopes, and to stimulate to continued exertions. [70]

The publication of the **Narrative** created a considerable stir. Reactions of all sorts were registered. One reviewer saw it as "a confession that Tractarianism is leading to Rome." [71] The Record, an extremely unsympathetic newspaper, carried a series of letters signed by "A Master of Arts" in which Palmer's writing was extensively and predictably criticized. [72] On the other hand, among High Churchmen, the **Narrative** received "a chorus of approval by all save the party against which it was directed." [73]

Second and third editions of the **Narrative** appeared in 1843, attesting to its popularity. The third edition was identical to the first and second except that it contained a postscript of two pages. The postscript was designed to counter some adverse criticism. The critic Palmer appears to have been answering was the anonymous writer of a letter, dated November 3, 1843, and printed for circulation by Baxter, Printer, Oxford. [74] A most judicious inquirer, the writer pressed Palmer at the point of his defence of some of the Tract-writers, Newman in particular. Had not Newman actually been more supportive of Romanizing ideas than Palmer wanted to admit? Palmer's response in the postscript was simply a re-affirmation of his conviction about Newman, despite whatever evidence to the contrary might be offered. Once again, his treatment of Newman was that of an affectionate and myopic supporter. [75]

Other readers of the **Narrative** made other charges. One called Palmer a "retractarian" for his views. [76] Edward Churton, Joshua Watson's biographer, belittled Palmer as "a man who [made] himself the hero of his own tale." [77] One critic even suggested that Palmer's criticism of the British Critic was a hoax, aimed at clouding the pervasiveness of the Romanizing tendencies throughout the Movement. [78] A very recent observer has suggested that Palmer felt and exhibited "bitterness and jealousy and even rage" at those who "snatched" leadership of the Movement from him in 1833, and that his warm language about Newman was used "lest the distaste he felt by this time for Newman should become too apparent." [79] There appears to be no evidence to support such claims.

By most accounts Palmer seems to have succeeded in exonerating himself from the taint of Romanizing. He was also rousingly successful in silencing the British Critic, whose last gasp was heard in October, 1843. (The death of the Critic re-directed the considerable energies of William George Ward to a full-length rebuttal to Palmer, **The Ideal of a Christian Church.**) He seems to have been less successful in communicating the delineation he sought to make between Church principles and Romanizing tendencies. Many of his critics appear to have missed his point, though it was surely well made. But the success of the **Narrative** may not be the best way to judge its importance.

For the historian of the Oxford Movement, the **Narrative** is a basic resource, as we have suggested earlier. In that it provides a systematic treatment of the early years, it is the first history of the Movement.

In 1883, the Oxford Movement marked its Jubilee. Of the original instigators, only Palmer remained both alive and Anglican. Newman was only alive. As a part of the Jubilee observance, Palmer was asked to write an article on the Movement for the Contemporary Review, which he did. [80] In addition, he republished his greatly augmented **Narrative.** The Contemporary Review article was essentially a condensation of the information and interpretation of the **Narrative,** 1843. In its own way, the augmented **Narrative** was both a new and an old creation.

In the 1883 edition, the first **Narrative** serves as pages 8-232. With the addition of a few explanatory notes, it is reproduced verbatim. Apparently, time had not altered Palmer's earlier perceptions. The rest of the volume contains a historical "Introduction" of eighty pages and a sixty page "Supplement to the Narrative."

For the present purposes, the "Supplement" must engage our attention. In it, Palmer sets out what had happened both to the Movement and because of the Movement during the years since 1843. After recounting the division of the Movement, and the fall of the "Romanizing Party," he gives himself to cataloging the advances made by the Church since that earlier time. What takes first place in his memory are institutional and organizational activities--synods, Convocation, the 1860 Congress of Churchmen, and diocesan conferences. Even when he speaks of "pastoral diligence," it, too, takes on an institutional definition. **[81]** Indicative of increased "diligence" are the twenty-six different kinds of clubs, classes, or organizations he lists, which can be found "going on quietly in parishes." **[82]** Finally, roughly one-third of the "Supplement" is given to identifying "Obstacles" to the Church--Romanism, Infidelity, Dissent, and Ritualism. **[83]** These obstacles are surely the predictable ones!

Both Owen Chadwick and Yngve Brillioth have observed that the most significant contributions made by the Oxford Movement to the life of the English Church were religious rather than theological. That is, its most lasting influence has been on the piety and worship of Anglicans. **[84]** In addition, though it has not "lasted" as some other has, the poetry of the Movement still provides it a prominent characteristic and an identifiable texture.

Granting the accuracy of this view, it is obvious that William Palmer, by aim or accomplishment, had little to do with the "religious" life of the Movement. It is certainly true that his **Origines Liturgicae** had a great deal to do with the revival of interest in liturgical study in the early nineteenth century and it is also true that such interest in turn may have generated a return to a deeper piety, but Palmer's intention in that work was not the enrichment of worship but rather the authentication of the English Church's claims to catholicity. If **Origines Liturgicae** affected the spiritual life of the English Church, it did so as an unintended consequence.

In addition to what one can say about **Origines Liturgicae,** it is a fact that Palmer vigorously opposed those later developments, like monasticism and the ritualist practices, which have most deeply influenced the continuing life of the Church. Even the romantic spiritual language of adoration, for example, which one finds in Pusey or Keble, is not to be found in either Palmer's work or his intentions. As close as he could come in this regard was to support the thought and language of others, as he did Pusey on the Eucharist.

What Palmer contributed to the Movement was decidedly theological and not religious. In his **Narrative of Events,** as well as **Origines Liturgicae** and the **Treatise on the Church of Christ,** Palmer's overriding concern was the Catholic Church as it was once and forever constituted. This Church he saw in England.

The mode in which Palmer cast his theological contribution was a predominately anti-Roman Catholic one. The stance he took was that of the controversialist and advocate, defending with great agility, what he believed to be the (true) catholic tradition.

When Palmer looked at the results of the Movement, his perceptions were of a particular kind. By 1883, he did not see that the Church's spiritual life, its piety and worship, had been enriched or improved. Rather, in his eyes, it was the institutional life which had been bolstered by the Movement. Signs of health and strength were found in organizational forms and increased numbers. Personal or corporate holiness or devotion--such notions, if noticed, were never mentioned.

After making this observation, one must be quick to say that the organizations which Palmer applauded and supported are best understood as the fleshing-out of the strong, heroic ecclesiology all his works present. Such activities were the embodiment of his views. They may also have been channels through which piety might seek expression, just as the episcopacy was a channel for the expression of tradition. In this way, what Palmer accounted to be the accomplishment of the Movement was quite consistent with his earliest intentions.

In the broad spectrum of Palmer's own work, the **Narrative** serves a double importance. First, in the most immediate sense, it provided a keystone for his anti-Romanizing writings, which continued beyond the **Narrative.** The early exchanges with Wiseman, the defence of Tract 90, and the Wiseman correspondence are all more intelligible when looked back upon from the perspective of the **Narrative.** Palmer's perceptions and the fears they generated flowered only falteringly until the **Narrative.** The self-understanding which necessitated his apologia, and which Palmer clearly articulated in its pages, provided a rationale not only for that work, but for that which preceded it and followed after.

Of even more significance, however, is the fact that the **Narrative** marked the finest hour of Palmer's life in the Movement, surely over-shadowing even his role in its inception. Although he had earlier claimed, rightly, that he had parted company with the Tract-writers after the early months of 1834, his interests, writings and correspondence attest to his continuing involvement, but in his own way. It was not as a Tractarian but rather as a controversialist and apologist that Palmer served the intentions of the Oxford High Church theology. In this light, the **Narrative of Events** stands as the epitome of his tenure as advocate.

NOTES

1. This essay is based upon my doctoral dissertation, "William Palmer of Worcester, 1803-1855: The Only Really Learned Man among Them," Princeton University, 1973, directed by Horton Davies.

2. All citations from the 1843 issue will be taken from **A Narrative of Events connected with the Publication of the Tracts for the Times, with Reflections on Existing Tendencies to Romanism, and on the Present Duties and Prospects of Members of the Church** (Oxford: John Henry Parker, 1843 second printing).

3. See the Preface to the 1883 re-issue, **A Narrative of Events connected with the Publication of the Tracts for the Times, with an introduction and Supplement extending to the Present Time** (London: Rivington, 1883), unpaged.

4. See, for example, correspondence between Newman and Froude: Newman to Froude, 13 Nov., 1833, **Letters and Correspondence of John Henry Newman During His Life in the English Church with a Brief Autobiography. Edited at Cardinal Newman's, Request by Anne Mozley** (London: Longmans, Green and Co., 1890), I, 420-421; and Froude to Newman, 17 Nov., 1833, cited in Piers Brendon, **Hurrell Froude and the Oxford Movement** (London: Paul Elek, 1974), 137.

5. Although neither is cited directly, general acknowledgement should be given to E. R. Norman, **Anti-Catholicism in Victorian England** (New York: Barnes and Noble, 1968), and Robert Greenfield, "The Attitude of the Tractarians to the Roman Catholic Church, 1833-1850," unpublished D. Phil. dissertation, Oxford University, 1956.

6. **Dictionary of National Biography**, ed. Leslie Stephen and Sydney Lee (London: Oxford University Press, 1959-60 reprint), XXI, 714-717 [DNB]. See also Brian Fothergill, **Nicolas Wiseman** (London: Faber and Faber, 1963).

7. "The High Church Theory of Dogmatical Authority," Dublin Review, III/VI (July, 1837), 43-79.

8. Ibid., 49.

9. "Tracts for the Times," Dublin Review, IV/VIII (April, 1838), 307-335, passim.

10. Dublin Review, V/X (October, 1838), 285-309.

11. Dublin Review, VII/XIII (August, 1839), 139-180. In his **Apologia,** Newman offered the following recollection of his reaction. In the face of Wiseman's argument, aided by Augustine's views on the Donatists, Newman said he thought "the theory of the Via Media was absolutely pulverized." **Apologia Pro Vita Sua,** ed. A. Dwight Culler (Boston: Houghton, Mifflin Company, Riverside Press, 1956), 123.

12. Tract 15, **Tracts for the Times by Members of the University of Oxford** (New York: Charles Henry, 1839, second edition), I, 91.

13. Dublin Review, V/X (October, 1838), 296.

14. Ibid.

15. Ibid.

16. Ibid.

17. **The Apostolic Jurisdiction and Succession of the Episcopacy in the British Churches Vindicated Against the Objections of Dr. Wiseman in the Dublin Review** (London: J. G. F. Rivington, 1840), 88.

18. Dublin Review, VII/XIII (August, 1839), 154.

19. This is the argument in the section on the English Reformation in Palmer's **A Treatise on the Church of Christ: Designed Chiefly for the Use of Students of Theology** (London: Rivington, 1838), Part II.

20. **Apostolic Jurisdiction and Succession,** 187.

21. **A Letter respectfully addressed to the Rev. J. H. Newman, upon some passages in his Letter to the Rev. Dr. Jelf, by N. Wiseman, D.D., Bishop of Melipotamus** (London: Charles Dolman, 1841).

22. The letters were published together as **Letters to N. Wiseman, D.D., on the Errors of Romanism, in respect to the Worship of Saints, Satisfactions, Purgatory, Indulgences, and the Worship of Images and Relics.** Citations here are taken from the first American edition, (Baltimore: Jos. Robinson, 1843).

23. Letter II, 4.

24. Letter IV, 23.

25. Marvin R. O'Connell, **The Oxford Conspirators: A History of the Oxford Movement 1833–1845** (New York: Macmillan, 1969) 336.

26. Manuscript holdings, the Oratory of St. Philip Neri, Birmingham, England.

27. Tract 90, **Tracts for the Times by Members of the University of Oxford** (London: Rivington, 1841), 4.

28. See **Treatise,** I/VIII.

29. Ibid., 23.

30. Ibid., I/VIII.

31. **Letters of the Rev. J. B. Mozley, D.D., Edited by His Sister** [Anne Mozley] (London: Rivington, 1885), 113.

32, Palmer to Newman, [March 18, 1841], Oratory, Birmingham.

33. Ibid.

34. "Bishop Jewel, His Character, Correspondence, and Apologetical Treatises," British Critic, XXX/LIX (July, 1841), 1-46. Authorship of articles in the Critic from January, 1836, to October, 1843, can be found in E. R. Houghton, "The British Critic and the Oxford Movement," **Studies in Bibliography,** ed. Fredson Bowers (Charlottesville, Virginia: Bibliographical Society of the University of Virginia, 1963), Vol. 16, 119-137.

35. DNB, XIV, 731-732.

36. Palmer to Newman, July 25, 1841, Oratory, Birmingham.

37. Manuscript holdings, Pusey House, Oxford.

38. **Narrative 1843,** 2.

39. Ibid.

40. Ibid., v.

41. Ibid., 9.

42. Ibid.

43. For text, see ibid., 11.

44. Ibid., 21.

45. Ibid., 22.

46. Palmer to Arthur Perceval, July 2, 1833, Pusey House Ms.

47. Palmer, "The Oxford Movement of 1833," The Contemporary Review, XLII (May, 1883), 654-655.

48. **Narrative 1843,** 23.

49. Ibid., 25.

50. Ibid., 33.

51. Ibid., 44

52. Ibid., 36.

53. Ibid., 47.

54. British Critic, XXXII/LXIV (October, 1842), 411.

55. **Narrative 1843**, 57-66.

56. Ibid., ix.

57. Printed in **Sermons, Chiefly on the Theory of Religious Belief, Preached Before the University of Oxford** (London: J. and F. Rivington, second edition, 1844), 311-354.

58. **Narrative, 1843**, 57.

59. "The Theory of Developments in Religious Doctrines," 321.

60. **Narrative, 1843**, 58.

61. Ibid., 60.

62. Ibid.

63. Ibid., 69.

64. Ibid., 70.

65. Ibid., 73.

66. Ibid., 74.

67. Ibid., 76.

68. Ibid., 85.

69. Ibid., 80.

70. Ibid., 87.

71. Unidentified newspaper clipping, Pusey House pamphlet 5564, Pa 280, 1837-43.

72. The Record, (October 26, 1843, to November 9, 1843 (Nos. 1667-1671).

73. Wilfred Ward, **William George Ward and the Oxford Movement** (London: Macmillan and Co., 1889), 246.

74. Pusey House pamphlet 3224, Pa 126, 1837-43.

75. Postscript, **Narrative 1843**, 3rd ed., 116.

76. W. R. Ward, **Victorian Oxford** (London: Frank Cass, 1965), 120.

77. **Memoirs of Joshua Watson** (Oxford and London: J. H. and Jas. Parker, 1861), II, 29.

78. Anonymous, "Secret History of Tractarianism," Pusey House pamphlet 5546, Pa 280, 1837-43.

79. O'Connell, **Oxford Conspirators**, 398.

80. Newman was given a chance to write in response to Palmer but refused, feeling that Palmer's treatment was satisfactory. P. W. Bunting to Newman, May 12, 1883, and Newman to Bunting, May 14, 1883, both Oratory, Birmingham, Mss.

81. "Supplement," **Narrative 1883**, 254f.

82. Ibid., 258-259.

83. Ibid., 269-291.

84. See Owen Chadwick (ed.), **The Mind of the Oxford Movement** (Stanford, CA: Stanford University Press, reprint, 1967), 58f., and Yngve Brilioth, **The Anglican Revival: Studies in the Oxford Movement** (London: Longmans, Green and Co., 1925), 37ff.

RELIGION IN THE WRITING OF AMERICAN HISTORY: RETROSPECTIVE ON THE SEVENTIES

John F. Wilson
Princeton University

Before Horton Davies immigrated to the United States he was already admired for his judicious study of the patterns of worship among English Puritans and for his critical assessment of new, and partial, versions of Christianity in the modern world. In the course of his three decades at Princeton, these subjects have continued to receive attention in his scholarship. Certainly his liturgical interests have flowered; who else in this generation has had the audacity to imagine--let alone publish--a study of worship and theology on the grand scale of five volumes? And while he has hardly announced sympathy for idiosyncratic religious movements, his religious inclinations have grown ever more catholic. The remarkable point, however, is that, in addition to these continuing themes in his work, Horton has developed--and shared with generations of students as well as colleagues and readers--an astonishing series of new interests: art (traditional and modern), architecture throughout Western history, literature (sacred and secular), pilgrimage as a phenomenon in European civilization, to identify only the best known. To remark upon the expanding sphere of Horton's interests is to indicate that his subject has become culture itself, albeit with an accent upon its religious aspects.

What fascinates a long-term younger colleague is that in the last decade the same enlarged range of sensitivity to religion and its location in the society and culture has been generally manifested in scholarship concerning religion in America. This body of work has evidenced both an increased variety of subjects and new kinds of approaches to them. Thus his adopted compatriots have, like Horton, displayed an expanded sense of religion, a greater appreciation for the kinds of claims it makes upon its adherents, and a marked appreciation for its cultural situation. This essay will review that extension and enrichment of the study of American religion, finding that it has paralleled a comparable development in the work of Horton Davies. In so doing, it suggests that scholarship may well be generational, and that in hidden and perhaps inexplicable ways, contemporary historiographies as cultural constructs manifest common characteristics.

* * * * *

In 1964, Henry May proposed that religious historiography, or at least its possibility, had been recovered in the preceding thirty years. [1] In important respects the literature produced in the decade of the 1970s demonstrates how correct his judgment was. The number of relevant studies, the range of particular topics they cover, and the variety of interpretations they advance all deserve comment. This state of the field is yet more striking because the same decade was relatively barren in areas which might be thought cognate, for example, constructive religious thought. This represents a reversal of roles, for when Sydney Ahlstrom reflected upon American religious history in the 1960s a decade ago, he noted comparatively few historiographical works but thought moral and theological writings the items of consequence. [2] Certainly for the seventies the situation is very different.

At the same time, however, the diversity of relevant studies makes difficult, if not impossible, identification of a predominant axis or even several overriding themes. Accordingly, attention will be given to noteworthy and representative studies in some important general categories. One obvious group is that of comprehensive interpretations. Other sets comprise monographs about regions, movements, figures, institutions, events, and the like. As specific as many of these monographs and books may be, often they contribute to a fuller understanding of religion in American history. A small but significant group of studies is directed to the interpretation of American culture but with religious materials as the means best suited to achieve that end. In no sense is it possible to discuss all relevant candidates for inclusion in this essay, and important publications are no respecters of arbitrary decades. One important point is to demonstrate the variety and range of an extensive literature as well as its important overall directions. More significant still is the implicit point that attention to its religious aspects has seemed increasingly important to an adequate interpretation of American history.

In certain respects the decade of the 1970s was framed by two very different overall interpretations of religion in American history, while a third major study punctuated the period and represented a third distinctive approach. Sydney Ahlstrom's **A Religious History of the American People** was initially published in 1972. [3] By any measure it is a massive book. With sixty-three separate chapters, comprising nine distinct parts, the over-sized text runs to some 1,100 pages. Its central theme concerns as indelibly puritan impulse at the core of three and one-half centuries of American cultural life. But the setting Ahlstrom sketches reaches back to late medieval Europe and forward to the post-puritan America which, in his view, decisively emerged in the 1960s. Within this framework any number of stories are recounted, episodes which make a glorious pageant out of this continuing experience of a people. The author's nominalism permits him to respect all the episodes--and to reflect and synthesize heterogeneous sources. So great leaders and institutions have their due along with lonely figures and dissenting and marginal movements.

It is interesting to place beside the Ahlstrom volume a slighter textbook published at the end of our period. **America, Religion and Religions**, by Catherine L. Albanese is explicitly written for classroom use and is much more selective. [4] Some fourteen chapters suffice for this project, and since the ideal of inclusiveness is clearly not possible, the author renders the necessity of selection a virtue. The first part stresses the "manyness" of religion in America: native American, Jewish, Roman Catholic, mainstream Protestant, Afro-American, as well as new religions and Eastern religions. By concentrating upon examples of diversity, and insisting upon the tenacity of traditions, Albanese yields nothing to Ahlstrom in terms of emphasis upon variety (though not his nominalistic construction of it). The shorter second part turns to the "oneness" of religion in American history--public Protestantism, civil religion, cultural religion--as a means of emphasizing the commonalities of the separate traditions and the positioning of each with respect to the cultural "center." Albanese's approach is informed by "history of religions" theories so that, far more than Ahlstrom, conscious selection and interpretation are at work throughout her writing.

If these two very different studies effectively frame a decade, beginning versus end, nominalist reading within an overarching theme versus inclusive interpretation on the basis of theoretical premises, a third overall study, published in the middle of the decade, also deserves comment. Robert T. Handy's project was more conventional, limited, and in some respects cautious. **A History of the Churches in the United States and Canada** is designed to take advantage of the possibilities for comparative study within the two North American national communities. [5] It is also primarily concerned with the shaping of Christianity, and that basically in terms of institutions. So comparisons, while explicit, are much less far-ranging than those implicit in Albanese's work. By the same token it is also less enamored of the particular than Ahlstrom's. In these terms it stands closer to the preceding traditions of scholarship while espousing a comparative program.

To comment that these three fine studies vary greatly is trivial. The point of juxtaposing references to them is that, taken together, they indicate that a spectrum of approaches is now routinely used in the study of religion in American history. Even more, this progression indicates that there has been a broad shift to social and cultural frameworks for the interpretation of religion. This suggests why so much of the literature of the decade is period and/or problem specific. To write of religion (not to speak of religions), or Christianity (or even some aspect of it), in American history necessarily raised searching issues about what the subject is as well as involving all the conundrums which generally characterize history writing. This point is illustrated in the provocative monograph by William Clebsch on **American Religious Thought.** [6] Its thesis is that in the move from Edwards to Emerson to James theology per se dissolves and more properly becomes designated by the alternative rubric of the title. To place beside each other the works by Ahlstrom, Handy, and Albanese forcefully poses this issue. Under these circumstances we are indebted to them all for the directness and vigor with which each ventured upon a separate approach to writing about religion in American history.

A large number of publications had directed attention to particular topics, turning to advantage and working to extend previous perspectives. A good example is at hand in the case of Puritanism. Here there has been a movement away from preoccupation with "declension," and several monographs have appeared that do not assume development across several generations as necessary devolution. Perhaps this is most evident in Robert Middlekauff's interpretation of **The Mathers.** [7] A comparable weighing of change with respect to institutions may be seen in several other unusually fine studies.

David Hall's **The Faithful Shepherd** is a full, careful, and highly nuanced analysis of the ministry in New England. [8] It reaches back to delineate the English and continental roots of the tradition, and treats the colonial elaboration and refinement of this Protestant office. The ministry in New World Puritanism has stood as a subject of inquiry for many decades. But only after the puritan tradition itself had been interpreted in a cultural framework, an ideal set out and begun by Perry Miller, was it possible for these old bones to take on new life.

Much the same point can be made about the subject of the sacramental life. Like Hall's study of the ministry, Brooks Holifield's monograph about the sacraments in the New England religious tradition derives its interpretive strength from the broader perspectives that have revitalized scholarship on Puritanism since World War II. **The Covenant Sealed** also traces the roots back into English and continental sources, thus showing New World developments with skill and analytical power. [9] In general these longitudinal studies focus on high cultural issues. A partial exception is a third example, Winton Solberg's discussion of the sabbath in early America, **Redeem the Time.** [10] Here too the earlier paradigm of declension has been dissolved so that cultural change is neutral.

At the same time that significant work like the above has enlarged an established subject like Puritanism, important studies have begun to suggest some of the variegation in the texture of religious life and practice that has marked different regions. This parallels recent emphasis in political and social history, and undoubtedly reflects late twentieth-century social and political developments. The most notable example of this genre is Donald G. Mathews' **Religion in the Old South,** which depends upon a sophisticated understanding of culture to analyze the levels of symbolization and action that structured the life of this region. [11] In many ways, Mathews' work provides a model for the historical study of religion as taking on a variety of cultural expressions. At the same time, it offers an example of "pay-offs" in fusion between theoretical reflection and empirical study.

A contrast can be drawn between Mathews' venture and other studies of regional subjects--which lack its methodological elegance. John Boles' **The Great Revival, 1787-1805** is an example of a rich and careful study that provides a useful summary of a noteworthy event. [12] But its interpretation is wholly narrative. Brooks Holifield's **The Gentlemen Theologians,** another study rising out of regionally defined subject matter, concerns the leading antebellum clergymen of the South. [13] It provides summary discussions of leading religious figures who were socially consequential but generally unappreciated--that is, they have eluded significant historical understanding. Like the Boles study, however, this one does not take full advantage of cultural perspectives in the manner of Mathews.

In the broad shift to social and cultural perspectives on religious subjects, increasing attention has been given to movements rather than institutions or particular bodies. A partial example of this is George Marsden's **The Evangelical Mind and the New School Presbyterian Experience.** [14] The "New School" was an influential group within the Presbyterian Church that in the nineteenth century came to form the basis for the "northern church." A broader study within the Reformed family (falling just outside the decade although it was widely consulted and used as a doctoral dissertation throughout it) is Fred J. Hood's much revised **Reformed America.** [15] This is an important analysis of the central Calvinist impulse that stemmed from Witherspoon's Princeton, which for too long was treated as if it were but a secondary extension of the New England Edwardsian tradition.

Religious movements in America have often been society-wide and not necessarily linked so directly to denominations. Some of the most significant recent gains in the historiography of American religion have been through studies of movements which had substantial cultural reality beyond a relationship to formal church bodies.

A good example of this is millenarianism. Recurrent throughout Western history, quests for the Millennium have been studied with care in Western historiography in recent decades. Historians of American religion gave it extensive attention in the 1970s. Especially noteworthy is James L. Moorhead's carefully delineated **American Apocalypse: Yankee Protestants and the Civil War, 1860-1869.** [16] Of interest also is a structuralist study by James W. Davidson, **The Logic of Millennial Thought.** [17] While primarily concerned with colonial phenomena, it reaches into the English background and draws conclusions about millenarianism that are very much more general.

Another significant movement is fundamentalism, which can be understood in terms of a spectrum that runs from interpreting it as a reduction of the Reformed tradition to absolute essentials to viewing it as a caricature of Thomas Paine in a religious mode. Early in the decade Ernest Sandeen analyzed the connection of fundamentalism with the Princeton theology of Charles Hodge and associates as well as with the tradition of "dispensationalism" rooted in the Plymouth Brethren. [18] A more recent study by George Marsden, falling at the end of the decade, is less concerned with origins and provides a fuller treatment that indicates the many sources and multiple appearances of this movement. [19] Such a discussion makes it clear that "fundamentalism" must be interpreted finally in terms of a social movement. The literature of the last decade confirms Richard Hofstadter's judgment that fundamentalism is the expression of a cultural style with deep sources in the structure of American society itself. [20]

If fundamentalism has been well served by recent literature so too has its counterpart, modernism. Never as shrill or strident as fundamentalism, probably because derived from liberalism, and perhaps without the effective organization that has given influence to its rival, modernism has nonetheless clearly been condensed into one or more religious movements. The Social Gospel, for example requires this larger context to be interpreted adequately. William R. Hutchison's **The Modernist Impulse in American Protestantism,** securely anchored in the discussion of individuals and groups, provides access to this setting. [21] One reason that the significance of modernism in American religion has been under-appreciated is the essentially polemical position taken against it by its successor movement in the interwar and postwar era--Neo-orthodoxy. With additional perspective on the latter, its dependence upon as well as modification of the former has emerged much more clearly.

Revivalism is another "movement" that has been interpreted in, if anything, even broader terms. William McLoughlin, who established the subject as peculiarly his own with earlier studies, [22] returned to the topic with an essay that views revivalism as the great heartbeat of American society. In **Revivials, Awakenings, and Reform, 1607-1977,** [23] he proposes that it was definitively established in the Great Awakening of the eighteenth century as a revitalization movement, and recapitulated not once but three times in the nineteenth and twentieth centuries. This extension has raised questions about the validity of studying revivalism as a repeated dynamic movement within the society. Without further analysis than the essay offers, doubt has been expressed about its historiographical usefulness.

Although emphasis properly falls on historiography that has broadened attention to religious movements, important studies have had a more restricted focus. Particular religious organizations that were in part defined by religious terms and dedicated to religious purposes have also received attention. An example is city mission societies. A fine case study of the New York city missions movement is Carroll Smith-Rosenberg's **Religion and the Rise of the American City.** [24] Another case study that calls attention to religious aspects, among others, of social institutions is Maren L. Carden's monograph on the Oneida community, a careful analysis of this most fascinating of the utopian ventures spawned in the nineteenth century. [25] Of course, case studies invite comparisons. With respect to utopian communities, Rosabeth Kanter's **Commitment and Community** indicates how sociologists can make use of historical data--and how the latter are interpreted helpfully by them. [26]

Case studies forcefully pose the issue of how religious aspects of, or elements in, a socio-cultural matrix are related to its other aspects or elements. Two recent publications are noteworthy examples of this point. Paul E. Johnson's meticulous analysis of the social components of the classical nineteenth-century revivals in Rochester, New York demonstrates the plasticity of religious symbols and behaviors in a period of social transition or change and shows how they work to make continuing community possible albeit in new forms. [27] In this connection the study of **Salem Possessed** by Paul Boyer and Stephen Nissenbaum also serves to suggest how religious elements are not abstract, remote, or other-worldly, but rather woven into the warp and woof of social life. [28] This is so much the case that, especially under conditions of social change or severe stress, their significance may be magnified. Religion may serve as a basis for attempting to create communities to resist, as well as to foster, the change or changes perceived to be taking place. Both of these books also indicate, however, that the cost associated with case studies is insufficient attention to longitudinal patterns, perhaps especially with respect to religious traditions.

Individual figures, or groups of them, who were noteworthy in the religious life of the society, were also studied in the decade. A few illustrations will stand for a much larger number. Samuel Willard, perhaps closest to a systematic theologian among the early American divines, has been well served in the biographical study by Ernest Lowrie. [29] The extraordinary Beecher clan has been brought into sharper focus by Marie Caskey's **Chariot of Fire: Religion and the Beecher Family.** [30] Woodrow Wilson's rootage in the religious traditions of the South is a prominent aspect of the biographical study by John M. Mulder that traces his career through the Princeton years. [31]

Any discussion of individuals must include mention of that towering figure, Jonathan Edwards, who at last seems to be receiving the sustained attention that, since Perry Miller, it has been thought he deserves. Four volumes of the **Works** came out in the decade under discussion, including one composed largely of previously unpublished manuscript materials, **Apocalyptic Writings,** edited by Stephen J. Stein. [32] Manuscript materials form at least a part of several other volumes, including **The Great Awakening** and particularly **Scientific and Philosophical Writings.** [33] With the attention he is now receiving outside the Yale Edition in numerous books like Conrad Cherry's **Nature and Religious Imagination,** and the major work by Norman Fiering, Edwards can no longer be judged a wholly "neglected" national figure. [34]

Typically, contemporary events serve to focus historical studies. The bicentennial celebrations of the beginning of the War for Independence occasioned several significant (as well as not so significant) books. One was a meticulous review by Nathan O. Hatch of preaching in the revolutionary era. [35] Hatch argued that the "civil millenarianism" which figured in the sermon writings of the new republic was a direct outgrowth of the struggle for independence. An even broader view of the revolutionary era as religiously generative was offered by Catherine Albanese in **Sons of the Fathers.** [36] Making use of interpretive categories drawn from the history of religions, the study analyzes, for example, the religious symbolism of the Liberty Tree, and the religious significance of the Masonic movement. In a partly comparable way, with the belated acknowledgment of a continuing Afro-American presence in the society, systematic attention was finally directed to the religious components that bulk so large in terms of cultural reality if not conventional social data. A strong study by Albert J. Raboteau, **Slave Religion**, was concerned with Afro-American practices in the South before Emancipation. [37] See also the fine study by Milton J. Sernett, **Black Religion and American Evangelicalism**. [38]

In general, studies of Roman Catholic subjects in American religious history have been cast largely as chronicles, usually based around diocesan archives and dominant ecclesiastical figures. In the 1970s two studies by Jay P. Dolan established that new directions were possible. **Catholic Revivalism** analyzes the strategies adopted by Roman Catholicism in the nineteenth century to retain the loyalty of migrating co-religionists. [39] **The Immigrant Church** is concerned with adaptations made by Irish and Germans in New York City between 1815 and 1865. [40] There is potential for much more work on this and comparably neglected traditional subjects.

The literature discussed above issued from the perception that religion had been thoroughly a part of American social history. At the same time, a growing literature has taken its departure from more strictly cultural perspectives. This distinction is certainly not absolute, neat, or sharp. Indeed, some of the studies already mentioned focus on cultural materials to a substantial degree. Albanese's **Sons of the Fathers**, as an example, is almost exclusively given over to analysis of cultural materials, but her larger framework derives from the politically defined period of the American Revolution and the social transformations associated with it. Some of the studies, an example being Mathews' **Religion of the Old South**, move virtually to define the religious subject as the central cultural aspect of the social system. So religion identified as a part of social history frequently has moved toward, and sometimes even approximated to, religion perceived as a cultural subject matter. This is certainly the case in David Stannard's **The Puritan Way of Death**. [41] Here a cultural perspective on New England is brought into focus by the broader historical interest in death developed by Philippe Aries. Where the shift to a cultural orientation has taken place there is typically less emphasis upon historical narrative or framework and more attention to the symbolic coherence religion mirrors or the dissonance it reflects within the society. Thus the dynamics of social change, if not the changes themselves, are accessible through religious mateials. Some examples of more strictly cultural studies may make this point clear.

One recent widely recognized study that depends upon a cultural understanding of religion is Ann Douglas' **The Feminization of American Culture**. [42] As the title suggests, the subject is a transformation of the culture worked through within an influential nineteenth-century subculture. In discharging her program the author draws heavily upon religious figures and institutions--specifically liberal clergymen and the symbiotic relationship they sustained with female authors. The outcome of this transformation is a progressive institutionalization of these new styles and values.

Another example of a study predicated upon a cultural understanding of religion is provided by an anthropologist. Dickson D. Bruce, Jr., studied the frontier camp meeting within the framework of symbolic anthropology. His book, **And They All Sang Hallelujah,** does not add to the specifics of our knowledge about the subject but it does identify the human dynamics and implications of this social institution which was perfected on and central to the Appalachian frontier. [43] The approach of cultural studies is complementary to that of social histories of religion--and offers the possibility of new dimensions in historiography because it attends directly to the power and influence exercised through religion.

It is not accidental that these two examples of recent cultural studies were written on the one hand by a professional student of literature and on the other by an anthropologist. For in the last decade both disciplines, cognate to the historical study of religion in America in different ways, have represented powerful resources for those involved in the field. On the literary side, the studies of those concerned with typology and figuralism have invigorated reading of puritan texts and demonstrated connections between religious and secular traditions which have until now been scarcely appreciated and little understood. The fruit of this interest is seen in Sacvan Bercovitch's **The Puritan Origins of the American Self and The American Jeremiad** (a reissue of his earlier "Horologicals to Chronometricals"). [44] Collaborators and associates in this effort have made contributions as well, for example, Emory Elliott's **Power and the Pulpit in Puritan New England,** a discussion of links between shifting literary forms and generational changes, [45] and Mason Lowance's **The Language of Canaan,** an analysis of the religious forms of expression in puritan culture. [46]

In this connection, attention should be called to narrower studies of American religious subjects that are more strictly cultural in focus. An example would be Sandra Sizer's analysis of hymns as a popular cultural form in nineteenth-century America. [47] A related project is Catherine Albanese's interpretation of the Transcendentalists in terms of the alternative religious worldview they espoused: **Corresponding Motion.** [48] Such studies indicate how placing religious materials within a cultural framework has opened significant possibilities for reinterpretation in American religious history.

The potential influence of anthropology upon the study of religion in American history is equally great. The Bruce monograph inevitably directs attention to anthropologists like Clifford Geertz and Victor Turner whose own studies suggest (even as their theoretical positions make possible) imaginative ways of interpreting religion within the cultural framework of understanding developed in their discipline. [49] One example of a religious historian using this perspective to chart little-traveled regions is Peter W. Williams' **Popular Religion in America.** [50] Understood by the author as in part a counterpoint and supplement to Ahlstrom's book, it suggests possible approaches to hitherto fugitive data and marginal groups in order to incorporate interpretation of them into religious historical writing.

As this discussion suggests, in the course of the seventies there was no single framework for the study of religion in American history. When it first appeared, Ahlstrom's discussion of a post-puritan, post-Protestant era gained wide assent. The implication was taken to be that pluralism and diversity were more pronounced from the outset of, and throughout, American history than has been allowed for in conventional judgments. Some of the titles cited suggest, and the studies themselves make it clear, however, that concern with unitive aspects of American history has in fact continued strong. In many ways, for example, Robert Bellah's discussion of "civil religion" seemed to offer a framework that was congenial to many--saving that when all was said and done it looked suspiciously like a dominant Puritanism redivivus. **The Broken Covenant** elaborated insights flowing from the original essay, "Civil Religion in America." [51] A discussion of the possibilities and limitations of such a concept with respect to its interpretive power and reach is my own **Public Religion in American Culture.** [52]

Thus a retrospective on historical writing about American religion in the seventies must stress its variety, which is impressive, and its vigor. If an overall pattern emerged, it was increasing reliance upon a cultural framework for interpreting religion. This meant that less attention was directed to specifically intellectual history or to studies controlled by institutions. Similarly, social interests and literary concerns tended to move toward, or resolve into, cultural questions. This overall reconstellation in the interpretation of religion was not accidental in a period when cultural studies generally increased in prominence and influence. For within a cultural framework religious subjects link popular as well as high cultural phenomena, direct attention to individuals as well as to corporate activities, and are sensitive to change as well as to stability through time. Thus recent studies of religion in American history and culture may be seen to parallel the expansion of subject matters that Horton Davies has explored in his own work during the same period.

NOTES

1. See "The Recovery of American Religious History," in American Historical Review, 70 (1964), 79-92.

2. See "The Moral and Theological Revolution of the 1960's and Its Implications for American Religious History," in **The State of American History,** ed. Herbert J. Bass (Chicago: Quadrangle Books, 1970), 99-118.

3. (New Haven: Yale Univ. Press, 1972). Subsequently republished by Doubleday in two volumes (Garden City, L.I., 1975).

4. (Belmont, Calif.: Wadsworth, 1981).

5. (New York: Oxford Univ. Press, 1977).

6. (Chicago: Univ. of Chicago Press, 1973).

7. (New York: Oxford Univ. Press, 1971).

8. (Chapel Hill: Univ. of North Carolina Press, 1972).

9. (New Haven: Yale Univ. Press, 1974).

10. (Cambridge, Mass.: Harvard Univ. Press, 1977).

11. (Chicago: Univ. of Chicago Press, 1977).

12. (Lexington: Univ. Press of Kentucky, 1972).

13. (Durham, N.C.: Duke Univ. Press, 1978).

14. (New Haven: Yale Univ. Press, 1970).

15. (University, Ala.: Univ. of Alabama Press, 1980).

16. (New Haven: Yale Univ. Press, 1978).

17. (New Haven: Yale Univ. Press, 1977).

18. **The Roots of Fundamentalism** (Chicago: Univ. of Chicago Press, 1970).

19. **Fundamentalism and American Culture** (New York: Oxford Univ. Press, 1981).

20. See especially, "The Paranoid Style in American Politics" in the collection so titled (New York: Knopf, 1965) and **Anti-intellectualism in American Life** (New York: Knopf, 1963).

21. (Cambridge, Mass.: Harvard Univ. Press, 1976).

22. **Billy Sunday Was His Real Name** (Chicago: Univ. of Chicago Press, 1955) and **Modern Revivalism** (New York: Ronald, 1959).

23. (Chicago: Univ. of Chicago Press, 1978).

24. (Ithaca, N.Y.: Cornell Univ. Press, 1971).

25. **Oneida: Utopian Community to Modern Corporation** (Baltimore: Johns Hopkins Press, 1969).

26. (Cambridge, Mass.: Harvard Univ. Press, 1972).

27. **A Shopkeeper's Millennium** (New York: Hill & Wang, 1978).

28. (Cambridge, Mass.: Harvard Univ. Press, 1974).

29. **The Shape of the Puritan Mind** (New Haven: Yale Univ. Press, 1974).

30. (New Haven: Yale Univ. Press, 1977).

31. **Woodrow Wilson: The Years of Preparation** (Princeton, N.J.: Princeton Univ. Press, 1978).

32. **The Works of Jonathan Edwards,** Vol. V (New Haven: Yale Univ. Press, 1977).

33. Respectively, Vol. IV, edited by Clarence C. Goen (New Haven: Yale Univ. Press, 1972), and Vol. VI, edited by Wallace E. Anderson (New Haven: Yale Univ. Press, 1980).

34. The Cherry study (Philadelphia: Fortress, 1980); the second, **Jonathan Edwards's Moral Thought and Its British Context** (Chapel Hill: Univ. of North Carolina Press, 1981).

35. **The Sacred Cause of Liberty** (New Haven: Yale Univ. Press, 1977).

36. (Philadelphia: Temple Univ. Press, 1976).

37. (New York: Oxford Univ. Press, 1978).

38. (Metuchen, N.J.: Scarecrow, 1975).

39. (Notre Dame, Ind.: Univ. of Notre Dame Press, 1978).

40. (Baltimore: Johns Hopkins Press, 1975).

41. (New York: Oxford Univ. Press, 1977).

42. (New York: Knopf, 1977).

43. (Knoxville: Univ. of Tennessee Press, 1974).

44. Respectively (New Haven: Yale Univ. Press, 1975) and (Madison: Univ. of Wisconsin Press, 1978).

45. (Princeton, N.J.: Princeton Univ. Press, 1975).

46. (Cambridge, Mass.: Harvard Univ. Press, 1980).

47. **Gospel Hymns and Social Religion** (Philadelphia: Temple Univ. Press, 1978).

48. (Philadelphia: Temple Univ. Press, 1977).

49. See especially Clifford Geertz, **The Interpretation of Cultures** (New York: Basic Books, 1973).

50. (Englewood Cliffs, N.J.: Prentice Hall, 1980).

51. **The Broken Covenant** (New York: Seabury, 1975); "Civil Religion in America," Daedalus, 96, No. 1 (1967), 1-21.

52. (Philadelphia: Temple Univ. Press, 1979).

LITURGY AND WORSHIP

Oil Portrait by Gordon Wiles

CHRISTIAN WORSHIP:
HUMAN AND DIVINE TRANSCENDENCE OF TIME

John Marsh

Sometime of Mansfield College, Oxford

An historically notable courtship of seven years was summed up in a single memorable sentence by the Elohist historian thus: "Jacob served seven years for Rachel, and they seemed to him but a few days because of the love he had for her" (Gen. 29:20). This brief but felicitous statement is pregnant with metaphysical as well as emotional implications. The seven long years of Jacob's courting servitude ticked their seconds, minutes, hours, days, months, and years relentlessly away, and doubtless Jacob often felt the sluggish tedium of his enforced wait. Yet, at the end of the seven years he felt as if he had but waited a few days. His love for Rachel gave him the ability dramatically to telescope the seven years, and so be more ready and resilient to embark upon his marriage. I want to plead that such a power is not uncommon, indeed probably universal among mankind, and is but one form of man's power to transcend time, which finds its consummation and fulfilment in the central acts of Christian worship.

First, time is commonly, if albeit unconsciously transcended in the experience of succession in certain visual phenomena. Thus if I write the three letters C and A and T, the reader will make three successive apprehension of letters. But if I write CAT, the reader will still have three successive (though more closely connected) apprehension of the three letters, but their transsuccessional unity as the one word CAT will simultaneously come in one moment of transcendent apprehension. A like analysis is applicable to words that constitute a sentence, or part of a sentence, a fact which is recognized in the now familiar method of teaching children to read by the "sentence" method.

More revealingly it can be claimed that the same is true of mature artistic literary forms. The words and lines of a Keats sonnet; the many lines of Bridges' "Testament of Beauty"; the pages of a George Eliot or Thomas Hardy novel; the plays of a Shakespeare or a Pinero; all provide an experience of words in relentless temporal sequence, but are also experienced in their unity as a sonnet, or poem, or play, or novel upon which judgement is passed as a unity, a unity that is experienced in and through the temporal succession of the printed or the spoken word.

Similar observations can be made about music. Were I to play a theme from a Bach fugue note by longish interval after note, the hearer would experience a number of separate and unrelated auditory experiences. But when I play them in their proper close and prescribed sequence, those same disparate sounds are now cognized as a unity, a theme from a Bach fugue. But the theme in turn becomes another unit which, as part of the whole fugue, is also part of an experienced unity cognizable only in and through the transcendence of temporal succession. The capacity to hear a fugue, concerto or symphony thus also involves human beings in a transcendence of time--the time it takes to convey to human ears the required number of temporally successive sounds. It is significant for our theme to note that the temporal succession is indispensable to the aesthetic unity: to play all the notes of one melodic theme, to say nothing of all the sounds of a symphony, together would produce sound, but not sense: it would not convey what belongs to and derives exclusively from time and succession--the melodic phrase and flow.

Human beings can also experience transcendence in another way--by meditation, contemplation or some other practice of mysticism. But in such experiences time, as succession, is not a constituent element of the subject, and for that reason they are not relevant to the theme of this enquiry.

* * * * *

"God created man in his own image; . . . male and female created he them" (Gen. 1:27). There has been prolonged, profound, and so far unconcluded discussion as to what the conviction expressed in this text implies for a Christian understanding of human nature. But in this essay the analogical relationship between God and man will be examined from the other side, and the question will be posed: Seeing that human nature experiences both the irreversible passage of time and its transcendence, what is thereby implied for a Christian understanding of the divine nature? But however much the image of God in human nature suggests that God experiences both the irreversible flux of time and its transcendence, the analogical relationship between God and man must not be allowed to become, or to be treated, as one of identity.

The scriptures clearly articulate an awe inspiring difference between God and man in relation to time. "Before the mountains were brought forth, or ever thou hadst formed the earth and the world, from everlasting to everlasting thou art God" (Psalm 90:2). God's "experience" of time is quite other than man's: "Before I formed you in the womb I knew you, and before you were born I consecrated you; I appointed you a prophet to the nations" (Jer. 1:5). Similarly Paul wrote of him "who had set me apart before I was born" (Gal. 1:15).

Man's experience of time is inevitably limited. He can know, or attempt to know, what has taken place in times past, and try to discern what went on in what took place. He can observe what takes place in his own present time. He can to some extent foresee and foretell what will take place in the future. But in all his knowledge, of past, present and future, he remains highly fallible. The scriptures themselves record what different historical judgements can be formed upon events that have taken place, e.g. in Israel's establishment of a monarchy (cp. 1 Sam. 10:1 and 2 Sam. 7:12-16 with 1 Sam. 8:10-22 and Hos. 13:11). They record differences of the interpretation of what was taking place at particular times (e.g. Jer. 20:7-12). They emphasize that the future, known to God alone, is fundamentally hidden from men, save for what foreknowledge God reveals to them by his prophets. (cf. Isa. 48:3-8). The overall picture that emerges from such an examination of scripture is that while man is firmly rooted in the temporal succession, and can only partially and imperfectly discern beyond his historical present, God is in a real sense a present participant in the present, but is also "beyond" and "outside" and "above" it. He is always related to the passage of time and in final and absolute control of events.

Yet that conception of a universal, transcendent God in complete control of his creation is known to be the outcome of a long process of development. In the earliest days of the people which came to be known as Israel, God was a tribal deity expected to provide victorious aid in the tribal struggle for existence. Later when the various tribes united first in a confederacy, and later in a monarchy. Yahweh became the God of a chosen and covenanted people. In this perspective Yahweh's activity was recognized as a critically decisive factor in Israel's history. It was he who defeated Pharaoh at the Red Sea (Exod. 14 esp. vv. 13f., 19-21, 24f., 29f.) and who was the real victor in Joshua's defeat of the Amorites (Josh. 10:8, 14, 42, cp. 23:3). By the mid-eighth century B.C. the great prophets were teaching that Yahweh was actively concerned not only with Israel's national behavior, but also with that of surrounding uncovenanted peoples; Syrians, Philistines, Tyrians, Edomites, Ammonites, and Moabites were all subject to his judgement and just retribution for wrong. By the time of the Babylonian captivity (Second) Isaiah could even see the Persian

Cyrus as "the Lord's anointed" (Isa. 45:1). Yahweh indeed exercized very wide sovereignty in the historical order.

Another, perhaps final, conception of God appears to derive through and from the Jewish experience of captivity in Babylon. For there, apparently, Jewish theologians became familiar with the Babylonian creation epic, which they adapted to their own use. Thus Yahweh, first known as a tribal God, and later to be recognized as exercising a very wide historical dominion, came to be revered also as the God of creation, the origin (and, in distinction from Babylonian myths, the only origin) of all that is. So in Judaism the movement has not been from a God who is the creator to one that is active in history, but conversely, from the God who is known as active in history to one that created and sustains the whole universe of being.

So to know and worship the Hebrew God was to be in relationship with one who both transcended the created order, and was acting decisively, in accordance with his own purposes, in the history of the universe he ordained and sustains. The Hebrew-Christian God is thus both transcendent and immanent: but his transcendence is not that of the Deist, whose God may create the world, but then leaves it to its own development; nor is his immanence that of the Pantheist, whose God is inseparable from his universe. The transcendence and immanence of the Hebrew-Christian God are joined in the historical order, as the worship of that God clearly reveals.

* * * * *

In the Old Testament Israel's worship of God contained elements which, whether from principle or impracticability, have not survived to the present day. There were Jews in the time of Jesus who, like the prophets before them (e.g. Amos 5:21), wanted drastically to reform the worship of the Temple. Jesus certainly so desired (Mark 11:15-18; John 2:13-22), and may well have been influenced by the sectaries, either directly, or through his kinsman John the Baptist. But what has remained as a revealingly distinctive feature of Hebrew-Christian worship has been its power to absorb history in its liturgy. The worship of the God who is so transcendent that "heaven and the highest heaven" (1 Kings 8:27) cannot contain him, reaches its most profound and potent point in the recital of a piece of Jewish or Christian history.

A significant point concerning the Hebrew use of history in its worship of Yahweh is its introduction into the already established worship of the great annual agricultural festivals, common to Israel and her neighbors in the ancient near east. These festivals were timed to coincide with certain climactic points of the annual rhythm of nature, so that at a certain point of the lunar cycle, at the spring and autumnal climaxes God was met and worshipped at the time when he could be known to be visibly active. The distinctive feature of Israel's incorporation of the Exodus story into its liturgical worship was not the kind of sacrifice thereby required, a paschal lamb or a basket of harvest produce, but rather that all Israelites of every generation came to this one historical, non-repeatable, once-for-all event, as the moment when God had made himself known in historic action, and provided his people with a "time" when he could be called upon, for he was "near". Historical man thus had through this one event a permanent access to his ever-living God.

Three further points can be added: First, the revolutionary intrusion of history into liturgical structure was as valid in the family celebration of the family as in the official cult of the Temple. Second, by the penetration of history into liturgical worship it was understood that worshippers, individual and corporate, of any and every generation, were enabled in a real sense, to participate in the actual Exodus itself. Third, the convert to Judaism was required to undergo a baptism, so that, like all other faithful members of the Jewish religious community, he too "had passed through the sea and . . . [been] baptized into Moses" (1 Cor. 10:1f.). The theological basis of this is that when the individual or community of Israel met its God, it met one who was not subject, as human beings are, to the temporal succession; but is, while active in it, transcendent of it. To encounter God at any point of the historical process is to meet him who is active in it all: but because he is particularly self-revealing at the Exodus (say the Jews) or at the Cross and Resurrection (say the Christians) his true worship is properly offered there, where he is to be known in his fulness.

* * * * *

Human being meet their God by voluntary encounter each time they choose, individually or corporately, to worship him. They come to God as mortal beings, sharing the limitations of all things that are "in process", or "becoming". The child of twelve is "in process" to become the sometimes unrecognizably different thirty-six year old adult; the worshipping community of 1914 will be vastly different from that of 1984! Experience in and of the passage of time is an unavoidable instrument of inevitable change.

By contrast, God does not "come" to meet men in worship; he is always "at hand" for such an encounter. Moreover, his being is eternal, not sharing in the limitations of time's passage, not "in process", not changed by his experience or his action in the passage of time. He is always fully himself, and so holds in his time-transcendent being the whole story of his created order. Language begotten in time is patently inadequate for a full and appropriate statement of the God who meets his creatures as they worship him. But something valid and valuable can be suggested by noting the contrast between human worshippers who can only appear before their maker with such self-knowledge and awareness of the world they have so far attained (as a child of twelve or an adult of thirty-six) through their temporal existence. But God, who receives his creatures' worship is always his self-same being in each encounter with his worshippers. In penetrating into time from his eternity he appears as the one who holds together in his time-transcendent nature the whole story of his creation. Man does not meet a God who can be "dated"; but a never-changing God, creator, sustainer and consummator of the whole universe.

* * * * *

What content do such considerations as these provide for a true appreciation of the assertion that "man is made in the image of God"? The ability of human beings to experience some transcendence of time, which was latent in Jacob's felicitous testimony to a much abbreviated seven years, led to an examination of Hebrew-Christian worship which suggested that human beings are able, within their inescapable confinement in time, actually to transcend time's passage as they hold communion with God who is infinite and eternal, holding in his timeless being the whole story of his universe. For the Christian community the worship of God finds its profoundest and most eloquent point in its sacraments, notably the two "Gospel sacraments" of Baptism and Eucharist.

Baptism and Eucharist (or Lord's Supper, Holy Communion or Mass) are so designed that worshippers can meet God at a point where his power and authority can be recognized, acknowledged and appropriated. At Baptism the Church approaches God at <u>the</u> point where the Father's authority and power were most conspicuously declared and conveyed to <u>the</u> believer, Jesus. Jesus was himself baptized by John in the Jordan, and heard a voice from heaven which affirmed, "You are my beloved son; with you I am well pleased": and as he came out of the baptismal water he saw the Spirit descend on him with equipment sufficient for his subsequent conflict, in and outside the desert, with <u>the</u> adversary. But the approach to God through the Jordan baptism cannot be made in isolation. The baptism by water itself was wanting fulfilment: "I have a baptism to be baptized with; and how I am constrained until it is accomplished" (Luke 12:50; cp. Mark 10:38f.). So to be baptized into Christ is to be baptized into his death (Rom. 6:3), and it is impossible to be baptized into Christ's death without realization that the God who worked his great wonder there, has done so only because his power and authority are universal and truly without temporal limit.

So when Christians assemble to celebrate the Eucharist they approach God at the point where, in the moment of his apparent impotence in the world, he in fact showed his full omnipotence. And if the cross be regarded as the baptism which fulfilled the baptism of John, then the resurrection is the "word" which God spoke at that time to his son-community; and the pentecostal outpouring of the Spirit can be seen as the descent of the Spirit upon the son's new body--the Church.

In a well known passage Dr. C. H. Dodd has made the point well: "Past, present, and future are indissolubly united in the sacrament. It may be regarded as a dramatization of the advent of the Lord, which is at once His remembered coming in humiliation and his desired coming in glory, but realized in His true presence in the Sacrament . . . In the Eucharist, therefore, the Church perpetually reconstitutes the crisis in which the Kingdom of God came in history. It never gets beyond this. At each Eucharist we are there--we are in the night in which He was betrayed, at Golgotha, before the empty tomb on Easter day, and in the upper room where he appeared; and we are at the moment of His coming, with angels and archangels and all the company of heaven, in the twinkling of an eye at the last trump. Sacramental communion is not a purely mystical experience, to which history, as embodied in the form and matter of the Sacrament, would be in the last resort irrelevant; it is bound up with a corporate memory of real events. History has been taken up into the supra-historical, without ceasing to be history." (C. H. Dodd: **The Apostolic Preaching & its Developments**, Hodder & Stoughton, London 1936, pp. 234, 235). Little needs to be added to that statement. But one last reflection may not be inappropriate. In the Eucharist we are joined, as Dr. Dodd rightly says, with the fundamental crisis of history in which the kingdom of God came. But we are joined to more than that, if we indeed meet the God and Father of our Lord Jesus Christ. We are joined to the God whose "son" was oppressed by Pharaoh (Exod. 4:22f.; cp. Hos. 11:1), who worked his victorious wonder at the Red Sea, who "spake by the prophets". We are joined with the God who created the universe, and placed human beings, made in his own image, within it, to love and serve him in freedom. We are joined with the God who will bring his whole creation to the end which he has purposed, which he has revealed and ensured in Christ. We are joined to him who is the only eternal, yet the one who, in and through Jesus Christ, has bestowed on mortal men the inestimable gift of eternal life. So in the moments of sacramental worship the Christian experiences a foretaste in history of that life which lies for him beyond history, to which he has already been admitted by his savior. For "he who hears my word and believes him who sent me, has eternal life" (John 5:24).

HOOKER'S UNDERSTANDING OF THE PRESENCE OF CHRIST IN THE EUCHARIST

John E. Booty

Richard Hooker (1554-1600), author of the Anglican *magnum opus*, **Of the Lawes of Ecclesiastical Polity**, defended the Elizabethan Settlement of Religion against Puritan objections and in the process described the fundamental teachings of the Church of England. His explanation of the presence of Christ in the Eucharist has attracted attention since its first appearing in Book V of the **Lawes** in 1597 and deserves close study now in the light of the growing understanding we possess of Hooker and his doctrine.

In chapter 67 of Book V of the **Lawes**, Hooker presents his own understanding of Christ's presence in the Eucharist. This doctrine is that upon which all, Hooker believed, must agree and, indeed, do agree, whether they teach consubstantiation, transubstantiation, or some other doctrine. Its essential meaning is this: that by means of the Eucharist there is a "*reall participation* of Christe and of life in his bodie and bloode" (V.67.2). [1] Where is Christ present? The "*soule of man* is the receptacle of Christes presence" (ibid.). What of the elements? "The bread and cup are his bodie and bloode because they are causes instrumentall upon the receipt whereof the *participation* of his bodie and bloode ensueth" (V.67.5). On such a basis it is possible to interpret Christ's words, "This is my body", in this way:

> *This hallowed foode, through concurrence of divine power, is in veritie and truth, unto faithfull receivers, instrumentallie a cause of that mysticall participation, whereby as I make my selfe whollie theires, so I give them in hande an actuall possession of all such saving grace as my sacrificed bodie can yield, and as theire soules do presently need, this is 'to them and in them' my bodie* (V.67.12).

This view is in fact "another doctrine" set in opposition to the teachings of Roman Catholics, Lutherans, and others. While attempting to sound conciliatory, Hooker is in fact polemical and his teaching is controversial. This becomes most apparent in the section of the chapter where he seeks to prove that the Fathers of the Early Church taught as he does. Because this has not been recognized as a crucial clue to Hooker's understanding heretofore and because the exercise is inherently beneficial, we shall examine this section with great care.

Book V.67.11 begins:

> Touchinge the sentence of antiquitie in this cause, first, for as much as they knew that the force of this sacrament doth necessarilie presuppose the veritie of Christe both bodie and bloode they used oftentimes the same as an argument to prove that Christ hath as trulie the substance of man as of God, because heere wee receive Christ and those graces which flowe from him in that he is man. So that if he have no such beinge, neither can the sacrament have any such meaning as wee all confesse it hath. Thus Tertullian, thus Ireney, thus Theodoret disputeth.

Having already appealed to reason and the Scriptures in laying down his theology of participation in long sections dealing with the sacraments and the Christology undergirding them (V.50.57), and in this section having reasoned on the basis of Scriptural citations which can be variously argued, Hooker now, immediately preceding his conclusion cited above (V.67.12), makes a statement purporting to report accurately the basic views of tradition as embodied in the teachings of the Fathers. Clearly, this section was meant to confirm and seal his argument, proving that Tertullian, Irenaeus, and others taught as he taught. That is to say, the Fathers were convinced that the significance of "value" [2] of the Eucharist necessarily presupposed the reality [3] of Christ's body and blood, for they relied upon this understanding as proof that Christ is in substance both man and God. And this is so because effects reveal the cause of a thing; the faithful, in the sacrament receive those graces or benefits which come from Christ as Incarnate ("in that he is man"). If Christ was not fully man, then, quite plainly, the sacrament could not be that which we know it to be by its effects.

How do the citations stand up in relation to this statement? Tertullian is arguing against the doceticism of Marcion in asserting that the bread is only properly a figure of Christ's body in that there was a true body (**Adv. Marc.** 4.40.3). Irenaeus was arguing against the Valentinians that the wine can only be the communion in Christ's blood if it is indeed blood which comes from "venis et carnibus," veins and flesh (**Adv. Haer.** 4.1). Theodoret is most to the point arguing: "If therefore the divine mysteries are types of the true body, the body of the Lord is now a body, not changed into the nature of His divinity, but filled with the divine glory." [4] The emphasis in these citations is on Christ's bodily presence, something which Hooker has stressed before (see V.56.9, V.53.1) citing Cyril of Alexandria, Irenaeus, Gregory of Nazianzus, and Theodoret.

Hooker is here arguing against all in his time who would so spiritualize Christ's presence as to nullify the effects of Incarnation in what he boldly calls the deification of human nature (V.54.5). Christ, as fully human, inaugurated a new humanity and it is that grace-transformed humanity which we enter in Baptism and grow in to perfection through the Eucharist. Hooker nowhere mentions names, but Thornton suggests that he has in mind some Reformed theologians and some "Anabaptists." [5] At any rate it is important to realize that he begins his appeal to antiquity by establishing the belief that Christ is present to the faithful not only in his deity but in his humanity.

It is also important to emphasize that as is often the case he follows the Aristotelian and Scholastic teleological way of locating proofs in effects. This is not to say that faith is grounded in experience, for experience witnesses to realities which are the actual grounds of faith. But this way of arguing does seem to indicate that the testimonies of Christian experience are more reliable than any metaphysical explanations unrelated to experience.

Hooker then proceeds to another argument, one which clarifies and modifies his first:

> Againe, as evident it is how they teach that Christ is personallie there present, yea present whole, albeit a parte of Christ be corporallie absent from thence . . .

This statement is a reiteration of Hooker's argument in chapter 55, especially section 7: "For the person of Christ is whole, perfect God and perfect man wheresoever, although the partes of his manhoode beinge finite and his deitie infinite wee cannot say that the whole of Christ is simplie everie where . . . " It is his contention that "somewhat of the person of Christ is not everie where": his manhood--so far as position is concerned--being "restrained and tied to a certaine place." Nevertheless, by way of "conjunction" that manhood extends as far as deity and "is in some sorte present."

In both places cited, Hooker was striving to affirm Christ's bodily presence ("the person of Christ is whole" and thus if he is personally present he is present in body as well as in deity), while guarding against the error of the ubiquitarians, who, while teaching that Christ's glorified body is not locally confined in heaven but present wherever His deity is present, seemed to confuse the two natures of Christ in a union such as that taught by the Monophysites. [6] Hooker in chapter 55 speaks of "conjunction" and in chapter 53.4 of "mutuall commutation." In the latter chapter, section 3, he lays down a rule for resolving all questions concerning the union of the two natures in Christ: "that of both natures there is a cooperation often, an association alwayes, but never any mutuall participation whereby the properties of the one are infused into the other."

Why does Hooker expend so much energy on this matter? Because he is earnestly concerned to affirm the presence of the whole person of Christ in the Eucharist--deity and manhood--without falling into the error of the ubiquitarians, and because he is here defending the doctrine of the **Book of Common Prayer** with its dual emphasis on Christ's local presence in heaven and His presence in His whole person in the Eucharist. [7] More of this matter when we come to speak of conclusions.

Hooker proceeds to the first of two "that" clauses in his extended sentence:

> that Christ assisting his heavenlie banquet with his personal and true presence, doth by his own divine power ad to the naturall substance thereof supernaturall efficacie . . .

That is to say, Christ by his presence ("personel and true") adds "supernaturall efficacie" or grace to "the naturall substance" of the Eucharist (bread and wine). Hooker has discussed this at some length, especially in chapter 58.1-4 (see also 50.3). In a sacrament it is grace which is offered, elements which signify grace, and the word "which expresseth what is don by the elemente" (58.2). As Thornton put it: "Sacramental things are channels and occasions of grace," [8] this is their import, and it is their limit. But again, Hooker is steering a careful path between errors, seeking to defend the sacrament and sacramental things as channels of grace while denying that they possess grace in and of themselves. In the Fragment prepared in response to the Puritan Christian Letter, Hooker directed his attention to those Roman Catholics who contend that the English Church ascribes no efficacy to sacraments, making them "bare signs of instruction or admonition; which is utterly false." He asserts: "For Sacraments with us are signs effectual: they are the instruments of God, whereby to bestow grace; howbeit grace not proceeding from the visible sign, but from his invisible power." [9] In support Hooker cited Bernard, Bellarmine, Gregory de Valentia, Henrieus Henriquez, and William Cardinal Allen, the latter four being post-Tridentine theologians of note.

How do the Fathers support this position? Hooker cites Cyprian in relation to "Christ assisting," or thinks he's citing Cyprian. In fact, the work which Hooker attributes to Cyprian was written by Arnold, Abbot of Bonneval (fl. c. 1144), as a part of his **de Cardinalibus Operibus Christi.** [10] The work does not belong to the age of the Fathers. Furthermore, Hooker got at the work, **de Coena Domini**, in an edition by the Genevan, Simon Goulart (1543-1628), a humanist, popularizer, and theologian "mais non des plus marquants," for whom religion was "surtout une question de morale et de sentiment." [11] Nevertheless, Goulart provided annotations of **de Coena Domini** running as long as Arnold's work itself. This too will be dealt with when we come to conclusions. Here it is sufficient to note that the citation reads: "Sacraments indeed, considered in themselves, must have their own power, and the majesty cannot absent itself from the mysteries," [12] the conclusion being that unworthy recipients receive condemnation--the point of the statement. Goulart comments that the author "aliud vult esse sacramenta, aliud propriam eorum virtutem." [13] How apt is the citation? If the citation is properly placed (and the manuscript which is the copy text indicates that it is) [14] then it may be concluded that it is not irrelevant, but neither is it impressive.

Two other citations are given in relation to "doth by his owne divine power." The first is from **de Coena Domini** (not Cyprian as Hooker supposed but the twelfth century Arnold of Bonneval): "The divine essence ineffably poured itself upon the visible sacrament that religious devotion might be concentrated around the sacraments." [15] The second citation is from Eusebius 'Gallicanus' (the Pseudo-Eusebius Emisenus) although elsewhere Hooker indicated that he believed the work cited to be by Salvian of Marseilles (c. 400-c. 480). At any rate the work does not have the strongest authority amongst the works of the Fathers. [16] The citation reads: "The invisible priest by His word changes by secret power the visible creatures into the substance of His body and blood . . . In the spiritual sacraments the virtue (virtus) of the word gives the order, and the result (effectus) follows." [17] The quotation does, indeed, support Hooker's statement--perhaps too forceably! It is difficult to believe that Hooker would agree fully with the statement that Christ "by His word changes (convertit) . . . the visible creatures (bread and wine) into the substance (substantiam) of His body and blood." He has renounced such theological language and in particular the understanding of it in his own time.

Hooker proceeds to emphasize and elucidate the change in the bread and wine:

> which addition to the nature of those consecrated elementes changeth them and maketh them that unto us which otherwise they could not be . . .

In chapter 67.5 Hooker explains that the bread and wine are recognized as the body and blood of Christ because we acknowledge them to be "causes instrumentall upon the receipt whereof participation of his bodie and bloode ensueth," but he is careful to point out that those elements exhibit but do not contain grace (67.6). In the passage which we are scrutinizing it must be noted that he says what he means quite carefully: the divine power added to the elements once consecrated changes them and makes them "that unto us which otherwise they could not be" (my emphasis), that is to say, causes instrumental.

Hooker's citations begin with one from Theodoret's **Dialogi tres**, wherein Eranistes, the collector of opinions, asserts: "The symbols of the Lord's body and blood are one thing before the priestly invocation, and after the invocation are changed and become another thing." Against this, Orthodoxos, who represents Theodoret and truth, replies that after the consecration the mystic symbols "do not recede from their own nature. They remain in their former substance, figure, and form, and are visible and tangible as they were before; but they are thought of and believed in as what they have become and worshipped as being what they are believed to be." [18] This important statement impressively supports and explains Hooker's understanding. Theodoret is saying that the consecrated elements are unto us (being thought of and believed in) that which they have become, without any change of substance, figure, or form.

The remaining two citations are taken from **de Coena Domini**. In the second we read: "The food of immortality is given, which differs from common foods in that it retains the appearance of corporal substance, but by invisible working proves the presence of divine power." [19] The first asserts that whenever the words "Do this in memory of Me, This is My flesh, and, This is My blood," are pronounced and faith employed, "that supersubstantial bread and cup, consecrated by a solemn blessing, profit to the life and salvation of mankind." [20] Theodoret's statement is most supportive of Hooker, this last from **de Coena Domini** is least, but the important point here is that these citations from the Fathers on the whole emphasize more emphatically the symbolic nature of the consecrated elements than the change which takes place in them.

Hooker continues his explanation of the consecrated elements:

> that to us they are hereby made such instruments as mysticallie yeat trulie, invisiblie, yeat reallie worke our communion or fellowship with the person of Jesus Christ as well in that he is man as God . . .

Concerning "mysticallie/invisiblie", see the distinction between the visible substance and the invisible meaning of divine ceremonies (50.2), his distinction between outward and inward (57.2), and his emphasis on the "life supernaturall" (50.3; see also 57.3-4). Here, in this quotation, Hooker seems to have most clearly in mind his statement "that this sacrament is a true and a reall participation of Christ" (67.7). The consecrated elements are moral instruments towards that end. As such they work our "communion or fellowship" with Christ, the meaning of which is first of all to be found in 1 Cor. 10:16 where the governing word is koinonia, a passage cited by Hooker in a central section of his discussion of the Eucharist in this chapter (67.5). [21]

In his citations here, Hooker leans heavily upon **de Coena Domini**. The first from that source asserts that the faithful are joined to Christ by a spiritual union, [22] the second asserts that "Our union with Him neither mixes the persons nor unites the substances, but it associates capacities and confederates will (sed affectus consectat et confederat voluntates)," [23] and the third is "Our abiding in Him is eating Him, and our drinking Him is a sort of incorporation in Him." [24] The final citation is from Hilary of Poitiers, de Trinitate, also cited in Goulart's annotation of **de Coena Domini** and the place from which Hooker doubtlessly got it. [25] "He is the Father by the nature of His divinity; we in Him by His bodily birth, He again in us, by the mystery of the Sacraments." [26] Taken together, these passages do seem to support Hooker, but it must be noted that those from **de Coena Domini** do so more convincingly than that from Hilary. The twelfth century theologian provides the chief basis upon which Hooker stands here.

The next section in the sentence under review is in some ways the heart of the matter, providing the most critical test of Hooker's use of the Fathers:

> our participation also in the fruit of grace and efficacie of his bodie and bloode, whereupon there ensueth a kind of transubstantiation in us, a true change both of soule and bodie, an alteration from death to life.

The emphasis here falls upon "a kind of transubstantiation in us" involving participation now in the "fruit of grace." Participation is a key word for Hooker, especially the understandings contained in the words koinonia and menō (menein), the first preserving the distinction between two entities, involving a two-sided relationship of giving and receiving, the second meaning to abide in or be in union with, and thus emphasizing the unity. The first comes to Hooker largely through 1 Cor. 10, the second through John 6. Both words are operative in the Prayer Book Eucharist. [27]

Hooker defines grace as the expression of divine favor, of God's mercy towards undeserving creatures. Grace is also the working of the Holy Spirit in us, the chief effects being the "saving virtues, such as are faith, charity, and hope." Finally grace is "the free and full remission of our sins." [28] It is as a result of this grace that "there ensueth a kind of transubstantiation in us." Hooker means here that a radical transformation occurs, defined in terms of the fruit of grace and also in terms of what he calls "a true change of soule and bodie, an alteration from death to life." There is a sense in which Hooker surrounds his central assertion of "transubstantiation in us" with definitions which are inter-related, for the "fruits" of grace include "change of soule and bodie" and "alteration from death to life."

Concerning the "change of soule and bodie" Hooker has said that "as our naturall life consisteth in the union of the bodie with the soule; so our life supernaturall in the union of the soule with God" (50.3; see 57.3). In 67.7 Hooker further explains his meaning as he says that the effect of the participation in Christ which the Eucharist affords us "is a reall transmutation of our soules and bodies from sinne to righteousness, from death and corruption to immortalitie and life." This is what Hooker means by "a kind of transubstantiation in us." [29]

How well do the patristic sources support this statement? Once more Hooker begins with **de Coena Domini**, thinking its author to be Cyprian. "This unleavened bread, a true and pure food, through the visible appearance and the sacrament, by its touch sanctifies, by faith illuminates, by truth conforms us unto Christ." [30] Next comes a passage from Pope Leo the Great, cited by Goulart: [31] "Participation in the body and blood of Christ does nothing else but unite us to that which we take, so that in all things spiritual and corporal we bear about Him in Whom we die, in Whom we are buried, in Whom we are raised up again." [32] The third citation is from Irenaeus, in which he says that in receiving the Eucharistic bread, now composed of "an earthly something and a heavenly something . . . our bodies . . . are no longer corruptible, but have the hope of resurrection." [33] The final citation, of considerable importance since Hooker has shown considerable reliance on the author in treating the Incarnation, is from Cyril of Alexandria commenting on John 6:53. "Since the redeeming flesh, joined to the word of God, which is by nature life, has become life-giving, when we eat it, then have we life in us, being joined to that Flesh which has been made life." [34]

These citations all support--to some degree--Hooker's understanding of participation in the fruits of grace, of the transformation of the Christian from corruption to incorruption, from death to life, but none of them supports Hooker in his central terminology ("a kind of transubstantiation in us") nor in that which it implies (the change is in the faithful receivers and not in the elements save insofar as they are instrumental in effecting change in the receivers).

Hooker has now concluded his citation of the Fathers and proceeds to a conclusion, rephrasing and expanding what has gone before:

> In a worde it appeareth not that of all the ancient fathers of the Church anie one did ever conceive or imagin other then onlie a mysticall participation of Christes both bodie and bloode in the sacrament, neither are theire speeches concerninge the change of the elements them selves into the bodie and bloode of Christe such, that a man can thereby in conscience assure him selfe it was theire meaninge to perswade the world either of a corporall consubstantiation of Christ with those sanctified and blessed elementes before wee receive them, or of the like transubstantiation of them into the bodie and bloode of Christ. Which both to our mysticall communion with Christ are so unnecessarie that the fathers who plainlie hold but this mysticall communion cannot easilie be thought to have meant anie other change of sacramentall elementes then that which the same spirituall communion did require them to hold.

Thus he concluded the section.

It is manifest that the Fathers did not teach consubstantiation or transubstantiation, concepts unknown to them, but neither did they teach Hooker's doctrine. E. C. Ratcliff discusses the views of the Fathers in terms of mystery, mimesis and representation: "The sacramental rites of the Church, as an ancient Christian regarded them, were drama; representaverunt; they 'made present again' to his sight, with all their saving potency, the divine acts from which those sacramental rites took their origin and their efficacy." [35] Even a Father such as Cyril, using terms such as metapoiein and methistanai to describe the conversion of the elements, was not so much concerned for that conversion as for the ramifications of the hypostatic union of the divine and human natures in Christ for the eucharistic liturgy. [36] Hooker is supported in his concern to focus on the effects of the Eucharist but the Fathers could not be expected to agree with his tortuous denials of doctrines with which they were not acquainted. The fact is, as Ratcliff says of Hooker's teaching on Confirmation in relation to Baptism, that "For all his judicious Anglicanism, Hooker stands . . . in the line of medieval tradition." [37] He is concerned to refute the doctrines of consubstantiation and transubstantiation--and also such doctrines as deny any actual importance to the consecrated elements--and to affirm a doctrine which is consonant with the meaning of the Holy Communion of the Elizabethan **Book of Common Prayer**.

From whence came Hooker's doctrine? Dugmore suggests the possibility of the reformed doctrine found in the **Consensus Tigurinus**, but while admitting that Hooker uses "Tigurine language when he speaks of the 'efficacy, force and virtue' of Christ, or of Christ by sacrament really and truly performing in us his promise" he does not teach "that the force of the sacrament resides in the promise." [38] In some ways Hooker's doctrine, especially in its emphasis upon participation, resembles that of John Calvin. I have in mind his **Of the True Partaking of the Body and Blood of Christ in the Holy Supper**, against Tileman Heshusius, for instance: "When I say that the flesh and blood of Christ are substantially offered and exhibited to us in the Supper, I at the same time explain the mode, namely, that the flesh of Christ becomes vivifying to us, inasmuch as Christ, by the incomprehensible virtue of his Spirit, transfuses his own proper life into us from the substance of his flesh, so that he himself lives in us, and his life is common to us." [39] This, and like statements, agree well with Hooker's teaching, but I find no direct evidence that he drew on Calvin for his teaching, a fact which is no convincing proof.

What we do know is that Hooker used and relied upon Arnold of Bonneval's **de Coena Domini**, believing it to be by Cyprian, and this in an edition heavily annotated by the unoriginal, humanist, Calvinist, Simon Goulart, Hooker's contemporary. In eleven conclusions, Goulart finds the Father who wrote **de Coena Domini**, teaching that on the one hand the bread and wine become, after consecration, the body and blood of Christ, [40] howbeit "Dicuntur autom panis et corpus Christi in mysterio, et pro Sacramenti ratione." Most important is this statement:

> "Quemadmodum coniunctio naturarum, in una Christi persona, illas naturas non confundit, neo humanam in divinam minime transformat: nec membrorum cum capite coniunctio, caput cum membris permiscet: ita nec panis est realiter corpus Christi, etiam si Christi maiestas non se absentat mysteriis: nec panem Angelorum sine sacramento manducamus in terris." [41]

Or we may look at the annotations themselves, especially in places where we know Hooker was reading Goulart carefully. In such places we find: "Panis ergo substantialiter manens panis, usu et conditione, hoc est, Sacramentaliter fit corpus Christi," and "Sicut in Christo invisibilis divinitas unita visibli humanitati, per hanc operans sese exerebat: sic in Sacramentis, invisibilis Divinitas, assistens visibilibus Symbolis, per ea operatur fidem in cordibus, et carnis Christi nos facit participes." [42]

Since Hooker was defending the **Book of Common Prayer** it is possible that he was influenced by the Prayer Book and by Thomas Cranmer. This is not the place to enter into the thorny subject of Cranmer's Eucharistic teaching. I am inclined to agree with Cyril Richardson that Cranmer entertained possibly conflicting doctrines, the one emphasizing a spiritual presence--influenced by late medieval nominalism--and the other emphasizing a mystical presence--influenced by John 6 and his inherent devotional attitude toward the sacrament. [43] While Hooker's terminology is not used by Cranmer, it is nevertheless true that his doctrine agrees well with the liturgy Cranmer devised (with the help of others), emphasizing as it does communion and the doctrine of consecration in the use of it. [44] Cranmer affirmed "that Christ is in all persons that truly believe in him, in such sort, that with his flesh and blood he doth spiritually nourish and feed them, and giveth them everlasting life, and doth assure them thereof, as well by the promise of his word, as by the sacramental bread and wine of his holy supper." [45] For Cranmer Christ is corporally in heaven, "and spiritually in them that worthily eat and drink the bread and wine." [46] There is no disjunction between such statements and Hooker's doctrine, although Hooker's teaching is more carefully and systematically presented with language not found in Cranmer.

It is quite possible that Hooker was influenced by all whom we have mentioned--and more besides. He relied heavily upon the twelfth century **de Coena Domini**, but he did not know that it was written some nine hundred years after Cyprian. For him it was a genuine work representing the thought of a major Father writing around the middle of the third century. It is also true to say that given his personal and historical limitations, Hooker could find support in the writings of Irenaeus, Hilary, Theodoret, Cyril, and others. But his opponents could also find support in such Fathers. Hooker was also seriously limited in that he concentrated on the mode of Christ's presence, even while arguing that that was not the main issue. He does not treat the doctrine of sacrifice at all here, a doctrine which might have set him on a different, more secure foundation. Struggling to be free of it, Hooker was confined by the nominalistic thought which harried Cranmer and many others in sixteenth century England.

There are at least two possibilities for viewing Hooker's doctrine more positively. The first is suggested by Olivier Loyer, an irenical Roman Catholic layman, who rightly acknowledges the importance of Hooker's teaching concerning mutual participation and in the light of it regards Hooker's eucharistic doctrine as receptionist. [47]

"Comme le virtualisme, le réceptionnisme est susceptible d'une interprétation pleinement réaliste. Bien plus, un véritable réalisme est réceptionniste, tout comme il est virtualiste. La présence est présence du corps, mais le présence du corps est nécessairement présence du Christ en nous et de nous dans le Christ. L'expression 'present to us', 'present to the worthy receiver' est désormais sans ambiguité. Elle n'enferme pas la présence dans une acception strictement subjective; l'opération visée n'est pas simplement imaginative ou mentale. Elle implique une double inclusion réelle. Être présent, c'est être présent pour quelque chose et dans quelque chose, c'est inversement recueiller la chose en soimême. Présence réelle et participation mutuelle, c'est tout un." [48]

This interpretation suggests Aquinas's conviction that "receiving is of the very nature of the sacrament." [49] In a sense, Hooker is right when he contends that he is simply asserting that which for all Christians is the irreducible heart of the matter, beside which all else is either erroneous or unnecessary. It is not surprising that Hooker was drawn to Cyril of Alexandria who viewed the Eucharist as the preeminent means of mutual participation. [50] Gebremedhin speaks of Cyril as understanding of the Eucharist to be transforming through participation.

In the Eucharist Christ enters the lives of the faithful and lulls the law which rages in the members of the flesh. He kindles their piety towards God and destroys their passions. He does not impute their transgressions to them but rather heals their sicknesses. As a Good shepherd, He binds up the one who is crushed and raises the one who has fallen. Cyril teaches: "Let Him then take hold of us or let us take hold of Him by the mystical eulogy, in order that He may free us from the sickness of the soul and from the assault and violence of demons." [51]

Concentration on the purposes and effects of the sacrament is not only justified but necessary and results in a view of the consecrated elements which does no violence to our common sense understanding of matter and spirit. But if we are to appreciate Hooker's doctrine in this light it is necessary to put aside his preoccupation with the views of others, both contemporary Roman Catholics and Lutherans, Anabaptists and Puritans. Such a positive attitude also requires dismissing his use or misuse of the Fathers and his lack of historical knowledge, whether on the basis of the circumstances of the time or some inherent blindness. It is, to say the least, difficult for the historian to dismiss such realities.

The second possibility requires that the student consider

Hooker's understanding in a context which is neither philosophical or strictly theological, but rather liturgical and poetic. It is of interest in the light of Ratcliff's statement about the liturgy in the early Church as drama, [52] and the emergence of modern drama out of medieval liturgy, [53] to consider Stella Brook's statement that "Liturgical writing calls for a simultaneous and balanced use of the physical and intellectual aspects of language which has something in common with the use of language in verse drama." [54] And there is a relationship between private prayers and meditations of a Lancelot Andrewes [55] and the public liturgy of the church. At the end of chapter 67 there is a passage which is prayer and meditation, such meditation as possesses dramatic qualities and impact. In it many of the main themes of the chapter are drawn together, themes involved with words such as "mysteries," "efficacie force and vertue," "soule and bodie," and the limits of human knowledge of things divine. Having called for an end to disputes which are the enemies of piety, Hooker writers: [56]

> the verie letter of the worde of Christ giveth plaine securitie that these mysteries doe as nailes fasten us to his verie crosse, that by them wee draw out, as touchinge efficacie force and vertue, even the blood of his goared side, in the woundes of our redemer wee there dip our tongues, wee are died redd both within and without, our hunger is satisfied and our thirst for ever quenched they are thinges wonderfull which hee feeleth, greate which hee seeth and unhard of which he uttereth whose soule is possest of this pascall lamb and made joyfull in the strength of this new wine, this bread hath in it more than the substance which our eyes behold, this cup hallowed with sollemne benediction availeth to the endles life and wellfare both of soule and bodie, in that it serveth as well for a medicine to heale our infirmities and purge our sinnes as for a sacrifice of thanksgiving, with touching it sanctifieth, it enlighteneth with beliefe, it trulie conformeth us into the image of Jesus Christ; what these elementes are in them selves it skilleth not, it is enough that to me which take them they are the bodie and blood of Christ, his promise in witness hereof sufficeth, his word he knoweth which way to accomplish, why should any cogitation possesse the minde of a faithfull communicant but this, O my God thou art true, O my soule thou art happie? (V.67.12)

This passage is comparable to Andrewes's devotions on "The Holy Mysteries," [57] it is also reminiscent of homiletic materials in any age, including the sixteenth century, for instance the "Homily of the Worthy Receiving and Reverent Esteeming of the Sacrament" in the Second Book of Homilies (1536) [58] and "A Briefe Homily" by Thomas Cooper, Bishop of Lincoln, especially:

> When our sight beholdeth on the Table, the Breade and Wine by Christes ordinaunce broken and powred out, for us to use, our faith is moved thus to thinke: as surely and truely, as my bodily eyes beholde upon the table of the Lord, the creatures of Breade and Wine, as the outward parte of his Sacrament, and see the same broken and powred out for me; so assuredly doe I with the eye of my faith, beholde the body and blood of Christ broken and shedde for me on the altar of the crosse, and the same my Saviour sitting now on the right hand of God . . . [59]

Such an understanding is influenced by the philosophical and theological discussions, but it proceeds from the person who partakes of the body and blood of Christ in the public liturgy of the church, and it surely cannot be denied that the experience of participation in and through the liturgy works on the mind and heart of the faithful. Thus it is possible that the mightiest influence working on Hooker as he formulated his view of the Eucharist was the **Book of Common Prayer** and its emphasis upon the sacrifice of Christ for us. In his homiletic/poetic conclusion to chapter 67 Hooker seems to agree more with the early Fathers than he does in the section wherein he seeks to expound their views and this is possibly so because the liturgy as known and participated in has its own power and effect.

NOTES

1. The quotations from Hooker are from the **Folger Library Edition of the Works of Richard Hooker**, W. Speed Hill, general editor, Vol. 2: **Of the Laws of Ecclesiastical Polity: Book V**, Hill, ed. (Cambridge, Mass.: The Belknap Press of Harvard University Press, 1977). The references in the text of this essay are to book, chapter, and section as found in this edition.

2. The word "force" here means "the real import or significance . . . the precise meaning or 'value" . . . the power or value of a symbol" (OED). See Bonner, **Profit. Doct.** (1555), sig. Miij: "Thyrde is to be considered, the vertue, force, and effecte of the sayd Sacrament." See also **Lawes**, V.50.3, 55.7, 57.3 ("force and virtue"), 58.1 ("naturall force"), and Fragments, Append. I.15 ("force or necessity").

3. I am interpreting "veritie" to mean "reality," although it could be either truth or fact (OED). See Tertullian, "Figura autem non fuisset nisi veritatis esset corpus" (my emphasis).

4. **Dialogi Tres** (1547), 38[r]; Ettlinger ed., 151. Note here the use of metablethen which I have translated as "changed". We shall deal with it later. Note also that Hooker has relied on this source for various quotations from the Fathers in his discussion of the Incarnation.

5. See L. S. Thornton, **Richard Hooker: A Study of His Theology** (London: S.P.C.K., 1924), 58.

6. Ibid., 60-63.

7. See below, 141.

8. Thornton, 85.

9. Hooker, **Works** (7th Keble ed., Oxford, 1888), 2:554; see **Folger Library Edition of the Works of Richard Hooker**, Vol. 4: **Of the Laws of Ecclesiastical Polity, Attack and Response**, John E. Booty, ed. (Cambridge, Mass.: The Belknap Press of Harvard University Press, 1982), 119.

10. Migne, PL 189:1641-1650. See also the note on "Ernaldus Abbas Bonaevallis," ibid., 1507-1512.

11. Leonard Chester Jones, **Simon Goulart, Etude Biographique et Bibliographique** (Genève: Georg & Cie, 1917), 293-294.

12. Cyprian, **Opera**, 1593, 501.

13. Ibid., 509.

14. Bodleian Library, Oxford, MS. ADD. C. 165, f. 144[r].

15. Cyprian, **Opera**, 1593, 501. See Goulart's note, ibid., 507.

16. See Eusebius 'Gellicanus', **Collectio Homiliarum**, ed. Fr. Glorie (Turnbolti: Typographi Brepolis Editores Pontificii, 1970), which is CCSL 100, vii.

17. **Homilia quinta de Pascha; Homiliae ad populum**, 1547, f. 44[v]; or Hom. 17 De Pascha VI in CCSL 100, 196-197.

18. **Dialogi Tres** (1547), 38[r]; Ettlinger ed., 152.

19. Cyprian, **Opera**, 1593, 500.

20. Ibid.

21. See my discussion of "participation" below and in my chapter on Hooker in **The Spirit of Anglicanism**, ed. W. Wolf (New York: Morehouse-Barlow, 1979), 17-21.

22. Cyprian, **Opera**, 1593, 501.

23. Ibid.

24. Ibid.

25. See Goulart's annotation, Cyprian, **Opera**, 508.

26. "Ille est in patre per naturam divinitatis, nos in eo per corporalem ejus nativitatem, ille rursus in nobis per sacramentorum mysterium" (**de Trinitate**, VIII.15; **Lucubrationes**, 1523, 136; PL 10:248).

27. For instance, in the Elizabethan Prayer Book, in sequence from the Sursum Corda through the post-Communion thanksgiving. Concerning the influence of the two Greek words on Hooker, see V.67.1-10.

28. The Fragment on the Sacraments, Append, I.16; Folger ed., 4:117. See the rest of this section in which Hooker expounds his understanding of grace in relation to remission of sins and justification.

29. See Append. I.16; Folger ed., 4:117-118.

30. Cyprian, **Opera**, 1593, 501.

31. Ibid., 512, but Goulart has a different version: "Hoc agit et efficit participatio corporis Christi, ut in id quod sumimus, hoc est in carnem ipsius, qui caro nostra factus est, transeamus." Compare with the next note.

32. "Non aliud agit participatio corporis et sanguinis Christi quam ut in id quod sumimus transeamus, et in quo mortui et sepulti et conresuscitati sumus ipsum per omnia et spiritu et carne gestemus" (Leo I, **de Pass. Serm.** 12; **Sermones et Epistolae**, 1482, sig. K5^{v}; PL 54:357).

33. Hooker cites the Latin of Irenaeus' **adv. Haer.**, 4.18.5: "Quemadmodum qui est a terra panis percipiens Dei vocationem ex duabus rebus constans terrena et Coelesti: sic et corpora nostra percipientia Eucharistiam jam non sunt corruptibilia spem resurrectionis habentia" (**Opera**, 1528, 237). For the Greek see **Sources Chrétiennes**, 100:610-613.

34. Hooker cites the Latin of Cyril of Alexandria's **D. Joannis Evengelium**, IV.14: "Quoniam salutaris caro verbo Dei quod naturaliter vita est conjuncta vivifica effecta est, quando eam comedimus tunc vitam habemus in nobis illi carni conjuncti quae vita effecta est." See the 1520 ed., 4.86^{v}; Pusey ed. (Oxford, 1872), 1:530, where it is ch. 2; the trans. in the Library of the Fathers (Oxford, 1874), 1:418; and PG 73:577.

35. E. C. Ratcliff, **Liturgical Studies** (London: S.P.C.K., 1976), 131.

36. See Ezra Gebremedhin, **Life-Giving Blessing" An Inquiry into the Eucharistic Doctrine of Cyril of Alexandria,** Acta Universitatis Upsaliensis, Studia Doctrinae Christianae Upsaliensia 17 (Uppsala, 1977), 69.

37. Ratcliff, **Liturgical Studies**, 118.

38. C. W. Dugmore, **The Mass and the English Reformers** (London: Macmillan and Co., 1958), 245. See Art. 10 of the **Consensus**: "Neque enim ad signa nuda, sed potius ad promissionem, quae illio annexa est, respicere convenit. Quatenus ergo in promissione illic oblata proficiat nostra fides, eatenus ista vis et efficacia, quam dicimus, se exserit. Ita materia aquae, panis aut vini, Christum nequaquam nobis offert, nec spiritualium eius donorum compotes nos facit: sed promissio magis spectanda est, cuius partes sunt nos recta fidei via ad Christum docere quae fides nos Christi participes facit" (Ibid., 220n).

39. "Quum substantialiter Chrisi carnem et sanguinem nobis offerri et exhibere in coena dico, simul modum designo, quod Christi caro novis sit vivifica: quoniam Christus incomprehensibili spiritus sui virtute ex substantia carnis suae vitam in nos transdunat, quae illi propria est: ut ipse in nobis vivat, eiusque vita nobis sit communis . . . " (**Opera**, Corpus Reformatorum 9:470; see the passage through p. 471: **Theological Treatises**, LCC, 267, see through 268).

40. Cyprian, **Opera** (1593) 512.

41. Ibid. The entire set of conclusions is worth more attention than is given to them here.

42. Ibid., 507. See the rest of the passage, especially: "Hac efficacia divina, vult author Sermonis, conciliari Sacramentis religiosam devotionem, hoc est, symbolarum reverentiam et legitimum usum, et rerum figuratarum fidelem et gratam meditationem . . . " And see p. 509.

43. Cyril C. Richardson, "Cranmer and the Analysis of Eucharistic Doctrine," Journal of Theological Studies, n.s., XVI, no. 2 (October 1965), 422.

44. On the doctrine of use, see C. W. Dugmore, **Eucharistic Doctrine in England from Hooker to Waterland** (London: S.P.C.K., 1942), espec. ch. 1.

45. Cranmer, An Answer . . . Unto a craftie and Sophisticall cavillation, devised by Stephen Gardiner, in **Works**, PS, 1:52.

46. Ibid., 1:54.

47. See Horton Davies, **Worship and Theology in England**, 1:83.

48. L'Anglicanisme de Richard Hooker, University of Paris Doctoral Thesis, 1977, 2:535. His entire chapter on the Eucharist is worth attention.

49. S.T., III.79.7 and 3; cited by Dugmore, **Mass**, p. 245.

50. Gebremedhin, **Life-Giving Blessing**, 90-91, discusses Cyril's understanding of participation in relation to key words.

51. Ibid., 91.

52. See above, 138-139.

53. See O. B. Hardison, **Christian Rite and Christian Drama in the Middle Ages** (Baltimore, Md.: The Johns Hopkins Press, 1965).

54. **The Language of the Book of Common Prayer,** The Language Library (New York: Oxford University Press, 1965), 122.

55. See **The Private Devotions of Lancelot Andrewes,** ed. F. E. Brightman (London: Methuen and Company, 1903).

56. Once again, Hooker is dependent on Arnold de Bonneval. See **de Coena Domini,** ch. 10.

57. **The Private Devotions,** 121-124.

58. **Certain Sermons or Homilies** (London: S.P.C.K., 1964), see espec. 476-477.

59. **A Brief Homily, wherein the most comfortable and right use of the Lords Supper, is very plainly opened and delivered** (London: Ralph Newberie, 1580), sigs. A.2^{v}-3^{r}.

WORSHIP AND DISCIPLINE: CONTEXT OF INDEPENDENT CHURCH ORDER IN THE WESTMINSTER ASSEMBLY

Robert S. Paul

Austin Presbyterian Theological Seminary

My friendship with Horton Marlais Davies goes back over forty years. It goes even beyond the time when, largely because of the fortuitous intervention of German buzzbombs, he introduced me to the English congregation that I served for nearly ten years, back to exciting days in Mansfield College, Oxford, when, inspired by a common ecclesiastical debt to the Congregational churches in Britain, we shared common interests in the Puritans, worship and liturgy and the wholeness of the One, Holy, Catholic and Apostolic Church.

Undoubtedly much of this interest was generated by the remarkable group of scholars who were our teachers, but in part it came from the Puritan material in which we both became immersed, and which we agreed had received a very bad press. It is my hope that in returning to the Puritan period and to these ecclesiastical roots, this article will pay tribute to the immense contribution that Horton Davies has made to the Puritans and to their worship. [1]

I

Horton Davies described Puritanism as a liturgical movement, [2] and with his inimitable learning and wit he was able to make a liturgical silk purse out of what many have been too willing to dismiss as an ecclesiastical sow's ear. Certainly, in the protest against the 'nocent' ceremonies and demands for a more reformed Prayer Book, liturgical issues were the most obvious expression of the Puritan protest, but as I suggested elsewhere, we could sell the movement somewhat short if we thought of this only in the negative terms of refusing to wear a surplice or finding new things to object to in the **Book of Common Prayer.** [3] It _was_ a liturgical movement only if we see that at its center there was a different doctrine of the Church, and if we therefore recognize the integral relationship of the liturgical issues with Puritan ecclesiologies: it was a movement in which the doctrine of the Church with ecclesiastical discipline at its center found explicit expression in the worshipping congregation.

This was particularly true for the Puritans who settled New England in the 1630s, and for the little group of supporters of the Congregational Way in the Westminster Assembly who--much to their own disgust--came to be known as Independents.

If we are to understand the seventeenth-century struggle in the Westminster Assembly, however, our denominational mythologies may need revision at two points:

(1) The documents of the Assembly have always raised problems for scholars of the period, because they were all written from the point of view of the successful party, and until recently the so-called 'Minutes' were not readily available [4]; but one of the curious ways in which the fresh study of the records forces us to revise the earlier denominational _apologiae_ is, we must now recognize that comparatively few of the divines came to Westminster with clear ideas about the future form of the Church of England. They were opposed to prelates, but apart from the Independents and a small group of convinced Presbyterians, the Puritan majority in the Assembly did not have many precisely formulated ideas about church polity beyond that point. [5]

Those Puritan divines were, however, firmly determined to preserve three things--the national character of the Church of England, strict ecclesiastical discipline to suppress the sects that were springing up, and their own status and authority as clergymen in the established church. The supreme political triumph of the Scottish Commissioners after they arrived at Westminster in the autumn of 1643, was in convincing the members of this Puritan majority that they had more likelihood of preserving these traditional forms of English churchmanship by throwing in their lot with Scottish presbyterianism than with the Independents; but the earliest form in which the ecclesiological struggle hit the Assembly was in the confrontation between the traditionalism of the Puritan majority and the radicalism they feared in Independency, and not between the presbyterianism of the Scots and the congregationalism of the Independents.

(2) Traditionally, the difference between the Independents

and other Puritans in the Westminster Assembly has been represented as a difference of polity--congregational vs. presbyterian church government. This is the denominational form in which this seventeenth-century struggle has been handed on to us, and obviously, there were decisive implications for polity in the differing interpretations of the scriptural evidence: one kind of Puritanism went to the Bible and found clear support for presbyterian church government, while the other kind of Puritanism became equally convinced that the scripture supported congregationalism. The disagreements hardened into differing forms of ecclesiastical government, and denominational historians have had good grounds for reducing the issue to one of polity.

At the same time, we suggest that polity was not the basic issue in the Assembly, although this was undoubtedly the pattern in which it appeared to the public. Behind that issue was a much more important difference concerning the way in which the Independents and the Presbyterians understood the spirit of government in the New Testament church.

II

This is to be seen in the distinction Independents draw between two kinds of authority under which people should be governed--'magisterial' authority represents the coercive power appropriate to the civil magistrate in the punishment of those who transgress the law, while 'ministerial' authority, they affirmed, is the only form appropriate within the church and it is essentially persuasive.

Philip Nye gives us a hint of this distinction during the debates early in March, 1643/4, when the divines were discussing the power with which the apostles acted in the New Testament church. Nye pointed out that although the apostle Paul might have commanded Philemon regarding the treatment of his slave Onesimus, in fact he did not, but preferred to entreat him in the spirit of the gospel. [6] Thomas Goodwin put the matter very frankly. In the course of a debate on Acts 15, he insisted that the declaration of the church of Jerusalem on that occasion was "not coercive but persuasive", [7] while later in the debates he and Nye described the kind of 'non communion' that they practiced in church discipline as a censure but not a judicial sentence. [8]

This distinction was at the heart of the Independents' refusal to permit the excommunication of a covenanted congregation by superior ecclesiastical authorities, or of an individual christian by external clerical authority or without the participation of the congregation in which he or she was covenanted: if a church member was to be disciplined, it must be done _coram populo_, in the presence of the people.

Other congregations and synods were responsible for calling erring parties to account for questionable beliefs or actions whenever there was cause in ministers or in individual churches, but that did not amount to juridical power: "it is their duty to send for them", said Jeremiah Burroughes, but, "it is not their power." [9] The Independents were convinced that in the New Testament church no such plenary power was vested either in the clergy as clergy or in superior ecclesiastical courts because it would be contrary to the spirit of the gospel.

"That which is a coercive power those assemblyes have not", declared William Carter, but in the system being proposed, he stated, "this is a coercive power". [10] He was therefore opposed to it, for in the view of himself and his friends, authority appropriate to the church is of a radically different quality from that which operates in civil society.

Throughout the debates this emphasis by the Independents on the distinctively spiritual or 'ministerial' character of authority in the Church emerges as a major point of difference between them and most of the Puritan majority. They may not have been wholly consistent in their understanding of this principle, [11] and they may not have been the only ones to see the distinction. Stephen Marshall, one of the few we can probably identify as a convinced Presbyterian when he arrived at Westminster, insisted that the apostles had used their power "not _ad modum imperii_, but _ministerii_". [12]

He was an exception. Most of the divines, like Lazarus Seaman, were looking for ecclesiastical authority that went beyond "moral persuasion" and was closer to "a political power" in the church, [13] but perhaps Richard Vines expressed the view of the Puritan majority most clearly, in response to one of Goodwin's speeches. In John Lightfoot's **Journal** of the Assembly, Vines declared that "the ground of obedience is founded upon office" [14], while the Minutes exegete his speech more comprehensively:

> the reason of obedience lyes in the office[;] if it be a part of the office & principall to preach the word[,] yet the ground of it lyes in the office[.] [15]

It is clear throughout the debates that the Puritan majority was very much concerned with the _office_ of the ordained ministry, and with the traditional authority that had been exercised by clergymen in the established church.

III

The conviction about the kind of spiritual authority appropriate in the Church is seen in the Independents' emphasis on the worshipping unity of a covenanted congregation and its ministers as the only proper context for church discipline. Richard Baxter was not a member of the Assembly, but he seems to have studied the issues between the parties very carefully, and he noted that one of the Independents' principles was that "A Worshipping Church and a Governed Church is and must be all one." [16] Despite his very critical attitude to some of the Independents' beliefs and practices, he became convinced that this insight belonged to the gospel, for he says that he "found in the search of Scripture and Antiquity, that in the beginning a Governed Church, and a stated worshipping Church, were all one; and not two several things." [17]

The issue appeared in many different forms. There was, for example, one occasion in the Spring of 1644 when the discussion of what the Independents understood as a synod seemed to offer a real possibility of agreement. They had pointed out that in defining doctrine a synod had real if still persuasive authority--i.e., a spiritual influence that went far beyond that of the local church--but they continued to deny that it possessed jurisdiction.

Some of the Puritan majority were impressed, and Thomas Case had observed that although the Independent view did not include, in the strictest sense, what the rest of the Assembly regarded as jurisdiction, yet the authority they granted to one of their synods virtually amounted "to all those purposes for wch Jurisdiction proprie dicta serves". [18] There appeared to be a real chance of agreement, and a movement was made to reach an 'accommodation.'

It was no use, because the Independents were wholly unwilling to remove church discipline, especially in the extreme case of excommunication, from its normal setting of regular worship which alone, they felt, permitted the exercise of proper ecclesiastical censures. William Price, one of the lesser-known members of the Puritan majority recognized the basic problem when he wistfully observed that the debates suffered from "want of accurate distinction between authority [i.e., spiritual authority] and jurisdiction." [19]

The issue naturally surfaced during 'the Grand Debate' whenever the question of jurisdiction arose. Right at the beginning of his argument against the presbyterian system, Thomas Goodwin laid down the congregational principle that the "extent of a pastor's power is to one flock as his whole flock". That appears to be a clear statement of Independent polity, but then Goodwin went on to establish the spiritual principle on which that was based--a pastor was to have power as pastor in a single congregation because for ministers, "pastoral ruling is founded on their preaching", and the jurisdiction they have as church governors must be "founded on order, so that the one can be no larger than the other."

Reformed divines had opposed prelacy on the sound ecclesiastical principle that "he that feeds me not should not rule me", [20] and his objection to the presbyterian system was therefore because it placed disciplinary power in the hands of those within the presbytery or classis who could not bear any direct pastoral relationship to the persons being disciplined.

George Gillespie, possibly the ablest debater among the Scots Commissioners, has left us his private notes on these debates, and he summarized the thrust of Goodwin's argument like this--that "A church for discipline [i.e., an ecclesiastical court that exists for discipline alone] cannot have the notes of a church that divines give from word and sacraments, yea, the people of that church do not communicate, but only the elders." [21]

So too, in one of Goodwin's most important speeches during the debates, on 14th February, 1643/4, he claimed that "presbyterian government makes two sorts of churches: one merely for discipline, the other for worship", and he contested that "discipline doeth not constitute a church, nor is it a note of a church." [22]

Naturally, he backed his position--as, indeed, they were all required to do by the terms of the Assembly's call and its own rules--with a panoply of proof texts, and in this case Goodwin presses the implication in Hebrews 12:7, 17; I Thessalonians 5:12, 13; and I Timothy 5:17 that those who had been given governance in the Church were also those who had labored among the believers in teaching and preaching. He also argued that pastors have authority over their congregations in very much the same way as fathers have authority over the children they have begotten. [23] Goodwin and the rest of the Dissenting Brethren were trying to maintain the ecclesial unity of pastoral discipline, preaching the Word and participation in the sacraments, and just as he had insisted that church discipline should not be separated from regular pastoral preaching, so he also insisted that where the apostles preached, "ther[e] they had the sacrament." [24]

One senses that often the positive theological principles to be found on both sides of the argument were better than the literalism on which they tried to base their arguments. In this particular case, in maintaining the essential unity of Word and Sacrament in the New Testament church, Goodwin went to almost bizarre lengths to suggest that the thousands of converts brought into the church of Jerusalem after Pentecost must have had their celebration of the eucharist in the courts of the Temple! The argument did not impress the majority in the Assembly.

But that was an aberration caused by the literalism in which the whole work of the Assembly was cast. The basic theological insight, for which we must give the Independents credit, was their desire to maintain the unity of Word and Sacrament, and the integral relationship of worship and practice. We know from that indefatigable correspondent among the Scots Commissioners, Robert Baillie, that the Independents tried to get the others in the Assembly to agree to weekly Communion in the Church, [25] but they were no more successful in that with the Puritan divines than Calvin had been on this issue with the syndics of Geneva.

IV

The issues of spiritual authority and of worship as the proper setting for church discipline appeared in several different guises during the later debates of the Assembly regarding the Lord's Supper and the reasons for excluding certain kinds of people from the sacrament.

The majority of the Puritan divines at Westminster, whether Independent or Presbyterian, had something of an obsession about maintaining the purity of the sacrament by excluding known sinners from participation. They all took I Corinthians 11:27-29 with intense seriousness, and in protest against the 'mixed' character of communicants in the English parish churches, were determined to exclude all those regarded as 'unworthy'. With the possible exception of the few Erastians in the Assembly, the English Puritans and the Scots Commissioners were no less insistent on this than were the Independents, and the only question on that particular issue between the latter and the rest of the Assembly was about the best way to achieve the objective.

The Independents insisted that no mere catalogue of sins carrying automatic exclusion would meet the case, and that only the pastor and 'presbytery' (consistory) of a local, regularly worshipping community could exercise the kind of pastoral oversight that was required. However, a radical difference very soon became apparent because behind their ecclesiological assumptions about church discipline there were questions about the Church itself--was the Church to be undersood as a 'gathered' and covenanted body of believers, or could it be validly expressed in terms of traditional geographical parishes? Obviously the pastoral oversight that represented effective discipline for the former might be totally ineffective for the latter, and the more formal relationship and people in the latter might demand a very different approach from that of a minister in a gathered church. But this underlying difference never seems to have been seriously faced.

So on April 15th, 1644, during the protracted debates on the church in Jerusalem, Thomas Goodwin, on the basis of his Independent assumptions about the Church, asked how there could have been any proper pastoral oversight and a proper 'fencing of the tables', if, as the majority argued, the church in Jerusalem simply represented a number of 'mixed' parishes, in the pattern of the national churches in seventeenth-century England or Scotland, with an eldership that was common to all of them. [**26**]

Behind his question was the Independent view that only the shared experience of Word, Sacrament and pastoral care could provide the proper churchly context for maintaining the purity of the sacrament. Robert Baillie was so exercised about this and similar issues, that he urged his relative, William Spang, who was a minister in Holland, to persuade the Dutch theologians to write in support of the Scots position against Goodwin and his friends on the questions of ecclesiastical power and jurisdiction. [**27**]

The questions had a habit of re-surfacing. On October 24 of the same year, arguing against the intrusion of an ecclesiastical power over many congregations, Goodwin declared "the presbytery [i.e., classis] have not the power of word and sacrament" [**28**], and this was the Independents' basic reason for refusing to allow a presbytery (classis) the right of excommunication.

The contrast may best be illustrated by the Scots. Robert Baillie expostulated in a letter to William Spang about how he regarded excommunication and the rights of presbyteries in this matter: "We count it a causa communis, and of so high a consequence as can be, to cut off a member, not from one congregation only, but [from] the whole church and body of Christ." [**29**]

The point at issue may have had overtones in terms of polity, but beyond that it seems to have arisen from a different understanding of the way in which the churches in the New Testament had been governed, not simply in terms of structures but in terms of spirit. No member of the Assembly was more rigorous that Philip Nye on the qualifications he required for admission to the Lord's Supper [**30**], and yet there is a profound difference of attitude when one compares Baillie's words above with Philip Nye's expression of uneasiness about using the word 'authoritative' in respect to church courts and exclusion from the sacrament. He suggested that perhaps the exercise of discipline should be regarded as "rather a suspension of the ordinance from the person than of the person from the ordinance." [**31**]

That debate took place only a month or two before the Dissenting Brethren began to enter their dissent from the Form of Government that was presented to Parliament on November 7th, 1644, but it must be remembered that this dissent did not prevent them from continuing to participate in all the other phases of the Assembly's program. So the issues surfaced again when the Assembly began to discuss the question of Excommunication in the following January.

At first, even the Scots Commissioner, Samuel Rutherford, who had read John Cotton's **The Keyes of the Kingdom**, thought that agreement should be relatively easy, since the two sides appeared to be so close to each other on that matter. [32], but it did not work out like that, because the Scots wanted a list of clearly defined 'sins' that would automatically invoke the sentence of excommunication, whereas the Independents wanted to leave room for pastoral discretion.

They seem to have thought not only that the Scots' list was too long, but they disagreed with the assumption that culpability centered in specific sins, rather than in the impenitence of the sinner. In the debate on December 31st, 1644, Philip Nye declared, "We grant that if any sin comes to obstinacy, it is liable to excommunication", but he was dubious about imposing the sentence simply because some sins were considered 'atrocious'. Then with an insight that would do credit to a much later age, he commented "There may be a fundamental error in one age, that is not a fundamental error in another, as the resurrection to be denied now is a fundamental error." [33] The crucial element in excommunication from his point of view was not the atrociousness of the sin, but whether it was maintained obstinately and without repentance. A month or so later on the same subject he insisted that "sin is not bound in heaven unless impenitently persisted in", while the Scots wanted the sentence to be automatically imposed "by sufficient evidence and testimony of the fact." [34] From these positions neither of the parties would budge.

However, the Scots stubbornness on this occasion would come back to haunt the Assembly, because in the Spring of 1645 the House of Commons would ask the divines to draw up precise and comprehensive lists of the sins that warranted excommunication. As the parliamentarians became more insistent that the list should be made absolutely comprehensive, the divines began to realize that all ministerial discretion was being taken from them: the issue was being interpreted so legalistically that the Church would lose control over its own sacraments. The Independents' principle of holding pastoral discipline together with the ongoing worship of the congregation had at least this wisdom in it, it did not allow extraneous influence like the state to control that which properly belonged only to the Church itself.

V

In this essay we have inevitably concentrated on the Independents, but it would be a mistake to think that everything of positive worth came from one side of the debate. Goodwin may have had a good deal in his favor when he argued that ministers should stand in a full pastoral relationship of Word and Sacraments to those whom they were responsible for disciplining, but on the other side of the debate, Gillespie argued that presbyters held their jurisdiction over the congregations in the presbytery, not because they were presbyters, but because they were presbyters corporately gathered in presbytery--non quatenus presbyteri, sed quatenus presbyteri in presbyterium collecti. [35] Against Goodwin's position he said that just as by baptism the individual is made a member of the Church Universal, "so by ordination, we are made ministers of the general church, and need not a new ordination when we go to another church, no more than a new baptism." [36]

There were positive insights into the gospel on both sides of the debate. Presbyterian polity rightly wanted to preserve the Church's catholicity and to emphasize that if we are to say with John Donne that 'no man is an island', the same should be true for christian congregations. On the other hand, the Independents were trying to ensure that church discipline should never be removed from the context of a regularly worshipping community, and that mutual ministry to each other in the community committed to the gospel cannot be divorced from the Word and Sacraments through which that gospel is proclaimed.

The very pressure of the Grand Debate, however, was pushing the Independents to new ecclesiological positions, and it tended to move them from an exclusivism that even threw doubts on whether the Church of England could be regarded as a true Church, to positions that were much more inclusive.

In a debate on April 17th, 1644, Nye and Goodwin insisted that they held the Church of England to be a true church, and Nye reminded the Assembly that even those who were prepared to justify the Reformation could still "defend separation from a true, yet corrupt church", while Goodwin declared that he "would keep communion with all churches in the world, and separate from none." [37] Some time later, in one of the committees trying to reach 'accommodation' with the Independents, Robert Baillie heard him state publicly "that he cannot refuse to be members, nor censure when members, any for Anabaptisme, Lutheranisme, nor any errors which are not fundamentall" [38]. The Independents were obviously on their way to an ecclesiology far broader than that with which they had entered the Assembly.

Almost as soon as he arrived at Westminster Robert Baillie described the Independents as 'very able men', men full 'of grace and modestie', [39] and his grudging admiration shows in the letters he penned home and to William Spang in Holland. He was so anxious to win the friendship and cooperation of Thomas Goodwin that very early in the proceedings he invited the Independent to dinner to get to know him better, "and spent the afternoon with him verie sweetlie." He was so impressed that he exclaimed in a letter home to Scotland, "It were a thousand pities of that man; he is of many excellent parts: I hope God will not permitt him to goe on to lead a faction for renting of the kirk." [40]

We agree. But then, something very similar might be said of the leaders on both sides in that particular dispute. How good and pleasant, and how very much better it would have been for later church history, if these particular brethren had been able to dwell in unity.

NOTES

1. Cf. Horton Davies, **The Worship of the English Puritans** (London: Dacre Press, 1948), and **From Cranmer to Hooker, 1534-1603**, and **From Andrewes to Baxter and Fox, 1603-1690;** [volumes 1 and 2 of his superb five volume study of **Worship and Theology in England,** Princeton: Princeton University Press, 1970, 1975, etc.]

2. Cf. Horton Davies, **The English Free Churches** (London: Oxford University Press, 1957), 6, and in the books cited above.

3. Cf. "The Accidence and the Essence of Puritan Piety", Austin Seminary Bulletin [Faculty Edition], Vol. XCIII, No. 8 (May 1978), 9f.

4. The main accounts of the Westminster Assembly by those who participated all came from the Presbyterian side of that event: John Lightfoot's **Journal of the Proceedings of the Westminster Assembly of Divines: From January 1, 1643, to December 31, 1644,** (which appears as vol. XIII of his **Works,** edited by John Rogers Pitman, London, 1824); George Gillespie's **Notes of the Debates and Proceedings of the Assembly of Divines and other Commissioners at Westminster, February 1644 to January 1645,** edited by David Meek (Edinburgh: Ogle, Oliver & Boyd, 1846); and in Robert Baillie's **Letters and Journals, 1637-1662,** edited by David Laing (Edinburgh: Robert Ogle, 1841).

Gillespie and Baillie were Scots Commissioners to the Assembly, and Lightfoot, although an Erastian on matters of church discipline, was a strong supporter of the majority party in matters of church government.

Only the 3rd volume of the 'Minutes' has appeared in print, and this does not begin until session 324 (18th Nov. 1644). It was edited by Alexander F. Mitchell and John Struthers (Edinburgh: William Blackwood and Sons, 1874). [This volume is hereafter cited as 'Minutes III'.] The original manuscript volumes are in Dr. Williams's Library, London, and as Mitchell and Struthers pointed out, are little more than barely decipherable notes by the scribes [Minutes III, viii.] There are large gaps in the 'Minutes", and punctuation and capitalization are almost non-existent.

Recently, however, a transcript of the three volumes made by E. Maunde Thompson at the end of last century and housed in New College, Edinburgh, and also the ms. originals, have become available in microfilm, and this has made serious revision of the history of the Assembly possible. [The Transcript is cited as 'TMs' and the manuscript as 'Ms.' in the notes of this essay.]

5. This is the conclusion of Ethyn Williams Kirby and Jack Rogers, and it is fully substantiated by my own independent study. Cf. Ethyn Williams Kirby, "The English Presbyterians in the Westminster Assembly", Church History, XXXIII, No. 4, (December, 1964); Jack Bartlett Rogers, **Scripture in the Westminster Confession** (Grand Rapids: William B. Eerdmans, 1967) 124; Robert S. Paul, **The Assembly of the Lord,** (Edinburgh: T. & T. Clark, 1984), 26ff., and Parts I and II passim.

6. TMs. I. 703 (Ms. I. f.363b).

7. TMs. I. 738 (Ms. I. f.381.).

8. Cf. the debates and in particular Nye's comments on March 8, 1643/4; TMs. I. 719 (Ms. I. f.371b), and Lightfoot's **Journal**, 205.

9. October 4, 1644, TMs. II. 466 (Ms. II. f.241); cf. Gillespie, **Notes,** 87.

10. TMs. II. 469f. (Ms. II. ff.242b-243).

11. E.g. Marshall's protest voiced in the note below was against Philip Nye's unguarded description of church censures as inflicting a 'misery'. TMs. II. 475 (Ms. II. f.245b).

12. Lightfoot, **Journal,** 196. Cf. also Marshall's comment on October 8, 1644, when he protested that church censures should be regarded more as a medicine than as a punishment. TMs. II. 475 (Ms. II. f.245b).

13. TMs. I. 726 (Ms. I. f.375).

14. Lightfoot, **Journal,** 159.

15. TMs. I. 580 (Ms. I. f.302).

16. **Reliquiae Baxterianae: of Richard Baxter's Narrative of . . . his Life and Times,** edited by Matthew Sylvester, 1696, Book I, Part II, 143 (#13).

17. Ibid., 140 (#5).

18. TMs. I. 720 (Ms. I. f.372).

19. Ibid., 726 (Ms. I. f.375).

20. Gillespie, **Notes**, 10f.

21. Ibid., 18f.

22. Lightfoot, **Journal**, 151; Gillespie, **Notes**, 18.

23. Gillespie, **Notes**, 20f.

24. TMs. I. 650f. (Ms. I. ff.337, 337b).

25. Baillie, **Letters and Journals**, I. 148f.

26. TMs. II. 21 (Ms. I. f.12b).

27. To Spang, July 12, 1644; **Letters and Journals**, II. 205.

28. TMs. II. 539 (Mx. II. f.277b).

29. **Letters and Journals**, II. 170.

30. Nye's rigor with regard to the Lord's Supper was attested by Baxter, both with regard to his earlier unwillingness to take communion in the established churches, and also the strictness of his policy when he followed Dr. Featley as minister of the parish of Acton. Cf. **Reliquae Baxterianae**, III. 19, 67f. (##41, 143).

31. TMs. II. 541 (Ms. II. 278b).

32. February 17, 1644/5, Minutes III. 60; cf. 31ff.

33. Ibid., 45.

34. Samuel Rutherford, ibid.

35. Gillespie, **Notes**, 11f.

36. Ibid., 12.

37. Gillespie dates this as April 17, 1644, but it is more likely to have been stated on the afternoon of Friday, the 16th, since the Assembly did not normally convene on Saturdays and neither Lightfoot nor the 'Minutes' record any session on that particular date; ibid., 53, but cf. Lightfoot, **Journal**, 163, and TMs. I. 593 (Ms. I. f.308b).

38. Written to Spang probably at the end of January, 1645/6, Baillie, **Letters and Journals**, II. 343; cf. ibid., 342n.

39. Ibid., 110, 111.

40. Ibid., 123.

SOME NOTES ON THE USE OF THE LECTIONARY IN THE REFORMED TRADITION

Howard G. Hageman
New Brunswick Theological Seminary

A Common Understanding

In the study of Reformed liturgics one of the most common and unquestioned assumptions is that following the example set by Zwingli in Zurich in 1519, Reformed worship abandoned the use of the lectionary in favor of the ancient custom of *lectio continua*, the consecutive use of a book of the Bible. It was on the first Sunday in Lent, 1519 in the Münster in Zurich that Ulrich Zwingli began to preach consecutively from the Gospel according to Matthew. Hitherto he had preached from the liturgical gospel each Sunday as all preachers who used the *Prone* were required to. Zwingli's custom was soon followed by other preachers, most notably Martin Bucer in Strasbourg and perhaps most influentially by John Calvin in Geneva. It should be underscored that in making the shift to *lectio continua* Zwingli was not innovating but returning to what had been the usage of the church centuries earlier.

One of the results of the change was that in those churches which followed the Zwinglian practice the observance of the Christian Year was reduced to the celebration of its major dominical days such as Christmas, Circumcision, Good Friday, Easter, Ascension and Pentecost. There is some evidence that Calvin was not entirely comfortable with these observances and it is well known that John Knox rejected them entirely. The great seasons of Advent and Lent disappeared in Reformed liturgical custom, replaced by weekly preaching from a Biblical book. Generally speaking, however, in the Reformed Churches on the continent of Europe, the major festival days mentioned above continued to be observed.

The liturgical situation just outlined is so commonly

presented as Reformed custom and usage that it would be idle to try to document it. Decisions by one Synod after another could be cited, all saying the same thing. In Reformed churches the traditional Sunday pericopes were no longer used but were replaced by lectio continua, the consecutive reading and preaching from a book of the Bible. In Reformed usage the celebration of the Christian year as a total pattern was abandoned. At most six dominical days were celebrated, although in most places the observance lasted for two days, e.g. Christmas and the day after, Easter and Easter Monday etc. No question has ever been raised about the accuracy of such an assertion.

Evidence to the Contrary

a. The first indication that this statement might not be universally true came to my attention some years ago when I was presented with a copy of the so-called **Marburg Hymnal.** This book is of interest to American bibliographers because it was one of the first hymnals with musical lines to be published in North America. Reprinted from a German original by Christoph Saur in 1763 in Germantown, Pennsylvania, its title page is worth looking at. (See facing page)

The title page has been fully quoted to establish the authenticity of the Reformed pedigree of this volume. The exact origins of the book are not clear, but it was designed for use in the Reformed Churches in Hesse, Hanover, the Palatinate and Pennsylvania. It must have had wide use in the latter since my 1763 copy is listed as a second edition. The fact that it begins with the 150 Psalms in Lobwasser's translation set to the traditional Genevan tunes would indicate its design for Reformed worship as would the inclusion of the Heidelberg Catechism. The inclusion of such a large number of hymns is surprising, although pietistic influence had begun to introduce hymn singing in the German Reformed Churches early in the eighteenth century.

The most startling part of the book comes at the end for here is to be found a collection of gospels and epistles for each Sunday in the year as well as for all the saints' days. In addition to the gospel and epistle (printed in that order) the volume contains what are called the church prayers for each Sunday which while not the same as the traditional collects certainly reflect the content of the Sunday lessons. These seem to be entirely from the traditional western lectionary.

The question which immediately came to mind was why Saur, usually a rather sharp business man, would have printed seventy-five pages of lectionary material for congregations in which a lectionary was never used, and do it in a second as well

Neu vermehrt unt vollstandiges

GESANG-BUCH

Worinnen sowohl die
PSALMEN DAVIDS
nach
D. AMBROSII LOBWASSERS
Uebersetzung hin und wieder verbessert
als auch
730 auserlesener alter und neuer
GEISTREICHEN LIEDERN
begriffen sind

Weiche anjetso samtlich
IN DENEN REFORMIRTEN KIRCHEN
der Hessisch, Hanauisch, Pflatzisch, Pennsylvanischen
und mehreren andern angrantzenden landen zu singen
gebrauchlich in nunlicher ordnung eingesheilt

auch
mit dem Heydelbergischen Catechismo und
erbaulichen Gebatern versehen

as a first edition. To say the least, the discovery of the so-called **Marburg Hymnal** somewhat shook one's faith in the traditional view of the rejection of lectionaries in the Reformed Church.

That original question led to a second one. When the Mercersburg party published its **Provisional Liturgy** in 1857, there was a liturgical storm in the German Reformed Church in America. Though just about every feature of the book was called into question by its opponents, there was little or no opposition to its complete lectionary, gospel, epistle and collect for every Sunday and festival day. Could it have been that German Reformed people in 1857 were sufficiently accustomed to them that their appearance in the new liturgy did not seem radical?

b. The next piece of contrary evidence is a small but rather surprising one. A German Reformed congregation was organized in New York City in 1758 to minister to the needs of a growing number of people. From its inception it was closely connected with the local Dutch Reformed Church which took supervision of it. On May 6, 1795, the German Reformed Church issued a call to George Philipp Milledoler, a son of the congregation. Most of the terms of the call were typical of the time, two services each Sunday, four celebrations of the Lord's Supper a year, instruction of the young in the Heidelberg Catechism etc.

But slipped in with this list of duties was an unusual one.

> Every (Sunday) morning there shall be a German sermon and the minister shall, after having read a verse or two of the hymn, read the Gospel for the day in front of the altar. [1]

To have that happen under the shadow of the Dutch Reformed Church in New York was sufficiently surprising to force a little research. Milledoler's predecessor in New York (and his theological preceptor) had been John Daniel Gros who had served several congregations in Pennsylvania before moving to New York State in 1773. No record of his call to the New York City congregation could be found, but neither the call issued to his predecessor, John Gabriel Gebhard, in 1774 or to his predecessor, Christian Frederick Foering, in 1772 contained any reference to reading the Gospel for the day in front of the altar. One may fairly deduce, therefore, that it was a custom which Dr. Gros had introduced in the New York congregation.

It seems possible that during the days of his Pennsylvania ministry (if not earlier in Germany) Gros used the **Marburg Hymnal** and began the custom there of reading the Gospel for the day in front of the altar, a term which was not unknown in eighteenth century German Reformed circles. Evidently the congregation liked it so well that they made it a requirement for the next minister.

c. James I. Good was one of the few American historians to have written about the history of the Reformed Churches in Germany. Often his history is unreliable because he used it to justify his own rather narrow pietistic views, but his work is worth consulting because it does contain much information which otherwise is not easily available.

One of Good's theological heroes was Theodore Untereyck, the Dutch Reformed pietist, who accepted a call to St. Martin's (Reformed) Church in Bremen in 1670. Good describes what Untereyck found when he came to Bremen.

> . . . after the Lutheran fashion, the Reformed ministers preached on the pericopes of Scripture lessons, gave private communion, the congregations used hymns as well as psalms, celebrated the Lord's Supper weekly. [2]

Anyone who knows anything about John Calvin (which apparently Good did not) may smile at the dismissal of a weekly eucharist as <u>after the Lutheran fashion</u>, but it is interesting to learn that in the Reformed churches of Bremen the lectionary was still in use in 1670. What Good does not say is whether Untereyck was successful in doing away with the pericopes. He does state that the St. Martin's pastor "preached on free texts instead of texts taken from the Scripture lessons" [3], but that does not necessarily mean that the pericopes were not read as part of the liturgy. Although Good tried to conceal the fact, there is good evidence that whether used for preaching or not, the pericopes continued to be read every Sunday as part of the liturgy for some years after Untereyck's time.

d. Up to this point all of the evidence to the contrary had been of German origin, leading to the uncomfortable suspicion that Good may have been right in dismissing the survival of the lectionary in Reformed churches as a Lutheran hang-over. But then a Dutch volume came to my attention, a rather stout book with the imposing title **Praxeos Populariter Concionandi Rudimenta**, published in Groningen in 1657. Its author was Johannes Martinus, one of the ministers of the city. He had been born in Germany and had had his early education there, but was a graduate of the University of Franeker in Friesland where he had studied with such Reformed stalwarts as Amesius (Ames) and Maccovius.

After his graduation in 1627 Martinus was unable to return to his native Danzig and accepted a call to a Dutch Church. In 1637 he was called to Groningen where he remained until his death in 1665. He was no insignificant person in the life of the Dutch Church in his time. A correspondent of the celebrated Concceius and the father-in-law of Abraham Trommius, another leading figure in the Dutch Reformed Church in the 17th century, as well as a minister in an important Dutch city, Martinus occupied a position of leadership in his church.

Praxeos is interesting to the historian of homiletics because it is really an early textbook in that subject, dealing with such subjects as invention, elocution, memorization and pronunciation. To use a phrase common in the 19th century, it is a textbook in sacred rhetoric. Into this rather standard kind of work, however, Martinus slipped two pages of unusual material. He listed additional texts (not in the pericopes) which could be used as preaching texts for the Christian year. The list is sufficiently interesting to warrant its reproduction here.

Advent I	- Revelation 22:17
Advent II	- II Peter 3:14 or Hebrews 2:28
Advent III	- Malachi 3:1
Advent IV	- Luke 3:4-6 or John 1:16-17
Christmas	- Isaiah 7:14 or Micah 5:1
Christmas I	- I Peter 2:4-5
New Year	- Matthew 1:21 or Galatians 5:6 or Ezekiel 18:31 or Ezekiel 36:25-6
Christmas II	- Psalm 34:20-21
Epiphany	- Micah 5:1
Epiphany I	- Psalm 42:3-4
Epiphany II	- Song of Songs 7:10 or Isaiah 49:14-16
Epiphany III	- Jeremiah 10:24
Epiphany IV	- Isaiah 43:1-2
Epiphany V	- I Peter 5:8-9
Epiphany VI	- Ephesians 5:8
Septuagesima	- Ephesians 2:8-9 or Philippians 2:12-13
Sexagesima	- Romans 1:16 or James 1:21
Quinquegesima	- Song of Songs 5:2-7 or II Corinthians 5:14-15
Lent I	- Matthew 26:41
Lent II	- Psalm 42:12 or Romans 4:20-21
Lent III	- Psalm 51:17 or II Thessalonians 3:3
Lent IV	- Psalm 33:18
Lent V	- John 5:24
Easter	- Job 19:25 or Ephesians 5:14
Easter I	- Ephesians 2:4-6 or II Chronicles 30:18
Easter II	- I Peter 2:25
Easter III	- Psalm 73:25-26, Jeremiah 14:7 or Matthew 5:4
Easter IV	- Matthew 5:3 or Matthew 5:6
Easter V	- Revelation 8:3-4
Ascension	- John 20:17
Easter VI	- Matthew 5:10-12

Pentecost	- Psalm 143:10 or Luke 11:13 or Romans 8:15-16
Whitmonday	- Romans 5:8-9, II Corinthians 15:5 or Ephesians 1:3
Trinity	- Psalm 51:12-14

Martinus also gave suggested texts for twenty-five Sundays after Trinity, but a listing of his choices for Advent through Trinity Sunday is sufficient to indicate what he had in mind. Evidently he was trying to suggest alternate possibilities for those who had used the traditional pericopes too often. His frequent use of Old Testament texts, especially from the psalms and the prophets may have been done for those who felt that the traditional pericopes were too exclusively from the New Testament.

Praxeos was followed in 1662 by a second volume, **Analytica et Topica Dominicalia Tripertita.** This was a series of sermon outlines on the gospel and epistle lessons for all the Sundays and major festival days. The lectionary which Martinus used is the traditional western one, used by Lutherans, Anglicans and Roman Catholics alike. In its general format Martinus' **Analytica** is surprisingly like the flood of exegetical and homiletical commentaries which came on the market after the new lectionary made its appearance in our own time. He could be said to be an ancestor of the **Proclamation** series.

And presumably he wrote these works for exactly the same reason that **Proclamation** was written. Ministers in the province of Groningen in the mid-seventeenth century were using the old lectionary and either wanted to learn how to use it more effectively or to find alternate preaching texts for use with the lectionary. Johannes Martinus was no crypto-Catholic or closet Lutheran trying to foist new ideas on the Dutch Reformed Church in Groningen, but a concerned domine who was seeking to help his colleagues do a more satisfactory job.

Well, all that came as something of a shock about a church the earliest synods of which had strictly forbidden the use of the lectionary. One could possible accuse Martinus of Lutheranizing by reason of his German birth, but obviously he was doing it in an area in which it was welcome because the use of the traditional lectionary had never disappeared. In at least one Dutch province, it was still regularly used.

By now the evidence had begun to mount: Pennsylvania and New York (German churches therein), Bremen, Groningen, all of them exceptions to the rule which everyone had said was universal. No lectionary or lectionary preaching in Reformed Churches. The time had come to do some investigating as to just what was happening here.

Some Possible Explanations

So far as the Pennsylvania Hymnbook is concerned, that may be the easiest to explain. Our friend Dr. Good pointed out that with one or two exceptions, the Reformed Churches in Germany did not come directly from Roman Catholicism but had first experienced a Lutheran period. One of the outstanding examples of his assertion is the story of the Church in Hesse.

Hesse had been Protestant ever since 1524. Denominational labels at this point are somewhat irrelevant, but under the long leadership of its celebrated Landgrave, Philip, the country could fairly have been call Lutheran. After Philip's death in 1567, it was divided between his two sons, one of whom was Melanchthonian in point of view while the other was more rigidly Lutheran. Ultimately the country was reunited under Philip's grandson Maurice, though the religious differences remained. Finally in 1607 Maurice called a Synod to resolve these differences.

The Synod of Hesse generally allied the Church with the Reformed cause, but as one concession retained the use of the lectionary and its pericopes every Sunday. Dr. Good accepted the decision of that Synod with some difficulty.

> Hesse thus became a Reformed land. But there was always a slight tinge of Lutheran influence in a few of her customs, as in her liturgy and the use of Scripture lessons which none of the other Reformed Churches revealed. [4]

To say that no other Reformed Church used the lectionary is obviously a Goodism since we have already found some others that did, as our pietistic author knew perfectly well. But let that go for the moment. The **Marburg Hymnal** lists the Church in Hesse first in its reckoning of those which used this book. The use of the lectionary in it is therefore no surprise since the church in Hesse voted to retain it after its further reformation in 1607. So far as Gros is concerned, he may have found the use of the lectionary in Marburg, and brought it with him to the new world or he may have become acquainted with it in one of his Pennsylvania pastorates and carried it with him to New York. If Hesse and its dependents were the only Reformed Churches to have retained the lectionary, our problem would be solved.

But what about Bremen? Does the thesis of a retained Lutheranism apply here as it apparently does in Hesse? The theological history of Bremen seems to afford little parallel to that of Hesse. For one thing, it was a free city and therefore not subject to the cuius regio eius religio which had divided Hesse.

It was much more closely connected with the other free cities, Hamburg, Lubeck and Danzig and with northwest Germany, especially East Friesland, to say nothing of the northeastern part of the Netherlands. In fact, many of the names connected with the reformation in Bremen are Dutch including the celebrated preacher Hardenberg and Van Buren, the city councillor who was one of Hardenberg's chief supporters.

Once again, in the earliest time after the reformation, terms like Lutheran and Reformed would have been inapplicable. There was always a more rigidly Lutheran party which occasionally gained control. But generally speaking this party was a minority and with the adoption of the **Bremen Confession** in 1595 the official position of the town became Reformed. The continued use of the lectionary in Bremen cannot be explained as an unwilling compromise with the Lutherans, but as something which the Reformed Church in Bremen did deliberately.

And surely the same is true in Groningen where there were hardly any Lutherans with whom to compromise! In Groningen, as well as in its sister province Drenthe, the retention of the lectionary seems to have been a deliberate decision on the part of the Reformed Churches and a decision which lasted until the usage was swept away in the pietism of the 18th century. To explain these retentions we obviously must look for something more than a lingering Lutheranism.

Further Investigations

The only discussion of the Groningen use of the lectionary is a brief essay by Dr. A. C. Honders, Director of the Instituut voor Liturgiewetenschap in Groningen University. Dr. Honders' article is primarily concerned with Martinus, but in the opening section Honders summarizes the very mixed-up situation which obtained in the Netherlands regarding the use of pericopes, some synods discouraging it or forbidding it, while others, especially Drenthe and Groningen, tried to advance it. His conclusion follows.

> It is clear that in this connection, as also with what the congregation sang, people in the northern part of the country went their own way for a long time after the Reformation. [5]

Jan Koopmans provides even more specific information. After describing the situation in other synods, Dr. Koopmans writes:

> The strictest was the situation in Groningen and Drenthe. The Ommeland Church Order of 1595 provides that a

> Gospel text must be used on Sunday mornings. Until 1818 when preaching for a call in Groningen, the candidate had to take his text from the Sunday pericope. The Drenthe Synod of 1643 also reaffirmed the use of the old Sunday lectionary. [6]

Evidently the use of the lectionary was not confined to these two provinces. Koopmans tells that the Synod of Utrecht ordered its use in 1590 and when in 1606 the Synod sent out a questionnaire about the state of the churches, the domine in Wijk reported that he held three services a week; Sunday mornings he used the evangelia dominicalia, Sunday afternoons the Heidelberg Catechism, while on Thursdays he was preaching lecto continua from I Corinthians. In the same survey the domine in Veenendaal stated that he used the pericopes on Sunday mornings. [7]

The Synod of Overijsel, on the other hand, took action against the use of the lectionary as early as 1587 and strongly urged the Calvinist custom of continuous reading and preaching, but in spite of the synodical injunction, the Church in Zwolle continued to use the traditional pericopes. As late as 1618 the Classis of Zwolle registered a complaint against their abandonment. [8]

Ypeij and Dermout, the almost classic historians of the Reformed Church in the Netherlands, state that although most of the early Reformed ministers followed the Zwinglian-Calvinist custom of reading and preaching lectio continua, there were some who retained the old custom of preaching from the lectionary, despite the best efforts of many provincial synods to dissuade them. By the middle of the seventeenth century apparently the matter had ceased to be controversial and the choice of scripture for preaching was left to the freedom of the minister. They suggest that by 1675 the use of the pericopes had largely died out, except of course in Groningen and Drenthe, where, as we have seen, they enjoyed a much longer life. [9]

Having been struck by the similarities between Groningen and Bremen, I wrote to Dr. Honders to see whether there were any historical connections of which he was aware. His reply was brief but suggestive.

> I think what is important is that the northeastern area of the Netherlands (Friesland, Drenthe and especially Groningen) and Northwest Germany (East Friesland and the direction of Bremen, Hamburg and Lubeck) were a whole, culturally, geographically, with many of the same customs, including church customs. It was in this area of Dutch and German Reformed Protestantism that they followed their own ways. For example, they sang

> not only the psalms but in Friesland and Groningen Lutheran hymns as well. With them the following of the church year was not unusual. In short, I am convinced that there is a definite northern Reformed Church type. [10]

Dr. Honders remark about the use of Lutheran hymns in Groningen is further explained in his essay on Martinus who had the old chorale O Lam Godes onschuldich sung by the congregation at every communion service in his Groningen church. Honders also gives a hymn on the seven last words from the cross which Martinus wrote. Since he set it to the same tune as Psalm 100, Martinus evidently expected his congregation to sing it during Lent which he considered one of the most important parts of the Christian year.

The remark about the use of Lutheran chorales reminded me that my old friend, James I. Good, in listing the Lutheran sins of the congregation in Bremen had mentioned hymn-singing among them, though he is not so specific as Honders as to what was sung. Evidently here is another similarity between Reformed Church life in Groningen and in Bremen, bearing out Honders' thesis about a northern Reformed Church with a life of its own.

A Northern Reformed Church?

It is well known that from its very beginning the Reformed Church has existed in two types, closely related as they may have been in many ways. The earliest was the Zwinglian Reformation which became the type in the German cantons of Switzerland and in certain parts of southern Germany. The second was the Calvinist Reformation which prevailed in the French cantons of Switzerland, in France, Scotland, the Netherlands and ultimately in English Puritanism. Though there were obvious differences between them, in the question before us, i.e., the use of a Sunday lectionary, they were in complete agreement in its rejection.

It is clear, however, that the northern Reformed Church described by Honders fits with neither the Zwinglian or the Calvinist Reformation though it has obvious affinities with each of them. Is it possible that there was still a third type of Reformed Reformation with which the Groningen-Bremen type at which we have been looking would fit and if so how can it best be described?

The leading 19th century historians of the German Reformed Church insisted that there was and they called it Melanchthonian. Here, for example, are some sentences from August Ebrard, a mid-nineteenth century Reformed professor at Erlangen.

> Melanchthon, the greatest of the learned coadjutors of Luther in the Reformed in Saxony, is rightly claimed by the Reformed Church, beside Zwingli and Calvin, as the third of her Reformers, and especially as the founder of the German Reformed Church . . . The rest of the German Reformed Church which . . . sprang up in opposition to the exclusive Lutheranism circumscribing itself in the Form of Concord are in reality nothing else than Melanchthonian elements which were violently thrust out of the Lutheran Church; which, however, with their separation from the latter and connection with the Reformed Church naturally experienced the new and moulding influence of Calvinism. [11]

Heirich Heppe, a Reformed professor at Marburg at the same time, puts it even more vigorously.

> The historical and dogmatical root of the German Reformed Church is not Calvinism but the German Reformation with its confessional writings.
>
> The origin of the German Reformed Church was the secession, beginning . . . in 1561, of exclusive "Genuine Lutheranism" from the Old evangelical communion of the Evangelical states of Germany . . .

Heppe goes on to say that it is his opinion that the Calvinizing of the German Reformed Church did it some harm. "The Calvinizing of worship and the whole church discipline must have plainly appeared in the conviction of contemporaries as a breach with history and this did severe injury to the productive power and vigorous life of the Church." [12]

Theodore Appel of Lancaster, a second generation leader in Mercersburg theology, has perhaps the strongest statement of all especially in view of the subject which concerns us. In comparing the German Reformed Church with other Reformed and Presbyterian churches in America, he also invokes the Melanchthonian thesis but puts it to this use.

> When, therefore, we claim for the German Reformed Church a more churchly character than what inheres in the strictly Calvinistic churches, we believe that we are fully sustained by history; and the language of a celebrated divine in our own communion (J. W. Nevin) is by no means too strong when he says that the "proper historical relations of the (Heidelberg) Catechism as they are presented to us in the German Church include the altar, the organ and the gown; church lessons and a church year with its regular cycle of religious festivals". [13]

It is easy to quarrel about the accuracy of the term Melanchthonian to describe this third style of Reformed Reformation, but it seems clear that there was a third style growing out of the struggles within German Lutheranism which found Calvinism's teaching on the real presence in the eucharist much more congenial than what was being advanced in more rigid Lutheran circles. The degree to which it bought into the rest of Calvinism obviously varied. In fact historians of theology are still in disagreement of many aspects of that question. But that this third style of Reformation brought to the Northern Reformed Church different liturgical customs which in some instances it was unwilling to surrender seems abundantly clear.

The theory which I have been describing will account for what we have found in the German part of our Northern Reformed Church, Bremen, Hesse etc., but what about the Dutch sections? After all was not Calvinism completely triumphant in the Netherlands? Surely there was no Melanchthonian influence there.

My much despised Dr. Good points the way to an answer, though, as usual, with maddening incompleteness. Pointing out that there was a Reformed Church at Emden in East Friesland almost before there was a Zwingli and certainly before there was a Calvin, he writes:

> . . . Emden and East Friesland became the model for the Dutch and German Reformed Churches; as Geneva had been for the French, English and Scotch Churches. [14]

The foolish part of that statement, apart from its odd chronology, is the way in which it assumes that the Netherlands was not influenced by Geneva. It is common knowledge that the surge of Calvinism into the Netherlands was largely from the French speaking south. Almost all of the early Calvinist leadership was Walloon. But in those early days the Netherlands was hardly a nation; it was a league of provinces united only by opposition to Spanish tyranny.

And therein lies the truth of Good's observation. Culturally and linguistically the northern provinces looked not to the French speaking south but to their German neighbors to the east. For them the model would have been not only Emden but Bremen, Hamburg and the other areas in their immediate orbit. This was the old area of the Brethren of the Common Life. Political necessity may have brought them to accept Calvinism theologically and organizationally but not necessarily in terms of liturgy and Sunday church practice.

There may be historical reasons as well for the conservatism of Groningen church customs. The city had abstained from joining the Union of Utrecht in 1579 because of its implicit anti-Roman Catholicism. As historian Pieter Geyl has described it:

> Rennenberg (the Stadtholder) and his provinces who had taken part in the first discussions in Arnhem abstained now that matters had taken this turn. Only the Ommeland (rural Groningen), always at variance with the ultra-Catholic town of Groningen, at once participated. [15]

A year later Rennenberg withdrew completely from any association with the other Dutch provinces and returned his provinces to Spanish control. Groningen was therefore not part of the earliest years of the Dutch Republic; in fact, it had to be taken by force in 1594 by Prince Maurice, William the Silent's son.

Geyl's description of what happened after the surrender of Groningen may contribute to our understanding of what happened with the lectionary.

> In all conquered towns and districts the Reformed Church organization was introduced without delay. The Protestantization of the people was considered as an indispensable guarantee of their loyalty to the States regime . . .
>
> In all towns that fell into the power of the States the exercise of the Catholic religion was at once suppressed and the churches were seized for the Reformed and "purged" in accordance with their ideas. [16]

If it be asked how such a rapidly reformed church found an adequate supply of clergy, the answer is that former priests were given the choice of either "holding their peace" or of submitting to an examination for admission to the Reformed ministry. Geyl says that in Groningen Province this worked very well, leading us to conclude that the majority of Reformed clergy there were former parish priests. It happened so quickly that there was never any chance for a counter-reformation in the Dutch northeast.

> It is evident that the majority of the North Netherlandish people only abandoned Catholicism under the pressure of public authority . . . It should not be forgotten that the substratum of the people's life was still in the main Catholic. [17]

Given all of these factors, it is more readily understandable why the province of Groningen and its sister province Drenthe (the smallest and weakest of all the Dutch provinces) should have retained the use of the Sunday lectionary. At a time when so many of the common symbols of the old religious way, altars, images, crosses, crucifixes and pictures, were suddenly and violently removed, here was something of the old way which could still be retained. And once the dust had begun to settle a bit, it was only natural that the newly Reformed church in the northeastern Netherlands should look in its traditional German direction and discover there that all Reformed Churches did not follow Zwingli and Calvin in their prescriptions for preaching.

But whatever may be the full explanation for the fact, the common statement that the use of a lectionary in preaching in the Reformed churches ceased with Zwingli and Calvin needs to be modified. There may be more churches than those which I have been able to identify, but even those which have been identified, while a minority, are a not inconsiderable group. They include some of the most celebrated and influential churches in Reformed Christendom. While the custom of the use of the lectionary died out at different times in different places, it is possible that its revival in the mid-nineteenth century was at least partially continuous with its use in an earlier time.

NOTES

1. **Ecclesiastical Records of the State of New York** (Albany, 1905), VI, 4371.

2. James I Good, **History of the Reformed Church in Germany** (Reading, 1894), 325.

3. Ibid., 329.

4. James I. Good, **Origin of the Reformed Church in Germany** (Reading, 1887), 365.

5. A. C. Honders, "Kerkelijk Jaar en Zondagse Pericopen," **Mededelingen**, (Groningen, 1982).

6. J. Koopmans, **Onder Het Woord** (Amsterdam, 1949), 333.

7. Ibid.

8. Ibid., 334.

9. A. Ypeij and I. J. Dermout, **Aanteekeningen op de Geschiedenis der Nederlandsche Hervormde Kerk** (Breda, 1819), I, 234-5.

10. A. C. Honders in private letter to author, 21 October, 1983.

11. **Tercentenary Monument** (Chambersburg, PA, 1863), 89-90.

12. Mercersburg Review V, 205-6.

13. **Tercentenary Monument**, 332-3.

14. **Origin of the Reformed Church in Germany**, 88.

15. P. Geyl, **Revolt of the Netherlands** (London, 1945), 170.

16. Ibid., 228.

17. Ibid., 231.

PRESBYTERIAN WORSHIP IN TWENTIETH CENTURY AMERICA

Julius Melton
Davidson College

The late twentieth century brought American Presbyterians a host of anniversaries to celebrate. In 1983 the 300th birthday of Francis Makemie arrived, and honor was paid to a man considered the founder of American Presbyterianism for his mission work, establishing of presbyteries, and sacrificial work in securing toleration for Christians of this persuasion in the Colonies. There have been a number of bicentennials for individual congregations and institutions, picking up the theme the nation heralded in 1976. Nearing its 250th birthday is the earliest prominent academy of Presbyterian origin, Princeton University. Theological seminaries came on the scene somewhat later, but one or two of them are well through their second century of influence in the denomination.

The 500th anniversary of Martin Luther's birth, which occurred in 1983, gave an indication of the relative youthfulness or age of the Protestant movement; while the 350th anniversary of the Westminster Assembly, which will occur in the 1990's, helps place English-speaking Presbyterianism in historical perspective within Protestantism.

The mention of these several anniversaries serves as a backdrop for some remarks on the public worship of American Presbyterians. Makemie's struggles for toleration in the early eighteenth century, as well as the literally revolutionary character of the Westminster Assembly during England's Civil War of the 1640's, make clear that the worship being examined is that of a group marked off from the liturgical Church of England. However, it is a group of people clearly within mainstream Protestantism, who had a profound respect for order and for an educated clergy, as their venerable academies testify.

Another anniversary, likely to be noted by the recently

reunited Presbyterian Church (U.S.A.), occurs in the late 1980's. It is the bicentennial of the first Presbyterian General Assembly in what was then the new United States of America. Among the first acts that unifying national church body took was to revise and adopt documents to govern and guide the denomination.

The "standards" chosen by that first American General Assembly were those initially written at Westminster about a century and a half earlier. They were revised to fit life in a new democracy. The Confession of Faith, **Book of Order,** and Catechisms usually come to mind, but another "standard" was the Directory for Worship. It might be called, however, the least of the standards. The politics of the new General Assembly and the diversity of worship practice already present among American Presbyterians influenced its wording in the new denomination. Suggestions of including pattern prayers--a rudimentary liturgy--were rejected, even though proposed by some of the distinguished urban pastors of the day, and its directions were almost always made as suggestions.

Public worship among Presbyterians was officially ordered only by this less than directive Directory for Worship for a century and a half. Of course, experimentation in worship was not unheard of although wild extremes were generally avoided, and controversy over what was and was not "Presbyterian" were often met in the nineteenth century. Finally the church took official steps to provide more specific directions and even examples. In 1906 the General Assembly of the Presbyterian Church in the U.S.A. issued a **Book of Common Worship.** This was anything but an imposed liturgy. "For voluntary use" was required to be printed on the title page. The Directory for Worship remained the formal, but largely unknown, document to govern worship practices.

The quickened pace of the twentieth century becomes evident when a few more recent events are recalled, related to American Presbyterian worship documents. The Directory for Worship itself, untouched since 1788 when first revised for American use, was brought up for extensive and impressive revisions by both major branches of the now reunited (as of 1983) Presbyterian Church (U.S.A.). This occurred in the 1950's and early 1960's. It happened again in the 1980's in advance of the reunion, and a formal effort to write a new directory continues. Of more interest, because of the more specific nature of their content, have been five different editions of the denominationally-provided book of liturgical materials which have appeared in fewer than 80 years, including one now in progress.

Reviewing certain influences on these books and their editors and certain effects of the several volumes brings with it an understanding of how American Presbyterians have worshipped and what developments have affected their worship in the twentieth century.

One influence is apparent from a glance at the arrangement of the elements of the Sunday service in the five manuals produced by the principal Presbyterian denomination in the U.S., including a volume circulated in 1983 for "field testing." (See the accompanying outlines.) The most recent two of the the five combine the celebration of the Lord's Supper into the normal Sunday service, considering a service without it to be out of the ordinary rather than the normal pattern. While this does not reflect the actual practice in most Presbyterian churches, it indicates that denominational leaders, when expressing themselves officially, have agreed with the expressed desires (although again not the practice) of their founder John Calvin. This change is in harmony with a revision made in the Directory for Worship in 1961, and not accidentally so, for the Directory is meant to state principles for worship, while the manuals add flesh to that framework. This is but one result of what has been called the liturgical revival, which has been influential in both Protestantism and Roman Catholicism in the twentieth century.

The location of the sermon earlier in the service in the 1970 and 1983 arrangements is also not without significance. It denotes a shift in emphasis. At one time in their Puritan and frontier experience Presbyterians spoke of going to "preaching" or referred to all but the sermon as the "preliminaries." The revised Directories for Worship of the 1960's definitely took an important step away from that concept as they sought to emphasize the vital importance of the people's participation in prayer and praise. The view that the worship of God by his people should normally conclude with their gathering around the Lord's Table also calls for placing the proclamation of the Word earlier in the service. The old custom of placing the sermon last fitted well, of course, an earlier time when, starved as they were for entertainment and socialization, many--even more--"unchurched" attended service than did church members themselves, if proportions were calculated. That phenomenon turned almost all pastors into Sunday evangelists. Clearly that situation does not prevail today, when the church must compete with the media, professional sports events, and the modern "weekend" for the attendance of even its own.

This very brief analysis of one or two changes obvious from a quick look at the orders of service in the five manuals implied that more than one line of explanation might be taken regarding what has happened in the twentieth century to the worship of American Presbyterians. The Presbyterians, of course, provide an interesting subject for study because their denomination has sufficient size and spread so that studying its worship life may reveal much about influences in mainline American Protestantism

ORDERS OF WORSHIP IN FIVE DIFFERENT AMERICAN PRESBYTERIAN BOOKS OF WORSHIP

Book of Common Worship 1906	Book of Common Worship 1932	Book of Common Worship 1946	Worshipbook 1970	Test Manuscript 1983
				Assembling
Doxology, hymn or psalm	Call to Prayer	Hymn	Call to Worship	Scriptural Greeting
		Call to worship	Hymn of Praise	Announcements and Concerns of the Church
Call to Worship	Invocation	Prayer of Adoration		
Invocation	Confession of Sin	Confession of Sin	Confession of Sin	Call to Worship
Confession of Sin	Assurance of Pardon	Assurance of Pardon	Declaration of Pardon	(Music or silence)
Assurance of Pardon	Responsive Words of Praise			Sentences of Scripture
Responsive Words of Praise			Response	Hymn of Praise
		Responsive Reading of the Psalter		(Opening Prayer)
Responsive Reading or Psalter	Responsive Reading of hymn		Prayer for Illumination	Confession of Sin
				Declaration of Pardon
		First Scripture Lesson	Old Testament Lesson	The Peace
Scripture Reading (both Testaments recommended)	Scripture Reading (both Testaments)	Hymn or Anthem	Optional Anthem, Canticle or Psalm	
		Second Scripture Lesson		
		Apostles or Nicene Creed		Prayer for Illumination
Hymn	Hymn or Anthem	Hymn or Anthem	New Testament Lesson or Lessons	Scripture Reading
Creed	Creed (where customary)			Psalm
		General Prayer, closing with the Lord's Prayer (here or after sermon)	Sermon	Scripture Reading
General Prayer, closing with Lord's Prayer	General Prayer, closing with Lord's Prayer		Optional Ascription and/or Invitation	Hymn, Song, or Anthem
				Reading of Gospel
		Offering (here or after sermon)	Creed	Sermon
			Optional Hymn	

ORDERS OF WORSHIP IN FIVE DIFFERENT AMERICAN PRESBYTERIAN BOOKS OF WORSHIP (cont.)

Book of Common Worship	Book of Common Worship	Book of Common Worship	Worshipbook	Test Manuscript
1906	1932	1946	1970	1983
Announcements	Announcements	Doxology or Prayer of Dedication	Optional "Concerns of the Church"	Hymn
Offering	Offering			(Baptism, or Ordinance of the Church)
Anthem	Prayer of Dedication		General Prayer	
Prayer of Dedication	Hymn of Doxology		The Peace	(Creed or Affirmation of Faith)
Hymn		Hymn or Anthem	Offering	
Sermon	Sermon	Sermon	Optional Anthem	Prayers of Intercession
		Ascription	Optional Hymn or Doxology	Offering
Hymn (may be after Closing Prayer)	Closing Prayer or Hymn			
		Hymn	Invitation to the Lord's Table	Invitation to the Table
Closing Prayer				Great Prayer of Thanks-giving
Benediction	Benediction	Benediction	The Thanksgiving	
			The Lord's Prayer	Lord's Prayer
			The Communion	Breaking of Bread
			Response	Communion of the People
			Hymn	Hymn, Song or Psalm
			Charge	Blessing
			Benediction	Charge

generally. The remainder of this article will attempt to call attention to some of the stronger influences noted in the century and see a few of their particular effects in the worship of the people called Presbyterians.

When the 1905 Presbyterian General Assembly voted to produce a Book of Common Worship it did so in response to a two-year study prompted by overtures from several quarters of the church. Knowing that neutral or hostile factions from within the generally non-liturgical denomination would need to be sold before they would support the service manual, the committee which prepared it came armed with a persuasive explanation.

First they described in succinct terms the interesting blend of order and freedom their church stood for in worship:

> Among those Churches of the Lord Jesus Christ which follow the Presbyterian rule and order, Liberty of Worship has been esteemed a most precious privilege and inheritance; and while they have been both fearless and faithful to uphold it, against the intrusion of superstitious and burdensome ceremonies, they have also been diligent to seek, in the Public Services of Religion, the golden mean between a too great laxity and a tyrannical uniformity. Such things as are of Divine Institution they have observed in every Ordinance; and other things they have endeavoured to set forth "according to the Rules of Christian Prudence, agreeable to the general Rules of the Word of God". [1]

They continued by citing historical precedent for their work, referring to the liturgies of Calvin and Knox:

> Although the Books of Common Order, which were prepared for the Reformed Churches, at the beginning, in all countries, contained both prayers and other forms, yet were those books not so much imposed by way of inflexible regulation, as they were offered and accepted as profitable Aids to Worship; and they not only permitted but encouraged the exercise of Free Prayer. In a like spirit the Directory for Worship, adopted at a later time by the Church of Scotland, for the sake of unity with their brethren in the Church of England, so far from establishing an invariable form of Public Worship, expressly provided for a liberty of variation; and it did not in any way prohibit the use of prepared orders and prayers, conformable to the general directions given therein. [2]

The prayers, worship materials, and the order of service itself were defended as being in keeping with the church's biblical basis, as embodying the faith and experience of the denomination, as expressing elements universal in the experience of the ecumenical church, and as being expressly related to the realities of present day life. This defense mirrored instructions set down by the 1903 General Assembly. Four criteria had been laid down: The service was to be biblically based, expressive of Presbyterian theology, ecumenical in scope, and in tune with the times in which the worshippers found themselves. Whether intended or not, these four criteria became a dynamic influence and led quite naturally to the four subsequent revisions of the Book of Common Worship.

A provisional motto used in 1983 by the newly reunited Presbyterian Church (U.S.A.) recalled the denomination's commitment to constant reformation (Ecclesia Reformata Semper Reformanda). The motto fits the Presbyterian attitude toward liturgy. Although the church established a liturgy in 1906, it was not only voluntary but was supposed to be regularly restudied. Many developments have occurred since 1906 in each of the areas set out as bases for the criteria by which Presbyterians would judge effective worship: scripture, theology, the ecumenical experience, and life in the world beyond the house of worship.

Biblical scholarship, for example, has advanced along with advances in science, historical and archaeological research, and linguistic and literary analysis. To describe some worship practice as being scriptural means something quite different in a day in which a more sophisticated understanding of worship in the biblical period prevails.

The systematic theology of Presbyterians, the second criterion for ordering worship, has almost always been viewed as a dynamic enterprise, intended as it is to express the faith in thought forms of changing times and cultures. Therefore worship which fits the church's theology would have had to undergo changes. One example of rethinking their theology is the Presbyterians' decision in the 1970's to admit baptized but not yet confirmed children to the Lord's Supper. The implications of this theological readjustment are yet being felt in the worship and sacramental practices of the church.

With World and National Councils of Churches, the Consultation on Church Union, and other substantial ecumenical expressions having largely developed since 1906, the meaning of worship as expressive of elements universal in Christian experience, the third criterion, has clearly been broadened. Presbyterians, known for their presence in almost all ecumenical enterprises as well as the world missionary movement, have had their horizons extended considerably over the eight decades of this century.

As for the fourth criterion, relevance to the outside

world, examples of how twentieth century society as a whole has changed, passing as it has through two world wars, a world-wide depression, developments of all kinds in nuclear power, explosions of awareness through the electronic media and rapid transportation, and on and on--these do not need to be itemized to show how a style of worship tuned to the realities of the secular lives of church members would of necessity have faced manifold changes.

This article's opening glance at altered arrangements of service elements in the 1906, 1932, 1946, 1970, and 1983 versions of the Book of Common Worship revealed only the tip of an iceberg of change. Twentieth century influences on worship can be related not only to the four original criteria just discussed, which were set down for an ideal Presbyterian service. They can also be viewed as coming from pervasive change in experience, in idiom, and in relationships within the church.

Each of the volumes identified some of the interests of its day which had been influential in the choice of topics for prayers, in emphases, and in rearrangement of elements of the service, or when it did not these could be inferred by a study of the text. In 1906 efforts were made to introduce many congregations to responsive or unison participation, and the Christian year was cautiously espoused, while prayers were included for current concerns like temperance, Sunday schools, evangelism, family worship, and missions. The version of 1932 gave heightened emphasis to the Christian year and a rudimentary lectionary appeared along with prayers showing the importance attached to young people, peace, and justice in the social order. In 1946 attention was called to the results of liturgical research in the intervening years and the increased appreciation of the liturgies of the Reformers, a full lectionary was borrowed from the 1940 Scottish Book of Common Order, and special services for children and young people were added.

The church has thus been consciously handling the content of its service books, in several revision efforts and in congregational life, for almost eighty years. This has made the Presbyterians more sensitive than they were in the nineteenth century to their traditions. Many have felt a duty to use their heritage with care and sensitivity. "No matter how simple the form of worship to which our congregations may be accustomed," wrote one minister, "it is a tradition--in fact a ritual, a liturgy . . . and as such it deserves our respectful understanding." [3] For the most part changes in worship on local and national levels have been made with care. This is one positive effect of the experiences Presbyterians have had with liturgy in the twentieth century.

Ecumenical experience was something which grew richer and deeper for many Presbyterians as the twentieth century progressed, and all in the church were affected by it. The Second Vatican Council must be given some of the credit. It opened up the largest single Christian communion to new contact with people like Presbyterians. The new use of vernacular in Catholic worship gave Presbyterians and other Protestants colleagues they had not known before, in the enterprise of producing worship materials in English. Interest in academic study of liturgy, church music, and scripture overlapped denominational lines as never before.

One illustration of such cooperative efforts and their effects on worship is the work which has gone on with regard to a unified lectionary providing scripture readings for use in worship for a three-year cycle. Presbyterians adapted the Vatican II version of the lectionary--which itself had been an ecumenical project--and produced the "Lectionary for the Christian Year" which they included in their Worshipbook, published in 1970. The texts of the Apostles and Nicene Creeds and some other major worship texts which appear in the same book are the work of the International Consultation on English Texts, begun in 1969 as another outgrowth of the Vatican II experience. Representatives of a number of denominations make up yet another study group, the North American Committee on Calendar and Lectionary, which has developed a consensus lectionary now being included in Presbyterian worship materials. Two Presbyterian leaders have prepared helpful volumes of worship materials to supplement the lessons of the lectionaries and introduce them more widely in the denomination. Yet a third ecumenically-sponsored lectionary, the Inclusive Language Lectionary from the National Council of Churches elicited much interest and some controversy when introduced in 1983 with its edited scripture lessons. Since some 40% of Presbyterian ministers follow the lectionary in some manner in worship and preaching, these developments have had significance. [4]

In addition to lectionary and English texts, another set of movements brought Protestants and Roman Catholics closer together in worship theory and practice. Catholics began to place a higher value on proclamation of the Word, and Protestants on the sacramental side of worship. Catholics were also found enjoying singing hymns in English, many of them familiar to Protestants. And some Protestants made more use of responses and psalms familiar to Catholics. On both sides lay people took a larger part in planning services. [5] One writer was moved to hope that such mutual interest in liturgical renewal would facilitate greater understanding among churches, saying "The road to reunion starts more truly from altar, pew, pulpit, and font than from headquarters in Geneva or Rome." [6]

One reason for increased similarity among denominations, including the Roman Catholic Church, has been their having to face common problems. One has been the question of how to deal with or even retain their youth. For a host of reasons a youth "counter culture" developed in much of the Western world in the mid-twentieth century. Within it was an emphasis on spontaneity, participation, sensory involvement, informality, and energy. Many churches responded with specially designed worship events or "celebrations." In 1971 the magazine Presbyterian Life had a special issue on "New Ways to Worship." It told of several experiences of this emphasis. Even the United Presbyterian General Assembly of that year got involved, with a two-day workshop on church music and liturgy which included such innovations as role playing, clapping, stomping, whistling, humming, and group vocal prayer--and even cheers (e.g., for Advent: "Give me an 'A', give me a 'D'. . ."). "Most in attendance," the reader was told, "went away ready to inject more celebration in their home churches." [7]

All across the continent experiments were afoot to cast worship in the contemporary idiom. In Riverside, California, a carefully-planned half-hour early service was launched called "Contemporary Celebrations for Families." It included multi-media presentations, balloons, use of the autoharp and prayers in contemporary language. [8] In Cincinnati, a Celebration of Evangelism was held in September, 1971. Photographs in a story about it showed 3,000 worshippers raising their hands aloft, clapping, singing and tapping balloons in a "floor-shaking finale" planned by the "director of creative worship" from a California Presbyterian church. [9] In the small and "obviously unprosperous" community of Port Jervis, New York, an "experimental" and "festival" approach was used on Pentecost Sunday. All wore something red, symbolizing Pentecost. After stirring traditional hymns the pastor read the story from Acts.

> The people make sound effects: the noise of wind and the announcement "God is love" in phonetics of five languages. By holding quivering, open hands over their heads they all simulate the appearance of the tongues of fire over the disciples. That's followed by a calypso setting of "Glory be to the Father."

A birthday celebration for the church followed as part of the service, still in the sanctuary. A nonagenarian and a teenager blew out candles on a cake as the congregation sang "Happy birthday to the church," accompanied by organ, piano, cymbals, and xylophones, with handshakes all around. [10]

It is not without significance that one comment about the Cincinnati Celebration of Evangelism was that a widespread interest surfaced there in the charismatic movement. [11] The charismatic movement also has had an influence on worship, though not formalized in service books--an influence again overlapping denominational lines. To a considerable extent it has institutionalized the themes of the innovations of the 1960's and 70's and carried them further. One continuing challenge facing Presbyterians during the period of the 1970's and 80's has been communication difficulties between charismatics and non-charismatics. Clergy and congregations which might be characterized as charismatic developed their own sets of expectations and criteria for worship; and worshipers of the charismatic and of the non-charismatic sorts often took care to search out a compatible congregation when they wished to attend a service outside their home communities. Although much would be common to all Presbyterian services, the style would be noticeably different.

What was called "the trend"--innovative, energetic worship experiences--was analyzed by one of its exponents as containing four elements: First, celebration should be the rule, since the gospel gives cause for vigorous rejoicing. Second, worship should be related better than it had been to reality, hence images in hymns should be current rather than rural and pre-industrial, and eloquence and generalization should give way to direct language, honesty, and candor. Third, a variety of forms and styles should be used; the Port Jervis services sought to give lovers of "Bach, or rock, or Lawrence Welk, or folk, or country, or gospel songs, or soul" their "moment," and as often as possible. And fourth, participation should take the place of a spectator approach to worship, meeting a "demand by people to speak, move, and sing for themselves and to have worship represent their own feelings." [12]

By the end of the decade of the 70's, however, "the trend" had waned and problems within it were being pointed out. Liturgical experiments too often took the form of "can-you-top-this" events called "celebrations," wrote one critic. They had the values of loosening Presbyterians up, of bringing in some "fresh air," or involving lay people, recognizing spontaneity, and making use of art forms. But much was in bad taste, involved a de novo mentality, and fell into the neo-revivalistic trap of evaluating liturgical effectiveness by "meaningful experiences." [13] The main problem was the reappearance in new dress of a long-standing confusion of worship and evangelism which had surfaced several times before in the experience of American Presbyterians.

In spite of the questionable nature of some experiments in worship, they may have served to redirect attention of church people to what went on in the sanctuary. Quite a significant contrast was noted by one church architect between attitudes in the late 1970's and two decades earlier. In the late 1950's he had to drag comments about worship out of people with whom he talked about church building projects. They told him with much enthusiasm then about suppers, youth meetings, Scouts, and women's work, but "people weren't interested in worship in 1958, so far as they would tell me." He concluded "I think worship for them was dull, and dull because in worship people were usually passive." [14] By the late 70's, on the other hand, congregations focused much more on what went on in their services, and felt they ought to be doing "live things" with "clear purpose and deed devotion."

Responding to the increased interest and seeking to inject more order into the somewhat confusing scene, the two major Presbyterian bodies in the U.S. established in 1970 a Joint Office of Worship and Music. It was intended to advise congregations, agencies and meetings in the two areas mentioned in its title. On its 25-member advisory committee were some of the denominations' most liturgically well-informed people, and it secured a well-qualified director with good credentials in both fields. [15] The Joint Office soon took over the formerly independent journal Reformed Liturgy and Music, which furnished a forum for some of the more serious students of worship and church music. It produced materials and represented the denominations in ecumenical consultations, such as those described earlier. It sat somewhat outside the Presbyterian bureaucratic establishment, being located on a Kentucky seminary campus, and even somewhat outside the academic enterprises of the denomination. Yet is has done important pioneering work and has enabled concerns for improved worship to have a way to be focused better than ever before.

Liturgical studies were coming of age in the mid-twentieth century, as the creation of the Joint Office indicated. A young Presbyterian liturgical scholar explained in the Joint Office's journal that liturgical scholarship was neither oriented to the past nor tinged with romanticism. Rather it was future-oriented, he said, and stayed in touch with other branches of theology. The other branches, meanwhile--biblical, historical, ethical, etc.--had been rediscovering their own context, which is the worshiping Christian community. As for its relation with theology, he reminded Presbyterians that "good worship strengthens and increases faith; bad worship weakens or erodes faith." [16]

Music, another concern of the Joint Office, seemed also to be coming of age in Presbyterianism--a far cry from the "quavering discord" President John Adams had heard issuing from Presbyterian worship in his day or the fascination with potential bombast and psychological effects of pipe organs found in the writings of nineteenth century evangelist Charles G. Finney. Basing her views on the premise that art itself communicates ideas, one Presbyterian church musician pointed out how the place of music in worship was much too profound to allow it to be used as background for verbal communication. Strong objections were voiced by church musicians to using their ministry and that of choirs to create moods or effects. Pastors were called on to examine their operative philosophies and use their influence to educate worshipers to a greater range of musical appreciation and expression. [17] Music, argued another of its spokespersons, is primarily an act of devotion and praise to God, even though it has many secondary benefits in worship, such as comforting, inspiring, teaching, building community, and creating ties between the various ages and eras. [18]

While much of a positive nature was occuring, there yet was a rather bewildering diversity of understandings of the various elements which make up worship, within the Presbyterian fold. A church architect told of asking building committee members what the pulpit or communion table meant, and said he often got as many varieties of interpretation as there were members. He considered that to mean that they actually wanted that many different types of church buildings for their congregation, if indeed form should follow function and the interpretation of function should govern design. [19]

There was a general feeling in Presbyterian circles that steps should be taken in the direction of developing a firmer consensus regarding worship. One step was taken in 1955 when a committee was created to begin to work toward a new edition of the Book of Common Worship. It was begun by the more national Presbyterian Church, but soon was joined by the Southern Presbyterians and the Cumberland Presbyterian Church as well. The process was careful and measured, but by 1966 a preliminary service book was printed and marketed for testing, and a final version came from the press in 1970, called by a new name, The Worshipbook.

Since some of the challenges facing the church in the 1960's and some of the worship experiments of the period have already been described, it will come as no surprise to note that The Worshipbook was considerably different from the three versions of the Book of Common Worship that preceded it, as its new name sought to indicate. Its style was contemporary, meaning simply the "straightforward use of words and language in current, contemporary use in the last third of the twentieth century." [20] Oversight of the literary and liturgical efforts which went into its production was provided over the long period of preparation by a committee composed of as many as 47 able church leaders, not all serving at the same time.

The principal writer-editor for the services, David G. Buttrick, was mindful of how hard a task he had accepted. "Liturgical writing," he said, "is a delicate theological task involving an interaction of Scripture and public language" in a world where language is constantly changing. He found himself trying to "use ordinary language in an extra-ordinary way." [21] He had taken on, in a much more visible fashion, the problem every Presbyterian pastor faced weekly, of leading others in prayer or praise, taking care that the worshipers actually were able to participate rather than simply observe the leader (or writer) going through his or her own private acts of worship.

The Worshipbook "leapt into contemporary phrases more than other 'official' prayer books." [22] That was a bold leap, for many other such books were being produced about the same time. During a twenty year period in the 1960's and 70's almost every branch of the Christian community rewrote its liturgy. [23] What their editors faced becomes clearer when one learns that of the 450,000 words in the large Webster's Dictionary in 1934, only some 150,000 were in use by 1978, while another 200,000 words had invaded the language. "Our liturgical writing," concluded The Worshipbook's editor, "is at best make-shift: unstable words stammering in the face of Majesty."

Upon its appearance in 1970 The Worshipbook was greeted as "light in the darkness" of the current dissatisfaction with traditional ways of worship, on the one hand, and criticism of individualistic worship experiments on the other. The virtues of The Worshipbook were, some felt, its sound basis in theology and liturgical principles and its recapturing of early Christian and Reformed customs, even while using straightforward, contemporary English. It could be used without expensive, elaborate accessories such as were necessary for multi-media presentations, one writer pointed out. While it was generally admitted that most churches and ministers would use it selectively, it nevertheless seemed to offer a good, agreed upon focus and could stimulate lay involvement in planning and conducting local services. [24]

The cautious approach taken by the preparation committee testified to the degree of feeling and diversity of opinion in the church. During a thirteen year period the committee received "thousands" of communications, each of which was "photocopied" for every committee member. Personally the members possessed vocabularies in which "not only thee and thou, but even beseech and vouchsafe were familiar, but they were persuaded to go with contemporary English for the new manual out of a fear that "the ancient (and beloved) language of the church was serving to cut it off from students and the young and from a world which views the church as too often irrelevant," and out of a belief that other Christian groups, Catholic and Protestant, were taking similar steps. [25]

Criticisms of The Worshipbook, when they came, did not usually center on the contemporary vocabulary, at least not overtly. One critic found that the length of the service effectively reduced the time available for the sermon "by a half or more." It did that by adding to "the ritual" and by recommending weekly observance of the Lord's Supper. He found this troubling in a time when most church members were not pursuing other avenues than listening to sermons for gaining an understanding of scripture. [26] Another criticism was leveled at the hymnal portion of the complete Worshipbook. It had included innovative hymns, but "our young people" had grown tired of the ones included before the book every came out, said one observer. [27]

The heavy artillery was saved for the "exclusivist" language--what is called in secular society "sexist" language. The Worshipbook had been in the works for a number of years, but it arrived in the churches as a new and modern guide to Christian worship just as many Presbyterians were becoming sensitive to this issue raised by the women's movement. The Worshipbook gave no evidence of having been aware that male-dominant language was a problem.

Female clergy and staff pointed out that the generic use of masculine words and the "reality of sexism in the church" might well be connected. Many felt strongly that the Presbyterian Church, through its choice of words should "give a clear signal to people who walk through our door" of where the denomination stood on this issue. There was certainly no need to say "brothers" or "men" where "people" would serve as well, or "sons" where "children" would do. [28]

The reason for moving to substitute "inclusive" language was well stated by a seminary professor who pointed out: "By relatively easy changes in my own liturgical and homiletical language, I can more accurately convey what I and surely the gospel intended all along, and thereby cease to injure or insult persons who, whether we understand it or intend it, hear themselves addresses as less than whole." [29] But once it was recognized as a valuable undertaking, the task of reforming language in this inclusive direction proved complex. It led the church into problem areas such as language about God, language from scripture, language of hymns, and how to agree on what was objectionable. What, for example, about prayers of confession which identified forms of over-assertiveness as sins, thereby seeming to cast passivity as a virtue?

The problem facing The Worshipbook in this regard was exacerbated due to the fact that the 1971 United Presbyterian General Assembly ordered all generic use of masculine nouns and pronouns eliminated from official church documents. The Worshipbook appeared in its final form, including hymns, just after that. Although its status as an "official document" was not clear, it was to be the showpiece and pattern for Presbyterian worship. For it to be stamped by a continued use of masculine language as generic seemed "a further sign of the anachronistic character of much of church life," charged a female seminary professor. [30] The Worshipbook had avoided the problem when it referred to individuals, as in the baptismal service, and when it spoke of small mixed groups of people, but fell into using "men" or "brothers" for larger collections of persons.

The denominations had printed 300,000 copies of The Worshipbook, and a total revision and replacement would have cost over a million dollars. A special committee from both major Presbyterian bodies was formed in 1973 and worked on the problem of what to do, reporting its decision in 1974. It found 260 instances of the problem on 134 pages of the liturgical portion of The Worshipbook and recommended a "110,000 study guide project. [31] The cost factor likely proved persuasive, and the United Presbyterian General Assembly simply received the report, taking no action except to allow continued sale of the existing edition of the book. To fill a void, the quarterly Reformed Liturgy and Music of the Joint Office of Worship and Music printed the proposed study guide so that ministers could make the suggested revisions on their own. The Advisory Council on Discipleship and Worship was created about that same time by the United Presbyterians as part of their official program agency, partly to keep alert to how issues of this sort affect and can be addressed through worship. It produced a pamphlet version of the "Service for the Lord's Day" from The Worshipbook, revised to use inclusive language, as well as other aids to worship in the same style. [32]

The experience had been instructive and would definitely inform future liturgical work in the denomination. One thing it led to was a careful analysis and inventory of the content of The Worshipbook. Among its 334 hymns, 22 were judged to have problems of language too serious to correct, while 118 had minor problems easily rectified. However, 57 of these were under other agencies' copyrights. Of the total of 334 hymns, 70 were found to have problems with titles used of Christ and 123 problem references to the Deity. Miscellaneous problems affected a final 29: masculine/feminine sterotypes, masculine language for angels, military metaphors, and references repugnant to American Indians. [33]

The launching of The Worshipbook had not been auspicious. The "bad press" seemed to cause the denominations to take a step back from it. At least there seems to have been a practical demotion of its status. Whereas The Worshipbook's own preface calls it "the successor of the Book of Common Worship (1946)," a report written in 1983 speaks of "the two servicebooks presently in use in the church," as it describes materials being developed "to supplement The Worshipbook and the Book of Common Worship." [34] Possibly that explains why, after a decade in print, only 25% of the United Presbyterian congregations had bought The

Worshipbook, and use of it for purposes other than as a hymnal was spotty. By contrast the Lutheran Book of Worship, which appeared in 1978 and made careful use of inclusive language, had been bought by 92% of the congregations for whom it was produced in its first 41/2 years and was well integrated into their liturgical usage. [35] Lutherans, of course, had more of a liturgical tradition, and a pattern of uniformity in worship was more common among them. The difference between the dates of publication is significant, however--1970 versus 1978. There was, wrote one critic, an "uneasiness with transcendence" in the 1960's and 70's, which moved liturgical writers of those days too much toward colloquialism. Under the circumstances much liturgical language of the period possessed "all the stylistic flair of a wet potato chip." [36]

With this experience to build on, the Presbyterians have taken great care in developing a new service book for their now reunited denomination. The United Presbyterians began the process of developing "a new book of services for corporate worship" by a vote in 1980, and were joined soon thereafter by the Presbyterian Church, U.S., with whom they reunited in 1983, and by the Cumberland Presbyterian Church. The plan is for them to develop over a several year period "a variety of worship resources . . . for trial use throughout the church before any publication is finalized." The draft "Service for the Lord's Day" is the first of the series to appear. It had reached the stage of a manuscript circulated for field testing, by summer, 1983.

The draft "Service for the Lord's Day" is officially viewed as providing material to supplement The Worshipbook and the Book of Common Worship, "the two servicebooks presently in use in the church." However, it is clear that when the series is completed, the book which results will supplant the two former volumes. The date aimed at for completion of the full book is "shortly after 1990." [37] What might be expected of that manual can be inferred from the 1983 draft.

The sources of materials in the draft "Service for the Lord's Day" are carefully cited by its editors. Of some 200 liturgical items (prayers, blessings, charges, responses, affirmations, invitations, sentences, etc.) collected for the principal Sunday service, only 18% were cited as having been taken from the predecessor The Worshipbook. Almost as many (31 versus 36) came from the 1946 or earlier editions of the Book of Common Worship, or from the first revision of it which preceded The Worshipbook. Only 12 items had been written for the new service book itself. [38]

Clearly the tone of the proposed new service book is more mainstream and stately than that of The Worshipbook, and the use of the earlier material fits it will, although language alterations were not avoided. When alterations were made, by the way, one of the principal criteria for change was to remove any unnecessarily male-exclusive terms, following guidelines from the Advisory Council on Discipleship and Worship. As for other sources of the materials arranged for use with the Sunday service, the Bible itself was the source cited for 71 items--more than one-third of the total number. No doubt many of these scripture selections had also appeared in several earlier service books as well. Other denominations' worship books were turned to for about as many items as came from any single Presbyterian source--34 or 17%. Anglican prayer books furnished almost half of these; 5 were from Scotland's Book of Common Order, 4 each from the United Church of Canada and the Methodists, and a total of 6 from Lutheran, Roman Catholics and other sources. Seven versions of traditional creeds, prayers and psalms were borrowed from the International Consultation on English Texts. [39]

At this moment in their history America's major collection of Presbyterians are working out once again a formal pattern for their worship together, a fitting task for them to attempt as they work out the implications of their reunion after a separation of 122 years. No Presbyterian expects to see his or her denomination move to an imposed liturgy. Yet there is a normative shape to their worship which emerges from their theology and life together over the years. Likewise a better understanding of their life and faith emerges through an examination of the shape and content of their worship. [40]

Energies expended in the pursuit of a more effective ordering of a church's worship are not peripheral to what the church is about, nor are they the hobbies of the few. As the newest source book of aids to worship for Presbyterians states in its opening paragraph:

> Worship is of primary importance to our life as the people of God. It is the principal means by which the faith is formed within us and the most visible way we express the faith. Because of its centrality, the reform of worship is a major concern confronting the church today. Above everything else, the reform of worship is a concern for the renewal of the church. [41]

NOTES

1. **The Book of Common Worship** (Philadelphia: The Presbyterian Board of Publication and Sabbath School Work, 1906), "Preface."

2. **The Book of Common Worship**, 1906, "Preface."

3. David H. C. Read, "The Directions of Contemporary Worship," Scottish Journal of Theology, 8 No. 3 (1955), 272-287.

4. Presbyterian Outlook, 165, No. 41 (Nov. 28, 1983), 10-11. The books referred to are Horace T. Allen, **A Handbook to the Lectionary** (Philadelphia: Geneva Press, 1980) and James G. Kirk, **When We Gather** (Philadelphia: Geneva Press, 1983). Allen was first director of the Joint Office of Worship and Music and Kirk heads at present the Advisory Council on Discipleship and Worship.

5. Horace T. Allen, Jr., "Is There an Emerging Ecumenical Consensus Concerning the Liturgy?" Reformed Liturgy and Music, 10, No. 2 (1975), 7ff.

6. Paul W. Hoon, **The Integrity of Worship** (Nashville: Abingdon, 1971), 17.

7. Presbyterian Life, July 1, 1971, 32.

8. Presbyterian Life, March 15, 1970, 24.

9. Vic Jameson, "Three Thousand Assorted Presbyterians Come Together to Praise God," Presbyterian Life, Oct. 15, 1971, 22-27.

10. Richard K. Avery, "The Church Is Alive and Singing," Presbyterian Life, Oct. 15, 1971, 8-11.

11. Vic Jameson, 27.

12. Richard K. Avery, 8-11.

13. Jack M. Maxwell, "The Pastor as Liturgical Theologian," Austin Seminary Bulletin: Faculty Edition, 94, No. 8 (May, 1979), 22-29.

14. James L. Doom, "Where Do We Go From Here?" Reformed Liturgy and Music, 16 (1981), 58.

15. Its first director was Horace T. Allen, Jr., who worked in church music in the Princeton University chapel before entering the pastorate, and who had just returned from two years with Scotland's Iona Community Abbey.

16. Craig Douglas Erickson, "The Place of Liturgical Studies," *Reformed Liturgy and Music*, 17 (1982), 118ff. Erickson's having received a Ph.D. from the University of Notre Dame is itself revealing regarding how things have changed.

17. Linda Clark, "Toward a New Working Philosophy of Music in Worship," *Reformed Liturgy and Music*, 17 (1982), 105ff.

18. John Weaver, "Why Church Music," *Reformed Liturgy and Music*, 16, (1981), 134.

19. Robert Rambusch, *Your Church*, 27, No. 5 (Sept./Oct., 1981), 9ff.

20. **The Worshipbook: Services** (Philadelphia: The Westminster Press, 1970), 5-6.

21. David G. Buttrick, "Our Liturgical Language," *Reformed Liturgy and Music*, 15 (1980), 74ff.

22. Ibid., 81.

23. Ibid., 74.

24. Paul J. Milio, "Implementing the Service for the Lord's Day," *Reformed Liturgy and Music*, 7. (1972), 19ff.

25. "Service for the Lord's Day," *Presbyterian Life*, Oct. 15, 1968, 28.

26. John Elder, "Letters," *Presbyterian Life*, Dec. 15, 1968, 4.

27. James L. Doom, 59-60.

28. Ruth C. Duck, "A Movement of the Spirit," *Reformed Liturgy and Music*, 16 (1981), 131ff.

29. Jack M. Maxwell, "Inclusive Language in the Liturgy: Set Free to be a Daughter of God," *Austin Seminary Bulletin: Faculty Edition*, 98, No. 3 (Oct. 1981), 39-40.

30. Catherine Gunsalus Gonzales, "The Need to Revise the Language of the Worshipbook," *Reformed Liturgy and Music*, 8, No. 5 (1973), 7.

31. Lewis A. Briner, "Report of the Special Joint Committee on the Worshipbook," *Reformed Liturgy and Music*, 8, No. 5 (1973), 17-21.

32. Copies available from the Discipleship and Worship Program, Presbyterian Church (U.S.A.), 1020 Interchurch Center, 475 Riverside Drive, New York, N.Y. 10027.

33. Horace T. Allen, Jr., "An Inventory of Hymns in The Worshipbook Needing Changes Because of Sex-Exclusive Language," Reformed Liturgy and Music, 8, No. 5 (1973), 61ff.

34. "Field Testing Manuscript: The Service for the Lord's Day," **Supplemental Liturgical Resource — 1** (Louisville, KY.: The Joint Office of Worship of the Presbyterian Church (USA), 1983), 3-5.

35. Craig Douglas Erickson, 121.

36. Jack M. Maxwell, "Inclusive Language," 38.

37. "Field Testing Manuscript," 3.

38. Ibid., 107-119.

39. Ibid.

40. Jack M. Maxwell, "The Pastor as Liturgical Theologian," 28f.

41. "Field Testing Manuscript," 3.

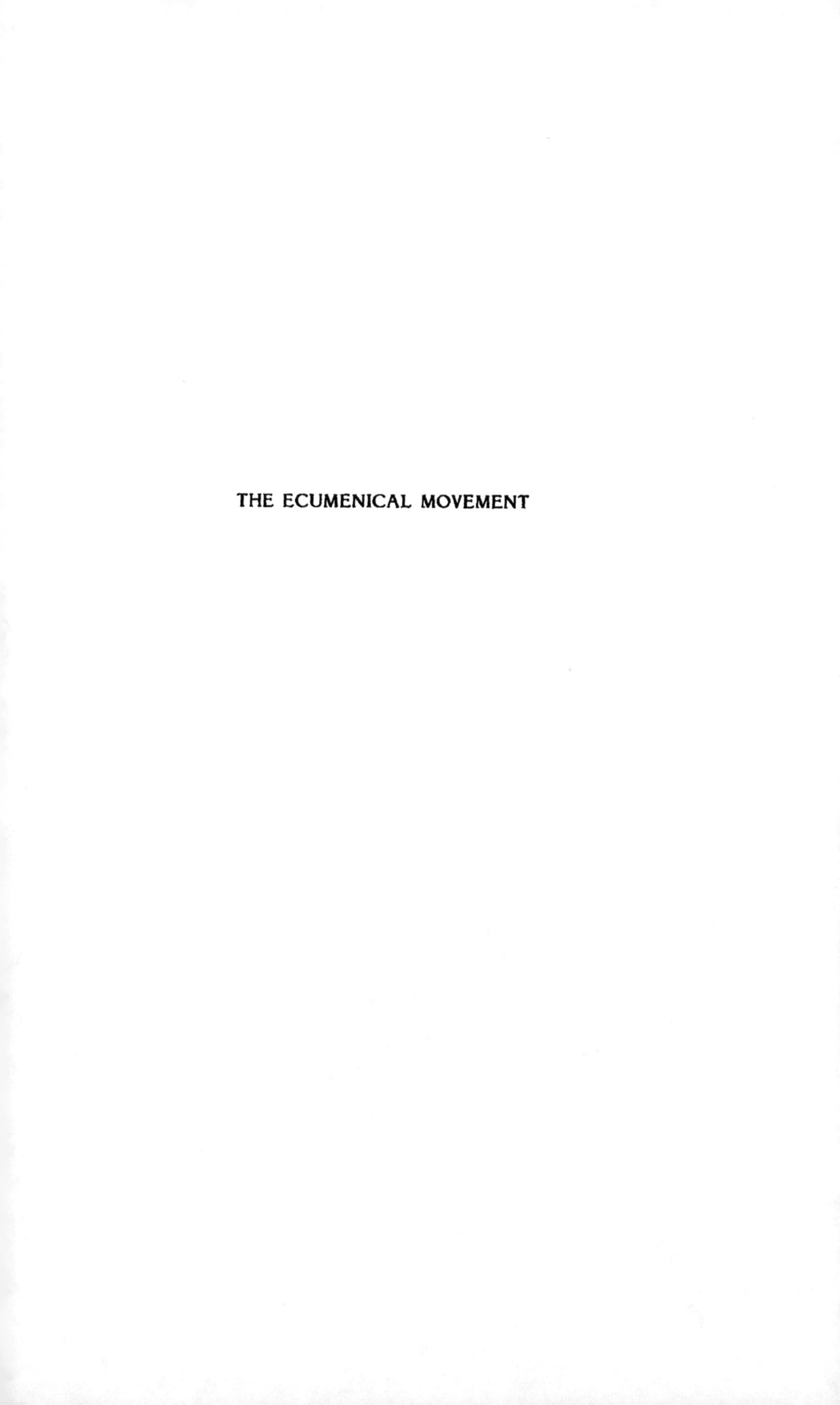

THE ECUMENICAL MOVEMENT

BIBLICAL EXEGESIS AND THE ECUMENICAL MOVEMENT

G. B. Caird

The Queen's College, Oxford

A meeting between old friends is a proper occasion for licensed reminiscence. I trust the license may be extended to cover the salutation of one old friend by another. It is over forty years since Horton Davies and I were fellow students at Mansfield College. During those years we have continued to share an interest in theology, churchmanship and ecumenism, while professionally our paths have diverged into church history and biblical studies. In this congratulatory volume it seems fitting that the biblical scholar should offer to the church historian some reflections on the way in which their two professional disciplines have impinged on their common interest in ecumenism.

I begin my reminiscence with 1963, when two events occurred in which I had some small part. In July of that year the Fourth World Conference on Faith and Order received a report entitled "Tradition and Traditions", prepared over several years by two commissions, one meeting in North America and the other in Europe; and I had been a member of each in turn. The burden of this double report was that, while all branches of the divided church held in common the one gospel tradition, to which the New Testament is the primary witness, each of them had preserved it as a denominational tradition, distinct from all the others; and that this was true even of those who claimed to be antitraditionalist and to rest their case on the sole authority of scripture. Ecumenists had long been familiar with the anomaly that, although all the churches claimed to derive their faith and order from scripture and to submit their practice to the critical judgement of scriptural authority, they had invoked that authority as warrant for conflicting and divisive conclusions. The rise of biblical criticism, with its dual emphasis on ascertainable historical evidence and on the normative force of a writer's intended meaning, had seemed to offer relief from the reciprocal artillery fire of proof texts projected from entrenched positions. The bombardment had indeed slackened, and the troops were leaving their foxholes to fraternize under an uneasy truce. But the long-expected peace treaty and act of union seemed as far away as ever. "Tradition and Traditions" was an attempt to discover why this was so.

What the report suggested was this. Just as the history of Europe written by a British scholar is different from one written by a German or a Russian, so each denomination has its own church history--not just a denominational history, but a denominational history of the church. The denominations are divided from one another by their divergent histories and by biblical exegesis carried out in the light of, and largely under the control of, their partisan tradition. Furthermore, each tradition was a compound of theological factors and all those social, political and economic factors which together make up human geography. The contrast between the commissions provided a startling illustration of this thesis; for the North American participants, from many church traditions, proved to have as much in common with one another in virtue of being American as they had with their European counterparts. Progress in ecumenism, therefore, might well depend on the emergence of an ecumenical church history in which all could share in virtue of being Christian.

Later in the same year I heard the Second Vatican Council debate the schema De Divina Revelatione. The Council of Trent in 1546 had laid it down that there are two sources of revelation, scripture and tradition. The wording of the decree was ambiguous, perhaps deliberately so. Revelation was contained in libris scriptis et sine scripto traditionibus, and much turned on the significance of the word "et". Was it to be understood that revelation was given partly in scripture, partly in tradition, or that what was fully revealed in scripture was also preserved in unwritten tradition? In the aftermath of Trent the former opinion prevailed, and in the strength of it the church of Rome proceeded, over four centuries, to promulgate the Marian dogmas without any need to provide them with scriptural warrant. The Second Vatican Council reverted to the other interpretation: there is one source of revelation, scripture as interpreted in the traditions of the church. Conservatives protested that this volte face would make the church ridiculous, compelling it either to renounce its dogmas or to discover strained scriptural justification for beliefs hitherto held on the ground of tradition alone. But the majority of the Council Fathers were undaunted. If the First Vatican Council had belonged to Manning, the Second belonged to Newman; and Newman had declared, against the massed choirs of Protestantism, that the Bible was not a self-explanatory book, but needed as commentary the tradition of the church.

What degree of convergence was achieved by these two parallel conciliar acts? Here were Protestants moving away from the intransigence of sola scriptura and admitting that they had a tradition which influenced their biblical exegesis; and there were Roman Catholics renouncing any claim to a tradition which had an authority independent of scripture. I suspect that both sides had been affected by the increasing part taken in ecumenical discussion by the Orthodox. For in Eastern Orthodoxy tradition has never been understood as a body of doctrine to be intellectually formulated and rationally analyzed, but as a living process in which scriptural revelation is assimilated and expressed throughout the life of the church. Professor Bonis, the Orthodox member of the European commission on traditions, would tell us, "Tradition is what we do." Although divine revelation is given in Holy Writ, the knowledge of it can never be mere book-knowledge. It is more like riding a bicycle or playing the violin, something learned in the doing of it. Similarly, Orthodox observers at the Vatican Council would dismiss the differences between Catholic and Protestant as unreal, because they were formulated in purely cerebral terms--an error they attributed to our common inheritance from Descartes. To them tradition was the embodiment of revelation in the whole life-style of the church, and above all in its worship; and this was the view while Protestants and Catholics were approaching from different sides.

No doubt they were influenced also by the New Testament, in which we may observe two opposite movements. On the one hand we see Jews and Christians in controversy, two communities divided by a common tradition which they differently interpret. Both claim to be God's chosen people, heirs to the Old Testament with its history and its promises. Each regards the other as failing in obedience to God's law and blind to the revelation of God's truth. On the other hand we see Gentile converts accepting not only the gospel, but with it the Jewish historical tradition to which it formed a climax. It was not enough that they should become sons of God, equal in all respects with their Jewish fellow-Christians; they must become sons of Abraham and adopt the Old Testament history as their history.

It is hard to estimate how far the rank and file of all the churches were aware of this growing consensus among their leaders or what response it might have evoked from them. One might have drawn the discouraging conclusion that all denominations were so imprisoned in their separate histories and exegesis of scripture that ecumenism was a lost cause. That was certainly not the intention of the two conciliar bodies. On the Protestant side unions had occurred in which each party had adopted the tradition of another denomination in addition to its own. In the United Church of Canada I can remember a former Methodist referring to "our inheritance from John Knox" and a former

Presbyterian acknowledging "our debt to John Wesley". On the Catholic side Pope Paul VI reminded the Council Fathers that certain elements in the common Christian tradition had been "well developed" among the "Separated brethren", clearly intending that this was a source from which the tradition of his own church might be enriched. Moreover the experience of these two great occasions confirmed the possiblity that Christians might grow together in spite of the gulf between their inherited traditions. At the American commission on traditions I recall one of our number saying: "Of course we here understand this, but how are we to explain it to them?"; and by them he meant the members of the churches we represented. We had reached a cohesion and mutual understanding hard to communicate to those who had not experienced the process. One important outcome of the Vatican Council was the effect it had on those who participated; and in particular the observers and their Catholic hosts undoubtedly grew into a deeper appreciation of one another.

The correct conclusion, therefore, is that the ecumenical movement must proceed by a living process in which Christians have a chance to learn an appreciation of other traditions than their own. During the last twenty years it has been encouraging to see such a process more and more in evidence. Theologians must, indeed, humbly recognize that, where their persuasion has failed, resistance has sometimes yielded to the arguments of necessity: a missionary necessity, because those who are united in their existing culture are not attracted to the prospect of being divided in Christianity; a social necessity, because the church cannot proclaim reconciliation to a divided world until it practices what it preaches; and the sheer economic necessity of survival. But the true ecumenist will not cavil at the means by which God achieves his ends.

Nevertheless divisions remain. There is wide agreement about the methods and results of biblical scholarship, and one may frequently read a scholarly book about the Bible without discovering the writer's ecclesiastical allegiance. There is agreement that in their past appeals to biblical authority all churches have employed methods of exegesis which any modern student would reject. Yet in their ecumenical stance the churches continue to read the Bible with the spectacles of their tradition, and to find other traditions than their own alien and opaque. Though some attempts at union have succeeded, others have failed. There is even a new division between united churches which have a pluralist inheritance and churches with a stubborn monoculture. The purpose of this essay, then, is to explore the reasons, reputable or otherwise, why progress has been slow. First, there are genuine difficulties in the way of mutual understanding. Secondly, there are points at which modern New Testament scholarship has unwittingly provided escape routes for those who find travel on the main highway too heady for their comfort. Thirdly, there are fallacies which have not even that meager excuse.

1. Genuine Difficulties

Some years ago I received, to my surprise, an invitation to become a patron of the Ecumenical Society of the Blessed Virgin Mary, a society whose members are drawn from churches, Orthodox, Catholic and Anglican, which accord to Mary a prominent place in their devotions. Equally to my surprise I accepted. How could a lifelong ecumenist refuse an invitation to penetrate the mysteries of a tradition which clearly meant a great deal to friends he trusted and respected, but which his Protestant upbringing had taught him to regard as dubiously Christian? The result of this exercise was that I came to recognize the existence of three levels of understanding. I could appreciate what members of the society said about Mary; I could follow the reasons they advanced in support of their practice; but what I failed to understand was what made them think this way and why they thought it so important.

If the ecumenical movement is to succeed, there must be room in the one church for great varieties of spirituality, and it is significant that my problem over devotion to Mary is one which exists within the Church of England, where some members share that devotion, while others find it either mystifying or repugnant, yet the unity of that church is not seriously imperiled by the difference. What is required for church unity is not total mutual understanding (otherwise we should all be locked in solipsist denominations of one member each), but mutual trust and respect; and the question we need to ask is how much understanding is needed for trust and respect to be reliable. It seems to require a higher degree of understanding to establish a new unity than to maintain an old one, because we are divided not merely by beliefs and practices, but by centuries of history. If we were already united, we should not regard any of our differences as grounds for splitting the church. The proof of this is that there are deeply felt differences which run down the middle of every denomination, such as the diverse beliefs about the authority of the Bible.

The point, however, of my reference to Mary is that the three levels of understanding which that experience helped me to identify apply to all matters of ecumenical debate. All three steps must be achieved in any genuine meeting of minds, and none of them is easy. In the past most Christians have failed at the first, the level of listening honestly to what the other person has to say and of reproducing it without distortion or caricature. We have naively assumed that truthfulness is commensurate with speaking the truth; but to listen truthfully is just as important and a good deal harder. The second level is a little easier, since it involves nothing more than hard thinking. But the third level is the crux. It differs from the second in that the reasons by which we justify our convictions are rarely identical with the causes that led us to hold them. I came from a tradition in which communion was a high and seldom festival, not to be trivialized by frequent repetition. Yet I have friends for whom daily communion is the necessary nurture of the soul, and to whom infrequent celebration is laxity tantamount to unbelief. The reasons given on each side cancel out. It is the causes that count.

The third level of understanding is permanently closed to the mere spectator. At this level a tradition can be understood only from inside. Part of the reason is that our convictions are based more than we commonly admit on association. Religious experience rarely, if ever, comes to us in naked simplicity. It comes clothed, even disguised, in borrowed garments, such garments as family loyalty and affection, moral decision, intellectual enlightenment, high public ceremony, or aesthetic appreciation, whether of natural or of artistic beauty. Much of the effect occurs below the surface of our conscious thinking, and we are therefore not likely to be fully articulate about it, supposing we are aware of it at all.

It is very difficult, for example, for an outsider to understand the Church of England. Horton Davies and I were brought up and ordained in a tradition which could properly be described as evangelical highchurchmanship. We could therefore with some justice claim to be theologically nearer both to the evangelical wing of the Church of England and to the high-church wing than they are to one another. The Church of England prides itself on being a comprehensive church. Why then could it not be a little more comprehensive by including the churches of our tradition, since we should provide a genuinely theological link between its extremes instead of the ecclesiastical adhesive tape which at present holds them together? If second level understanding were all-important, this argument would be unanswerable. The answer is of course that what I have mischievously dubbed "ecclesiastical adhesive tape" is in reality a bond of considerable tensile strength, but one which its adherents are as little able as I am to explain; and it has very little to do with the theological arguments by which they have been accustomed to defend their position.

Another difficulty, which overlaps with the first, is that in every church community there are subtle differences between theory and practice. In the negotiations between Presbyterians and Congregationalists which led to the formation of the

United Reformed Church, the break-through came when the Presbyterians recognized that the theoretical independence of the Congregational church meeting had never inhibited, nor had been intended to inhibit, the corporate responsibility of the churches for one another, their common action, or their common deference to synodical authority; and when it dawned on the Congregationalists that the supposedly authoritarian "ruling elders" of Presbyterianism were in the conduct of their office indistinguishable from their own deacons. Protestants may boggle at the dogma of papal infallibility, while Roman Catholics simply learn to live with it, perhaps noting with a wry amusement that, although no Protestant would admit that any of his beliefs were <u>ex sese irreformabiles</u>, and therefore exempt from that perpetual reformation in which the church must engage, in practice every Protestant church has some elements in its tradition which are not negotiable. The spectator of the Church of England may observe that those who are most vocal in their insistence on episcopacy are also those who most consistently disregard the leadership of their bishops. But he would be rash to accuse them of hypocrisy; it is just that he does not understand what episcopacy means to those who are inside the system. These tolerances, the ways in which a tradition, like an old and loved garment, moulds itself to the form of the wearer, constitute a major part of our problem.

Among genuine difficulties we must include those defense mechanisms which inevitably come into play when people feel that what they love and value is threatened by change. Some of the fears are indeed illusory or misdirected. There is a sin of fear, a refusal to follow where God leads, to be weaned from the milk of the word to its solid meat; and it is harder for institutions than for individuals to learn the lesson that to save one's life is to lose it, that what does not grow is moribund, that the Christian way is the way of death and resurrection. There is a fear which is a fragility of faith, the insecurity of those who cannot believe themselves to be right without constantly proving someone else to be wrong. Yet some fears are proper enough: the fear that uniformity will iron out distinctive qualities which are also distinctive strengths; the fear that union will turn out to be realignment into new and more intractable divisions; the fear that size will lead only to bureaucratic control. But whether the fears are well or ill founded, the defense mechanisms are always real, and they militated against third level understanding.

2. <u>Escape Routes.</u>

Biblical scholarship ought to have been the strongest ally of ecumenism. Yet only to a limited extent has this expectation proved true. Biblical scholars, however innocent and sincere their intentions, cannot avoid some share in the responsibility for our small progress. During the last hundred years one new trend has followed another, each bringing some fresh insight and advance in our understanding of the Bible; and yet each, either by overstatement or by insufficient clarity of definition, has provided an escape route for those churchmen whose commitment to ecumenism has been less strong than their commitment to an inherited and divisive ecclesiastical tradition. The three trends I have particularly in mind are those which have emphasized historicity, eschatology and development.

During the nineteenth century biblical studies had to win their independence from dogmatic theology. Till then theologians had cited the Old and New Testaments largely as scriptural warrant either for doctrines of the creed or for their own ecclesiastical institutions. The rise of historical criticism compelled them to look for a new source of security for the old certainties, and at the same time appeared to offer one. The authority of dogma could be replaced by the authority of historical fact. In the early stages of the movement attention was concentrated on the historical Jesus, in the later stages on the revelation of God in history. From the first there were warnings sounded that eternal verities cannot be made dependent on historical contingency, and that history does not deal in certainty but in probability; but the quest for secure authority went on. Even the scepticism of Wrede and Schweitzer's attack on the quest of the historical Jesus started from the premise that historical fact, if it were ascertainable by research and intelligible to the modern mind, would provide a bedrock of incontrovertible truth; and Bultmann's virtual severance of the link between Geschichte (history meaningful to me) and Historie (verifiable fact) was but the last in a long line of attempts to place the foundations of faith out of reach of the erosions of criticism. It is easy enough for us, with the wisdom of hindsight, to recognize that this movement was misleading, both in its first misplaced confidence and in its subsequent failure of nerve. My concern, however, is not with the protagonists, but with those who welcomed Bultmann's radical rejection of history because, by denying them the possibility, and therefore also the obligation, of tracing their tradition back to Jesus, it left them free to ground it firmly in the doctrine and practice of later centuries.

New Testament study in the present century began with a hypothesis which soon attained the status of an axiom: that the early church expected an imminent end of the world and believed that they had the authority of Jesus for their expectation. Some of the implications of this theory were explicit from the start in Schweitzer's discription of the teaching of Jesus as "interim ethics". But there were other pieces of embarrassing evidence besides the "impractical idealism" of the Sermon on the Mount which could be explained away in like manner. The New Testament provides no unambiguous support for any one form of church government. But that was surely inevitable if neither Jesus nor his disciples looked forward to a future in which the continuity of the church would need to be expressed in institutional form. Was not institutionalism the church's answer to the failure of the eschatological hope? It is now at last coming to be recognized that the eschatological school gravely misunderstood the nature of eschatological language, and in particular the purpose of the apocalyptic writings to which they made their primary appeal. But in the meantime the long dominance of the eschatological axiom has played into the hands of those who wished to exempt church order from the critique of New Testament authority.

The idea introduced by the History of Religions school, that Christianity ought to be studied as a historical phenomenon in its setting in the development of world thought, has an obvious attraction and an obvious propriety; and in practice it has proved immensely fruitful. We owe a vast debt to the labors of those who have collected and interpreted the evidence bearing on the background and environment of early Christianity. But the replacement of New Testament theology by a history of early Christian thought turned out to be especially attractive to those in which ecclesiastical tradition development already played an important role, since it appeared to supply the tradition with a scriptural origin without exposing it to an unwelcome scriptural critique. The term "development" is, however, notoriously problematic. The disagreement between rival proponents of Religionsgeschichte exemplifies one of its ambiguities. For while German Protestants held that the early period was a golden age, from which all subsequent development was a decline towards incipient catholicism, theologians of an opposition persuasion regarded the first century as a period of growth in the direction of second century maturity. An unbiased historian of this school might wish to argue that every sequel to the primitive beginnings is equally a part of the total Christian story, but this is a view of development which the major Christian traditions have been understandably reluctant to adopt.

If on the other hand we define development as the legitimate unfolding of that which was present in germ in the origins, we still have at least three difficulties ahead. A legitimate development may not be an adequate development. When a musician composes variations on a theme, he may choose to develop in any one variation a single melodic or rhythmic fragment of the theme, but we should not be satisfied if each succeeding variation explored only such elements as were already developed in the first. Thus we might hold that episcopacy or eldership or church meeting were legitimate developments of apostolic tradition, and yet find that they had been developed to the neglect of other elements. The second difficulty is that, once we have committed ourselves wholeheartedly to development, there is no reason why the process should stop. The fullness of development can lie only at the end, and, short of that, there can be no such thing as definitive development. There are three possible views: we may hold that development is a continuous process in which every stage is provisional and to that extent obsolescent; or that development is a contextual process, in which the validity of each stage is determined by its appropriateness to the needs of the time; or we may adopt some judicious combination of the two. The third difficulty is the need for criteria to determine legitimacy. All the churches in the ecumenical movement profess to find their criteria in the New Testament. But the one thing that all advocates of development have in common is a disregard for the New Testament canon. If you are writing a story of development, whether you believe its direction to be up or down, it is a single continuous process, not to be interrupted by arbitrary distinctions, such as that which discriminates between 1 Clement or the Shepherd of Hermas on the one side and Hebrews or Revelation on the other. One writer has even called the canon a historical accident, whereby some books were canonized and others were not. But to the churchmen of the second, third and fourth centuries the canon was no accident, no arbitrary distinction. They conceived the idea of a canon, debated its limits, and finally closed it precisely because they appreciated the need for criteria independent of any fiat of ecclesiastical authority. It is irresponsible to build on their traditions of creed and institution if these are divorced from the principle to which they gave precedence, that the tradition embodied in scripture is different from any other tradition, however preserved, and that it provides a norm by which the validity of all subsequent developments must be judged.

Thus each of these escape routes, when critically scrutinized, turns out to offer only a spurious security. But the preoccupation of New Testament scholars with their underlying themes has lent to them a regrettable plausibility.

3. Fallacies.

When I look back on more than forty years of ecumenical discussion, I can recall three frequently repeated arguments which have left me in a mood of frustration and despair. The first is an appeal to truth, the second to continuity, and the third to hope.

"Certainly," the first argument runs, "we are committed to the reunion of the churches, but not at the sacrifice of truth!" The "truth" referred to has usually been something to do with the nature of the church's ministry. Now I do not believe that the speakers would have been willing to excise from the Nicene

Creed the clause, "I believe in one holy, catholic and apostolic church." Nor would they have repudiated the dictum of Ignatius that "where Jesus Christ is there is the catholic church". The unity of the church is therefore an integral part of the truth which they themselves would uphold. Because there is only one Christ, there can be only one church. "You are the body of Christ" was admittedly first addressed to the local church in Corinth, and could as well have been addressed to the church in Philippi; but it would be questionable exegesis to infer from this that Paul believed Christ to have more than one body. Moreover, the unity of Christ with his people, however we may define it, and therefore their unity with one another, is central not only to the doctrine of the church but to the doctrine of salvation; it comes close to the heart of all that Christians believe. Thus any failure to act on the assumption that all Christ's people are one is itself a sacrifice of truth. The argument, then, needs to be restated. For how can that which is done in obedience to the central truths of the gospel be a sacrifice of truth?

There is, to be sure, one way: we may hold that the church of Christ is exactly coterminous with our own ecclesiastical tradition, so that to be outside the one is also to be outside the other. But that is a path of blind insolence which all churches have had the grace to abjure. To follow it would be to declare ecumenism meaningless, since there would be no other Christians with whom to unite. Yet if once I admit that another person belongs to Christ, I have thereby admitted that he belongs to me as a fellow member of the only church which has any existence; and if I think that there are truths which inhibit that admission, have I any choice but to question their truth value?

The New Testament contains examples of just such a questioning process at work. It is true that I am called to acknowledge my dependence on God in worship, but I cannot give expression to that truth without first being reconciled to my brother (Mt. 5:23-4). If I attempt to approach the central mysteries of the faith in a Eucharist from which, for any reason, my brother is excluded, then it is not the Lord's Supper that I celebrate (1 Cor. 11:20).

The appeal to continuity is somewhat more persuasive, since it is the nature of the Christian life that it is to be lived not only in community with one's contemporaries, but in the communion of the saints of all ages. But in this sense continuity is characteristic of every denomination. There is no Christian who is not linked with Jesus by an unbroken line of tradition. I did, indeed, once meet a chief of the Masai who had recently reconverted himself to Christianity and was busy converting his tribe with the assistance of his four wives; but he had not achieved this feat without a translation of the Gospels left behind by a colporteur of the Bible Society. Most Christians, moreover, are heirs to an institutional continuity, since neither they nor their fathers in the faith could be Christian without belonging to an institutional church. The question at issue, then, is whether some particular form of institutional continuity is required in order to symbolize and guarantee the unity of the church throughout the ages. Such a claim has been made for episcopacy, but it is a claim difficult to sustain in view of the divisions between episcopal churches and the failure of some bishops at least to be models of orthodoxy.

A much more fundamental objection, however, is that in the New Testament continuity is always associated with newness and surprise. God's promises are granted to his people from generation to generation, yet continuity is not guaranteed by pedigree, but by grace alone; for God can from the stones of the desert raise up children to Abraham (Mt. 3:9; Lk. 3:8). Those who rely on natural descent merely betray that they are the slave children of the earthly Jerusalem, not the free, spirit-born children of the Jerusalem above (Gal. 4:25-29). According to Matthew Jesus was son of Abraham and son of David, but only by a miracle of grace which broke with normal human expectation. He came to fulfill the whole law (Mt.5:17), but in ways which shattered every Jewish institution in which that law was enshrined and by which it was defended, so that in the end the kingdom of God was taken from the sons of the kingdom and given to a people that would produce the kingdom's fruits (Mt. 21:43). World mission is entrusted to the Twelve, but in the event the brunt of the work is discharged by an upstart to whom they have given no commission, who insisted that his authority came directly from God without human mediation, the arch enemy of the church transformed by grace into the apostle of the Gentiles (Gal.1:1, 15-16, 23). Paul himself could not plan his travels without having his plans overruled at every point by the Holy Spirit (Acts 16:6-10).

Continuity is maintained throughout, but only by a divine ruthlessness that transcends all human concepts of continuity; and an essential ingredient of that ruthlessness is its criterion of validity. The disciple of Jesus will be known by his love, and his love by the obedience to the master (Jn. 13:35; 14:15). The prophet will be known by his fruits (Mt. 7:16). The credentials of apostolicity are apostolic results (2 Cor.3:2; 12:12). Continuity with the past belongs to those who, like Abraham, are willing at the bidding of God to break with the past (Heb. 11:8). We do not honor the past by building the tombs of the prophets, but by following their example (Mt.23:29-32). "Remember Lot's wife" (Lk. 17:32).

Finally, there are those who would consign the hope of church unity to the indefinite, or even the eschatological, future. We may grant that they are realists. Throughout its history the church has never been free of divisive tendencies, and attempts to impose on it the unity of a power structure have been as divisive as any. The divisions of which we still feel the effects, the Great Schism of 1054 and the Protestant Reformation, were not the beginning of the story. The first signs appeared in Corinth in the fifties of the first century (1 Cor. 1:10-17), and by the end of the century the elder John was having to cope with the consequences of a walk-out in the churches of Asia (1 Jn. 2:19). As for the patristic period, it has been said that an examination paper on the subject could well consist of one question: List the heresies in order of preference, giving reasons for your choice.

If unity were indeed nothing more than a duty for our effort and a dream for our aspiration, we might well be disheartened by the sorry tale of human frailty and folly, ignorance and arrogance. But unity is also God's gift. It comes to us not merely in the imperative and optative, but in the perfect indicative. It is an essential part of what God has done for us once for all in Christ. The whole doctrine of salvation, in all its aspects and with all its adjuncts, is presented to us in the New Testament in three tenses: we have been saved, we are being saved, we hope for salvation. Part of the explanation is that salvation is a process, begun, continued and ended. But because the God with whom we have to do is Alpha and Omega, the First and the Last, the three tenses are always intermingled, and the end is already present in the beginning. In Christ God has already reconciled the world to himself (Col. 1:20). In this one representative person God's work is complete (Jn. 17:4). He has identified himself with mankind, and we share in his redemptive work in so far as we accept that identification by an act of faith. But we cannot be united with him without at the same time being united with one another. We cannot sit at his table without sharing it with every other guest whom he has invited. Unless we accept the unity of the church as a fact, we do not even belong to it. Unity is indeed both a duty and a dream, but it could not be either unless it was first a datum.

The church is one because Christ is one. Faced with self-assertive factions at Corinth, Paul asks, "Is Christ divided?" Those who find divisions tolerable even for a moment only display how little their thinking and their attitudes have been transformed by the Spirit of Christ (1 Cor. 1:13; 3:1). But the most serious threat to church unity that Paul faced came from the segregation of Jewish and Gentile Christians, the one group claiming to be bound by loyalty to an ancestral tradition, the other standing pat on a new-found freedom. Paul answers the threat, not with a statement of obligation or of hope, but with an assertion of fact. Divisions belong with the old, unredeemed humanity which died with Christ on the cross. "God forbid that I should boast of anything but the cross of our Lord Jesus Christ, through which the world is crucified to me and I to the world! Circumcision is nothing; uncircumcision is nothing; the only thing that counts is new creation!" (Gal. 6:14-15). "Gentiles and Jews, he has made the two one, and in his own body of flesh and blood has broken down the enmity which stood like a dividing wall between them . . . This was his purpose to reconcile the two in a single body to God through the cross, on which he killed the enmity" (Eph. 2:14, 16).

Too often in the ecumenical movement the dominant ethos has been set by the prayer of Jesus in the Fourth Gospel: "may they all be one". Wrenched from their context in the great prayer, these words have been used to give the impression that the Johannine Jesus regarded unity as a remote goal, faintly glimpsed in the mists of a far horizon. But in John's theology, as in Paul's, the union of disciples with Jesus is achieved on the cross. It is by dying that he, like a grain of wheat, ceases to be alone and bears a rich harvest (12:24). It is in being lifted up from the earth that he draws all mankind to himself (12:32). Unity, then, is his gift to his followers: "the glory you gave me I have given to them, to make them one as we are one" (17:22). The gift, to be sure, requires a human response: it is a gift of life, and the recipients must live it, making their unity and mutual love visible in the eyes of the world. Not the least part of the apostolic commission is that the world is to be won for Christ by observing the unity of his followers: "then the world will know that you sent me, that you have loved them just as you have loved me" (17:23).

"May they all be one", like "your kingdom come", is a prayer that looks to the future. But one of the most egregious errors of modern New Testament scholarship has been the quaint assumption that any reference to the future in the New Testament must be to the ultimate, eschatological future. No doubt both prayers will find their complete fulfillment only in the final consummation of God's purpose. But in each case the primary reference is to the immediate future, the future that ensues directly on the utterance of the prayer. Matthew at least leaves this in no doubt. God's kingdom is present wherever men and women accept God's sovereignty over their lives and allow it to take effect in their conduct, wherever his will is done on earth as in heaven; and when we repeat the Lord's Prayer, this is what we ask for. By the same token Jesus' prayer that his followers may be one is to be implemented in their immediate and continuous obedience to his commands. John makes it clear that the unity in question is a unity of will and purpose, such as already subsists between Father and Son. That is the unity that matters, and all other considerations must be subservient to it.

Among the heirs of the Protestant Reformation there are some who, justly apprehensive of that uniformity which is another name for death, have argued for what they call "spiritual" rather than organic unity. By "spiritual union" they appear to mean a general good will and bonhomie which will leave all of us free to relax into the familiar comfort of our separate traditions. But they too have misread the scriptures. The unity which Christ has bestowed on his church is indeed "spiritually discerned" (1Cor. 2:14), but it must show itself in common action and common worship, and must body forth in such institutions as will give effectiveness to the common life. The lamp is not lit to be placed in the bread-bin or under the bed. It is vital to the apostolic task of the church catholic that it should show itself to be holy, but no less vital that it should show itself to be one.

A PIONEER CONTRIBUTION TO ECUMENICAL THEOLOGICAL TRAINING IN SOUTH AFRICA

Leslie A. Hewson

Rhodes University College, South Africa

It need occasion no surprise that the mother system for South African education was the system introduced into the Cape Colony early in the nineteenth century. At that date the hinterland beyond the borders of the Colony was almost unknown to the western world; and the migrating masses of the population beyond the Orange and Kei Rivers, churned up in the early decades by the Mfecane resulting from the Zwide-Shaka wars, were illiterate. [1] The lore in which they were learned was written not in books but in veld and forest, in desert and mountain, and in the people who lived and warred there, and in the animals they tended or hunted.

It is surprising that, a century and a half later, after explorer, missionary, trek-boer, miner, merchant and manufacturer had ripped the sub-continent wide open, the mother system for English-medium theological education at university level should be introduced at Rhodes University College in semi-rural Grahamstown, and not in the mother city of Cape Town, or the industrial metropolis of Johannesburg on the Witwatersrand.

The present study examines the pioneer contribution to that development made by the Christian scholar in whose honor this Festschrift is gathered together.

For the colonizing whites, clustered in the western Cape Colony, education on European lines was introduced first by the Dutch administration, and after 1806 by the British governors at the Cape.

For the indigenous blacks, however, moving west and south from the hinterland, the pioneers in western education were the missionaries of the London, the Scottish, the Wesleyan, the American Boards, and the Anglican Missionary Societies. C. T. Loram states:

> The history of Native education in South Africa is the history of South African missions; for it is due entirely to the efforts of the missionaries that the Natives of South Africa have received any education at all. [2]

It is noteworthy that it was the successors of these five Societies who, building on their experience in the education of blacks, finally combined to initiate that joint scheme of theological training which is the subject of this study.

Theological education in the English medium has been a century-long pilgrimage from denominational mission school, to mission seminary, to ecumenical college, and finally to divinity school at university level.

Before we turn our attention to that pilgrimage due recognition must be given to ministerial training in the Afrikaans-speaking churches; for this has been of major importance in theological education in South Africa. These Churches were resolved to provide for their ministries theological training at university institutions in South Africa.

The oldest and largest of these Dutch Reformed Churches is Die Nederduitse Gereformeerde Kerk, which has developed into a federation of four independent provincial Churches. Since 1859 the ministry of this Church has been trained at a theological seminary established at Stellenbosch, which developed in time into the Stellenbosch Gymnasium (1866), Stellenbosch College (1886) and Victoria College (1887). This College became Stellenbosch University in 1918, with its own faculty of divinity. In order to meet the needs of this growing Church, there was established at the University of Pretoria in 1937 a faculty of theology, with two fully-staffed divisions, A and B. Division B provides ministerial training for the Nederduitse Hervormde Kerk of the Transvaal. [3] Die Nederduitsch Hervormde Kerk van Afrika, the Church of the Transvaal Voortrekkers, held its first general assembly at Rustenburg, Transvaal, on 8 August 1853. In 1917 the training of its ministry was introduced at the University College of Pretoria. As stated above, when a faculty of theology was established at Pretoria University in 1937, two divisions were fully staffed to serve the needs of two churches. Division A provides ministerial training for the Nederduitsch Hervormde Kerk. [4]

Die Gereformeerde Kerk in Suid Afrika came into being at Rustenburg, Transvaal, on 11 February 1859, and later established congregations in the Transvaal, Orange Free State and the Cape Colony. For the training of its ministry a theological school was established in 1869 at Burghersdorp in the Cape Colony. This was transferred to Potchefstroom University College for Christian Higher Education in 1908. This Church staffs the faculty of divinity at Potchefstroom University, which became autonomous in 1951. [5] Since "hervormd" and "gereformeerd" both indicate reformed churches, A. A. Louw provides the comment "In the Netherlands, the convention developed in the 19th century that "hervormd" indicated Reformed Protestantism in broader sense, while "gereformeerd" was associated with Calvinism in narrowed sense." [6]

These three Churches now have the same patterns of ministerial training, normally lasting six years for the Hervormde Kerk, and seven for the other two. The first requirement is a degree in Arts, which includes Latin and the Biblical languages as essential tools for the post-graduate theological training, in which the traditional fields of Old and New Testament, Systematic Theology and Church History are included.

For our study, Potchefstroom is of special importance. In 1947 the divinity department of this University College sponsored the embryo divinity department of another constituent college of the University of South Africa, the Grahamstown college of Rhodes.

I. Ministerial Training in English-speaking Churches

Theological education in the English-speaking Churches has developed in a different way. Until almost the end of last century the ordained clergy of the English-speaking Churches were trained in Britain or America where the parent Churches or Mission Societies were based. White men recruited for the ministry in this land were too few to warrant the establishment of denominational South African seminaries. They were therefore sent back to Britain to be trained. This same course was followed with the first black man from South Africa to be ordained to the Christian ministry. This was Rev. Tiyo Soga (1829-1871) who finally graduated from Glasgow University, and returned to South Africa as a Presbyterian minister to exercise a great influence on both black and white. [7]

White missionaries early realized the necessity to recruit black men to minister to their own people. First came the mission school to give blacks literacy in their mother tongue, and then in the English language--the essential key to make available their heritage in the learning of the Western world. Students with the requisite vocation and abilities were then grouped in seminaries associated with the mission school. For half a century, each of the mission Churches which are our concern endeavored to train its own clergy.

The first seminary to be established was located at Amanzimtoti by the American Board Mission in 1865, and named Adams Theological School after Dr. Newton Adams one of the original pioneers of the Mission. Adams has had an unbroken history linking the original seminary with the Federal Theological Seminary at Alice in the Eastern Province until expropriation compelled the removal of the Federal Seminary to its present location near Pietermaritzburg in Natal. [8] In 1867 the Wesleyan institution at Healdtown in the Eastern Cape Colony opened a theological department with four black ministerial students. Theological training was moved to Lesseyton institution seven miles north of Queenstown in 1883, and remained there until 1920 when it was transferred to the recently established South African Native College at Fort Hare. [9] In 1870, Dr. Stewart introduced a three-year theological course at Lovedale designed to qualify students to preach in the vernacular and in English. The Lovedale seminary is of special significance because it became ecumenical. A Congregational minister, Rev. T. Durand Philip, son of Dr. John Philip, the pioneer L.M.S. superintendent, raised the standard of training to a high level during the decade he was in charge, 1885-1895. In 1897 there were ten students from five Churches at this Presbyterian institution. [10]

The Anglican Church in South Africa took on a new lease of life with the arrival of Bishop Robert Gray at Cape Town in 1848. Education was given special prominence under his administration. The first attempt at the theological training of Africans was not a success. The most promising students were sent to St. Augustine's College, Canterbury, England; but did not fulfill their promise. It was therefore decided to train black Anglican ordinands in the environment in which they were to live and work. The Bishop of the diocese gathered suitable men round him; and C. E. G. Goodhall reports that at one time there were eleven of these small diocesan colleges in existence, domestic and patriarchal in character, the students closely in touch with the Bishop who would eventually ordain and license them. [11] Yet from these small beginnings eventually developed some of the best African schools in the country: St. Peter's College, Rosettenville, Johannesburg; Zonnebloem, Cape Town; St. Augustine's near Dundee, Natal; St. Matthew's, Keiskamma Hoek; and St. John's, Umtata. [12]

Nevertheless, as early as 1906 the Johannesburg Provincial Missionary Conference of the Anglican Church had resolved that, whilst recognizing the advantages of the existence of theological colleges in the several dioceses, the Conference considered that as soon as needful a central Native Theological College or Colleges should be provided for those capable of higher theological training. Action was eventually taken in 1934 to close the smaller colleges and concentrate on two: St. Bede's at Umtata, to serve the southern part of the Anglican Province of South Africa, and St. Peter's, Rosettensville, Johannesburg, to serve the northern part. Ministerial training had become a Provincial rather than a Diocesan concern. [13]

While the Anglican Church was thus pondering its training problems, a new development of major importance had taken place in South African Native education. To put this in perspective, we must review developments in the wider field of education in South Africa. In 1873 the University of the Cape of Good Hope had been established in Cape Town, not as a teaching, but as an examining institution. In 1916, a University Act was passed which established two teaching universities--Cape Town and Stellenbosch--and the University of South Africa to bring a brood of university colleges to eventual autonomy. [14]

As better provision was steadily being made for the higher education of whites in South Africa, so there arose a demand among blacks educated in the missionary institutions that they be given similar opportunities. The reasoned plea of the black elite, expressed in Lovedale's Christian Express, J. T. Jabavu's Imvo Zabantsundu, and the Mhala--A. K. Soga publication Izwi Labantu, prevailed over white prejudice and fears; [15] and in 1908 a Select Committee on Native Education reported in section 18:

> The establishment of a Native College has been recommended, partly in order to provide for the higher education of Natives, and partly to prevent Natives from going out of the country in search of it.

All fears and frustrations were finally overcome; and on 8 February 1916, the Prime Minister of South Africa, the Rt. Hon. General Louis Botha finally opened the South African Native College at Fort Hare, under the Principalship of Mr. Alexander Kerr, M.A. Its name was changed to the University College of Fort Hare in 1952.

The Churches were vitally interested in this new venture. Hostels were provided by the Anglican (Beda Hall), the Methodist (Wesley House) and the Presbyterian (Iona House) Churches. Each of these Churches provided the Warden to have spiritual oversight over the members of his own denomination in the College. The Methodist church transferred its theological training from Lesseyton to Wesley House in July 1920; and the Presbyterian and Congregational Churches transferred their ministerial students from Lovedale to Iona House at the same time. The Anglican Church of the Province had made other arrangements for the training of their Native clergy as stated above, and therefore Beda Hall at Fort Hare was not used for theological training of their ordinands. During the next two decades these four Churches gained invaluable experience in the training of black men for the ministry in co-operation at the level of a university college. This completed the pilgrimage of black ministerial training. It did more. It convinced these Churches that the time had come for a new venture in the training of white ministerial students.

The Minutes of the Annual Conference of the Methodist Church of South Africa record a process that clearly included the other Churches. In 1938, the Conference "affirmed the principle of co-operation with other Churches interested in a joint scheme of ministerial training." The outbreak of World War II halted further developments. The subject was taken up again in 1943, and the Conference resolved "that the future training of the European Ministry is a matter of urgency, and agrees to take adequate measures to provide such training . . . and approves a scheme for the creation of a Chair of Divinity at a University College." The reference to a University College implies conversations in progress with Rhodes University College in Grahamstown fifty miles from Fort Hare at Alice. Transvaal members of the Conference felt that the Churches would be better served at an autonomous university established in a major metropolitan center; and this possibility was considered. The Conference therefore resolved that a committee should investigate the possibilities of Johannesburg as a venue for the training scheme, and the establishment of a Faculty of Divinity at the University of the Witwatersrand. (Minutes, 56ff.). Nothing came of this attempt; and the Minutes of 1944 record the resolution of Conference that the authorities of Rhodes University College be approached concerning the formation of a Faculty of Divinity . . . and that the General Committee on Ministerial Training be given authority to bring to finality the details of co-operation with other interested Churches. (Minutes, 52).

Rhodes was a small institution, and looking for an increase in enrollment. More important, however, was the fact that the Master of Rhodes, Dr. J. Smeath Thomas, was an elder of the Presbyterian Church, convinced that the ministry of the Christian Church should be well educated, and thus he was sympathetic to the proposals of the Churches, which were parties to the joint scheme for ministerial training. As World War II drew to a close, the Churches and the College prepared for action. The Minutes of the 1945 Methodist Conference record four positive resolutions:

> to continue to consult with the other interested Churches and the representatives of Rhodes University College to enable the Faculty of Divinity to function at the beginning of 1947.
>
> to contribute £3,500 towards the endowment of a Chair of Divinity at Rhodes University College.
>
> to co-operate with the other interested Churches in the erection of a joint theological hostel.
>
> to appoint Rev. L. A. Hewson, M.A. as the Methodist tutor of the joint theological hostel.
>
> (Minutes 66, 67)

By 1946, the actual training scheme was taking more definite shape. The Conference of that year resolved:

> that the period of residence at College be three years, and that as an integral part of their ministerial training, such students be placed in Circuits or Missions during the long vacations.
>
> (Minutes, 63)

This insistence upon practical experience in worship and pastoral care in an active church is clear evidence that from the beginning of the scheme, the Methodist Church regarded pastoral care as an essential part of ministerial training. This led to important developments in the Rhodes scheme in later years.

The Methodist Conference of 1946 designated for theological training five white men. These were joined by two other Methodist students not yet accredited by the Church. The Presbyterian Church designated two men and the Congregational Church one. Rhodes had opened its doors. The pioneer group of students had been designated for training. The warden of the as yet non-existent divinity hostel had been nominated. One thing was lacking, and that was the key appointment. Rhodes University College, in consultation with the four Churches which had endowed the Chair of Divinity, turned its attention to the appointment of the first Professor of Divinity of an English-speaking university in South Africa.

II. The Post-war Situation

If the achievement of the first Professor of Divinity at an English medium university is to be justly assessed, the situation which confronted him must be clearly understood. It was an immediately post-war situation; for he was to take up his appointment at the beginning of 1947 in a country where among the Afrikaans-speaking people there had been strong opposition to the war effort of the victorious Allies. The potential weight of this fact will be seen more clearly below. There were already in existence four divinity faculties at South African universities; but all of them used the medium of Afrikaans; and all of them were closely identified with a particular Afrikaans-speaking Church. These faculties were those at the Universities of Stellenbosch and Pretoria and the University College of Potchefstroom. (See above, p. 221). There were two English-medium universities (Cape Town and Witwatersrand) and two English-medium University Colleges (Natal and Rhodes); but none of these had even a department of religious studies in 1946.

The only university institution that was sympathetic to the approach of the Churches seeking theological training at university level was Rhodes University College, which was one of the constituent colleges at the University of South Africa. There was, however, one such constituent college which did have a faculty of divinity, and that was the Potchefstroom University College for Christian Higher Education. Its name gave a clear indication of its theological outlook. This outlook is thus defined by one of it own members:

> Potchefstroom University College for Christian Higher Education is the only South African university without the conscience clause. This clause was deleted from the Potchefstroom University Bill; and the Council is obliged to maintain the University's Christian historical character. It is guided by the fundamental principle that the Word of God is the foundation of all knowledge. [16]

Any proposals affecting religious studies in any constituent college of the University of South Africa had perforce to come to the Senate of that University by way of the Faculty of Theology at Potchefstroom. Two of the partner Churches in the Rhodes proposals were Calvinist, but not fundamentalist in theology; and one of them was the stronghold of that evangelical expression of religion which was repudiated by the Gereformeerde Kerk which had founded the Potchefstroom institution. All the "Rhodes" Churches were English-speaking in a South Africa where conservative Afrikaaners were still striving for freedom from all forms of English domination--a struggle kindled to a new intensity by the world war recently concluded.

In addition to the religio-political factor there was a factor of some academic importance. All the Afrikaans-speaking churches were convinced that an acceptable standard for an educated Christian ministry required first a degree in Arts upon which could be based a second post-graduate degree in theological studies. To complete this course of studies, seven years were required by the Churches training their ministry at Stellenbosch and Potchefstroom and the B faculty at Pretoria; and six years by the Hervormde Kerk. Proposals to introduce a three-year scheme for ministerial training would inevitably be regarded as defective.

There was one further academic problem. The Methodist Church had accepted as candidates for the ministry some who lacked the qualification of matriculation exemption required for entrance to a South African university. As if he had not problems enough to cope with, the newly appointed Professor at Rhodes was being pressed to provide for the theological needs of these "non-matriculants".

Finally, in the immediate post-war period, the Government had perforce to impose restrictions upon building. The influx of ex-servicemen had strained Rhodes accommodation to the limits. The partner Churches in the divinity scheme were insistent that for the preparation of their ministerial students, community life in a divinity hostel was essential.

III. **The Pioneer Professor and His Work**

1. The First Professor [17]

The Divinity Chair Appointments Committee selected five applicants, all resident in Great Britain, and appointed as commissioners prominent academics representing the partner Churches to interview the five. Their unanimous recommendation was that Rev. Horton Davies, M.A., B.D. (Edin.), D. Phil. (Oxon) should be offered the Chair. The appointment was confirmed, and Dr. Davies accepted on condition that his wife and child should be able to accompany him to South Africa on the same ship. In post-war conditions, passages were not easily granted; but the High Commissioner for South Africa was able to secure them for Dr. Davies and his family. The partner Churches and Rhodes College were anxious to have the Professor in residence in time to launch the new Department of Divinity at the opening of the academic year in 1947. He sailed a week before Christmas in the Winchester Castle, and was in Grahamstown on 23 January.

2. The First Divinity Program

The new Professor was confronted with an apparently insoluble problem. The partner Churches to the Rhodes scheme wanted Rhodes to offer a three-year degree course for ministerial students. Permission to establish this degree course had to be obtained from the University of South Africa of which Rhodes was a constituent college; and this University recognized only a post-graduate divinity degree, based on a prior degree in Arts. The Arts degree required a three-year curriculum consisting of eleven courses. Professor Davies boldly determined to ask for the inclusion of six Divinity courses in the Arts degree. Supported by proposals of the Rhodes Senate, he had to plead his case at the annual meeting of the Senate of the University of South Africa meeting that year in Durban as guests of the University College of Natal. His route to the decisive Senate meeting was by way of the Board of Studies in Divinity to the Faculty of Arts. The first encounter was with the representatives of Potchefstroom University College. The anticipated difficulties confronting him there have been indicated above.

As an Appendix to this study a contemporary report describes Professor Davies' success in securing all that he had hoped to achieve. This was doubtless due in great part to the resolution and charm of his personality, and his conviction of the justice of the proposals he urged. Yet even this would not have availed without the co-operation of the Potchefstroom representatives. They responded to the appeal of this ardent young pioneer professor. They were convinced of his academic competence and Christian integrity. Forebodings that on grounds of principle and of prejudice the men of Potchefstroom would strangle the new-born English enterprise at birth were proved by the event to be nothing but nightmares. The theologians of Potchefstroom gave Dr. Davies the essential support that opened the door of a university education to ministerial students of the English-speaking churches.

The Rhodes University College Calendar of 1948 (p. 199) gives the first published official record of the infant Department, and of Professor Davies' success in bringing it into being.

DIVINITY

Professor Horton Davies

and Part-Time Lecturers

> Divinity courses may be taken for the B.A. degree, in combination with any other non-theological courses. Courses are also given in preparation for the post-graduate B.D. degree. There are two B.A. Divinity Majors: Biblical Studies (a course lasting three years) and Systematic Theology (a course lasting two years). In addition Ecclesiastical History may be taken as a minor course.

Rhodes University College, through its new Professor of Divinity had met the needs of the partner Churches in winning approval for an eleven-course Arts degree with six theological options. The standards of the parent University had been honored in providing a post-graduate B.D. degree for ministerial students qualified and permitted to complete a six-year scheme of theological training. Further, in order to meet the needs of non-matriculated students, a three-year Diploma in Divinity studies was soon to be introduced.

3. The First Divinity Prospectus [18]

This was a daring venture of faith for a department with the Divinity Professor as the solitary staff member. In 1948 he was granted a colleague, a senior lecturer in Biblical Studies. The prospectus of the Department showed both what he hoped to achieve and how he hoped to accomplish it.

The Staff of the Department

Head of the Department: The Rev. Horton Davies, M.A., B.D. (Edin.), D. Phil. (Oxon).
Professor of Divinity

Senior Lecturer in Biblical Studies: The Rev. William Cosser, M.A., B.D., (Glas.), B. Theol. (Strasbourg).

Part-time Lecturers:

The Rev. L. A. Hewson, B.A., (Wits.), M.A., (Cantab), Warden of the Divinity Hostel, R.U.C.

The Rev. J. MacDowall, M.A., (Glasgow), formerly Lecturer in Biology in the South African Native College, Fort Hare.

The Rev. C. R. Stephenson, M.A., (Cape Town and Cantab.), B.D. (Lond.).

The Rev. F. C. Synge, M.A. (Cantab.), Warden of St. Paul's (Church of the Province) Theological College, Grahamstown.

with the assistance of the Heads of the Departments of Classics, History and of Sociology, respectively, Professors K. D. White, B.A. (Liverpool), M.A. (Cantab.); M. Roberts, M.A., D. Phil. (Oxon.), and J. Irving, B.A., Hons. (Cantab.).

The Aims of the Department

The Chair of Divinity, as the nucleus of the new Department, was partially endowed in 1946 by the contribution of £10,500 from the Anglican, Congregational, Methodist, and Presbyterian Churches of South Africa, primarily to provide academic training for ordinands of those Churches. Training for the Christian Ministry is, therefore, its main, though not exclusive purpose. The

Department is ecumenical in origin and in purpose; its staff includes ministers of the contributing Churches, and its students belong to these four Communions; in addition it includes students of the Baptist and Disciples' Denominations. At the same time the Department of Divinity is prepared to give every possible co-operation in training candidates for the Ministry accredited by any Christian denomination.

The Department does not intend to limit its activities to giving theological training to candidates for the Christian Ministry, important as that primary responsibility is. It will welcome inquiries from teachers intending to specialize in Religious Instruction in Schools, and from intending Youth Leaders who will work for the Churches or allied Christian Youth organizations (such as the Y.M.C.A.) and Missionary candidates.

The Courses now offered are:

I. A B.A. Degree (with theological subjects included) of the University of South Africa.
II. The B.D. Degree of the University of South Africa.
III. An R.U.C. Diploma in Theology, (post-graduate and non-graduate).
IV. An R.U.C. Diploma in Social Studies with endorsement in Christian Youth Leadership or Missionary Leadership.
V. Religious Instruction (as a teaching skill).

In Conclusion, attention is drawn to the fact that Rhodes University College, with its inter-denominational Divinity Department, its residences accommodating nearly a thousand students, its proximity to the South African Native College at Fort Hare, and its Department of Bantu Studies, Professor Mrs. M. Wilson, M.A., Ph.D. (Cantab.) is admirably equipped for the training of missionaries. The Head of the Department will be pleased to advise missionary candidates from this country or overseas on suitable courses.

The Divinity Department regards its responsibilities as the provision of theological training for intending ministers and missionaries, Christian youth leaders and scripture specialists in schools. Its dominant emphasis is laid on the Lordship of Jesus Christ, and, therefore on the supreme relevance of the Christian Revelation to our contemporary situation, and on the need for devout and well-equipped Christian leaders in all spheres of life. It aspires to work ecumenically, in obedience to the Dominical intercession *ut omnes unum sint.*

After more than thirty years, reflection upon that prospectus shows two things that merit comment. The first is that Rhodes University College in 1947 through its first Professor of Divinity pioneered theological studies in English-medium universities in South Africa. Following approval by the University of South Africa of the Rhodes proposal to introduce divinity subjects into an Arts degree, Religious Studies are now recognized and provided in every South African university. The second is that that final paragraph formulating the aims of the Department still stands substantially the same through the administrations of the four Heads of Department and Deans of the Faculty of Divinity who have succeeded Dr. Davies at Rhodes. They still affirm, and aspire to practice the Lordship of Jesus Christ and the supreme relevance of the Christian Revelation to our contemporary situation; and they are still committed to work ecumenically, in obedience to the Dominical intercession, ut omnes unum sint.

4. Ecumenism in Action

"The great new fact of our era . . . " Those words were spoken in the dark depths of World War II by William Temple at his enthronement as Archbishop of Canterbury on St. George's Day, 1942. They describe "a Christian fellowship . . . the result of the great missionary movement of the last hundred and fifty years . . . extending into almost every nation . . . this world-wide Christian fellowship, this ecumenical movement . . . " [19] When those words were newly minted coinage, they came as an exciting challenge. The young Professor Davies conveyed that excitement and that challenge to his colleagues and his students. Events important to the Christian Church were taking place in South Africa, and in the wider world. Christian leaders were already preparing for the first meeting of the World Council of Churches in Amsterdam in 1948. In South Africa, in that same year, the Nationalist Government came to power with the policy of Apartheid which it has resolutely imposed upon the peoples of South Africa during forty years of rule. If the World Council of Churches had chosen to be, like the United Nations Organization, international instead of ecumenical, the architects of Apartheid might have found it more palatable. The distinction between these two terms is thus expressed by the early ecumenical leader, Dr. G. K. A. Bell, the Bishop of Chichester:

> The term international necessarily accepts the division of mankind into separate nations as a natural, if not a final, state of affairs. The term ecumenical refers to the expression within history of the given unity of the church. The one starts from the fact of divisions, and the other from the fact of unity in Christ. [20]

For the policy of Apartheid, divisions are the fundamental fact, and therefore must be made permanent. It was thus inevitable that Ecumenism in general, and the World Council of Churches in particular have been vigorously opposed by South African Government agencies. Attempts to get the South African members of the World Council of Churches to denounce that organization, and withdraw from it have been unsuccessful. One reason for this is undoubtedly the fact that during the last generation there have moved into leadership of the partner Churches in the Rhodes scheme men and women who were influenced during their ministerial training by Dr. Horton Davies himself, and by the Divinity Department and Faculty which he established.

On 9 June 1948, the first Professor of Divinity at Rhodes University College delivered his inaugural lecture, entitled Towards an Ecumenical Theology and a United Church. The opening paragraph is a fitting introduction to the lecture subject; but also to the pioneer venture in ecumenical theological training which he initiated in South Africa:

> The theme on which I have the honour to address you is controversial, but nevertheless appropriate. For in August of this year representatives of almost 150 different Communions of the Universal or Ecumenical Christian Church will be gathering from the ends of the earth to Amsterdam to inaugurate the World Council of Churches. This is thought by many to be the most significant development in ecclesiastical history since the days of the Reformation. It was, one may believe, a wave of the same ecumenical tide that reached the shores of South Africa, and established a Chair of Divinity here. This Chair was founded, in the main, by united representations and contributions of the Church of the Province, the Congregational Union, The Methodist Church and the Presbyterian Church of South Africa. Let it also be admitted openly that the present holder of it is an advocate of Ecumenism, who is not unduly perturbed by being termed an "Ecumaniac" since he believes that if "this is madness yet there is method in it", and remembers that the greatest of the Apostles was content to be thought a fool for Christ's sake.

In the course of his lecture the speaker dealt in turn with:

1. The Desirability of a Reunion of the Christian Churches.
2. The Potential Dangers of Ecumenism.
3. Designs for Unity.
4. Demonstrations of Unity.
5. Dedication to Ecumenism.

Much has been achieved by the Ecumenical Movement in the world beyond our borders; in South Africa, despite strong opposition, there has been steady advance towards a closer union of Christian churches. Yet "there remains much land to be possessed". For that reason, the words with which Dr. Horton Davies concluded his inaugural lecture are as timely to-day as they were when he uttered them in 1948:

> Re-union will come fully when the members of the severed branches of Christ's Church recognise that Ecumenism is not primarily a request for an intellectual or organisational reconstruction of the Church, basic as that is, but a sincere petition for the graces of the Holy Spirit. The aim of Ecumenism at its deepest level may be given in the words of the prayer:
>
> > May the Holy Spirit, the Spirit of forgiveness and love, so invade the Church that the broken mirror of Christendom will be renewed to reflect in full the glory of God in the face of Jesus Christ. **[21]**

APPENDIX

The Crucial Encounter

April 9, 1947 - Durban

The Senate of the University of South Africa met at Howard College, Durban. In the opening speeches of welcome, the Administrator of Natal approved the Matriculation standard of entrance for university courses, and ended by relating an anecdote told by General Smuts - banquet - London - Winston Churchill present - loud-voiced woman asked Gen. Smuts à propos of a statement made by Churchill quoted in press: "Is it true? Gen. Smuts replied: "Madam, what is truth? It is a gem very precious and rarely found; it is a thing so powerful as to be very perilous - too dangerous for careless use, and to be bandied about from lip to lip."

Ellis Brown, the Mayor of Durban, next read a halting speech of welcome; and in the course of it attacked the matriculation as a standard of entry, quoting the experience of business men with matriculants and non-matriculants, and quoted in his support Dr. Malberbe and his speech on intelligence tests.

Dr. Malherbe, called on next to speak as the Head of Natal University College, got out of the impasse by saying he would be greatly interested to hear a debate between the Administrator and the Mayor on the question of Matriculation.

During the lunch interval we met the Potchefstroom men and Horton had a long talk with du Toit. He is an old hand with eleven years experience, and put some searching questions, ending up with "What do you think of the Higher Criticism?" He said that in the absence of van Rooy, Jooste would take the chair of the Committee of Studies ("so that he can be free to fire all the shots if necessary" said Horton).

We met at the Parade Hotel, and Prof. Postma (the Principal) and Prof. Stoker (Philosophy) were added to the Committee of Studies. The introductions were very cordial. My little bit of Afrikaans, my South African birth and training, and strangely enough, the fact that I had once enquired of a Bloemfontein predikant about Kuyper's lectures on Calvinism all helped to prepare a congenial atmosphere for the discussion.

When our proposals came to be discussed, Horton gave a preliminary survey to show the background. It soon became clear that there was opposition to a plea for a B.A. in Theology. Prof. Postma quoted a discussion in the Senate this afternoon. The necessary basis for any professional degree must be a preliminary general degree. In effect this meant that while the Methodist Conference presses that the Matric. should not be the necessary preliminary standard for theol. training, the Senate was suggesting that B.A. should be.

Horton defended the Rhodes proposals splendidly. The course while primarily for ministers hoped to attract teachers and any Christian student concerned to know how to defend the Faith. There was an analogy in British Universities.

Slowly the tide began to turn. Biblical Studies won the approval of Prof. Postma. Then Ecclesiastical History as an alternative to History II was accepted. Then came the question of Theology. How could it be a major subject in an Arts degree? Would this not imply lowering the standard of Theology? Could it not be described by some other word? At this point we dispersed.

Outside, du Toit asked me if the Methodist Church would not agree to a lengthened period of training. I said that Confce had accepted three years; and that I had no authority at all to agree to an extended period. He appreciated that.

Then before we finally parted, Jooste said: "It's no use our standing apart, and pulling our hair out; we must help each other."

April 10

When we assembled for the Committee of Studies on Wednesday morning, du Toit and Jooste propounded a "new solution". Let the proposed course be called a Diploma in Theology. Horton rejected that inside half a minute. Then the old discussion was resumed again. How could Theology be a major subject in Arts?

After a while du Toit, Snyman and I went off to meet the Classics Board of Studies with a request about introducing a preliminary course in Greek, and its relation to Greek I, II and III. When we returned, Synge had appeared. We met him at the tea table, and he said: "I intend to be dumb." That was a shock and a disappointment.

After the Potch. members had made various other suggestions, du Toit returned from a meeting he had been addressing; and when actual courses wère outlined by Horton, the last vestiges of opposition finally disappeared. It was an unexpected triumph; for at two stages last night and today it had seemed that we had no hope.

April 11 - Meeting of the Faculty of Arts

Coming on early, our report was presented by Jooste, who left Horton to speak to the Rhodes proposals. The Chairman halted him on a question of procedure. Had there been adequate notice of motion? Horton had the answer to that. Then we waited for the reaction of the Faculty. First Finlay (Philosophy) then Hartmann (Music) and then Durrant (English) spoke warmly in favour of the new proposals, and the matter went through. Prof. Snyman of Potch. was seated beside me. He slumped down in his seat and whispered: "Ek is verbaasd." (I am amazed).

L.A.H.

NOTES

1. Leonard Thompson, The Difaqane and its aftermath 1822-36, being Chapter IX of **The Oxford History of South Africa**, Vol. I, (Oxford, 1969), 391-404.

2. C. T. Loram, **The Education of the South African Native** (London, 1917), 46.

3. **Standard Encyclopaedia of Southern Africa** (Cape Town: Nasua Ltd., 1974), Vol. 8. 132-156.

4. Ibid., 125-130.

5. Ibid., Vol. 5, 171-175.

6. Ibid., Vol. 8, 132.

7. J. A. Chalmers, **Tiyo Soga: A Page of South African Mission Work** (Edinburgh, 1977), passim.

8. D. Roy Briggs & Joseph Wing, **The Harvest and the Hope,** United Congregational Church of Southern Africa (Johannesburg, 1970), 9, 138ff, 298ff.

9. J. Whiteside, **History of the Wesleyan Methodist Church of South Africa** (London: Elliot Stock, 1906), 278, 285.

10. T. Simon N. Gqubule, An Examination of the Theological Education of Africans in the Presbyterian, Methodist, Congregational and Anglican Churches in South Africa, 1860-1960 (Unpublished thesis of Rhodes University, Grahamstown, 1978-), 73, 79.

11. C. E. G. Goodhall, The Church and the Ministry, quoted in Gqubule, op.cit., 175 as from Gray Centenary Pamphlets, first series, No. 2.

12. Gqubule, **op. cit.**, 173.

13. Idem., 188.

14. Idem., 119.

15. Idem., 121.

16. **Standard Encyclopaedia of Southern Africa,** (Cape Town: Nasua Ltd., 1974), Vol. 8, 140.

17. Rhodes University File 679/1 Divinity Department.

18. Idem.

19. William Temple, **The Church Looks Forward** (London: Macmillan, 1944), 2-3.

20. G. K. A. Bell, **Christianity and World Order** 118.

21. Prayer by Prof. L. Levonian in The International Review of Missions, Vol. XXXVI, No. 144, p. 558; issue of October 1947.

A CHRONOLOGY OF HORTON DAVIES

Born March 10, 1916, elder son of the Rev. D. D. Marlais Davies, Congregational minister, and Mrs. Martha Reid Davies (nee Davies) at Cwmavon, near Port Talbot, Glamorganshire, Wales.

Schooling: North Manchester Grammar School; Queen Elizabeth's Grammar School, Middleton, Manchester; and Silcoates School, Wakefield, Yorkshire.

University Education: Edinburgh University: M.A. *magna cum laude* in English, 1937; B.D. *summa cum laude* in Systematic Theology, 1940; Oxford University: D. Phil. 1943; dissertation "The Worship of the English Puritans," scholar of Mansfield College, Oxford.

Ministry: in the Congregational Union of England and Wales (now in the United Church of Christ, U.S.A.) served as Minister of the Congregational Church of Wallington and Carshalton, outer London suburb, from 1942-1946; with a year's leave of absence to serve as Director of Education of the 55 centers of the Y.M.C.A. with the British Army on the Rhine, 1945-1946.

Personal: Married, in 1942, to Brenda Mary (nee Deakin), divorced 1973; Children, Christine, Hugh and Philip; married, 1973, to Marie-Hélène (nee Baudy).

Theological Teaching: Founding Professor of Divinity at Rhodes University College (now University), Grahamstown, Cape Province, South Africa 1946-1953; Dean of the faculty of Divinity 1951-1953. Head of the joint Department of Church History at Mansfield and Regent's Park Colleges, Oxford University, 1953-1955. Professor of Religion in Princeton University, 1956-1984; Emeritus 1984.

Honors: 1934, English medallist, University of Edinburgh; 1940, Gunning Divinity Prizeman, University of Edinburgh; 1951, earned D.D. of the University of South Africa for dissertation "The English Free Churches"; 1952, Carnegie Travelling Fellowship to study American Theological Education; 1953, Coronation medal of Queen Elizabeth II for services to British Commonwealth education; 1959 and 1964, Guggenheim Fellowships; 1966, Honorary D. Litt. from LaSalle College, Philadelphia; 1970, earned D.

Litt. from Oxford University for volumes III, IV, and V of **Worship and Theology in England** (final volume appeared in 1975); 1979, given the Berakah Award by the North American Academy of Liturgy, with the inscription: "As historian of worship and theology in England, he has written a chronicle unequalled in scope and insight of the liturgical life and thought of a whole people over the course of five hundred years."

Ecumenical Pursuits: presently a member of the editorial board of the ecumenical and international quarterly, Studia Liturgica, published in Rotterdam, Holland; formerly associate editor of the American Benedictine journal, Worship; one of seven faculty members from New Jersey colleges and universities who teach in a cooperative ecumenical graduate program in liturgical studies inaugurated in 1978 which is administered at the campus of Drew University; May 1966, received an honorary degree of Doctor of Letters from LaSalle College, Philadelphia, a Catholic institution, for the ecumenical spirit displayed in his writings as a Protestant church historian.

Special Interest: study of the impact of Christianity on culture, especially in the areas of literature, the visual arts and music, as seen in his current research on over forty preachers to be called "The Witty Preachers: The English Metaphysical Pulpit, 1588-1645."

Major Works: **Worship and Theology in England** (five-volume series), **Worship of the English Puritans** (1948), **The English Free Churches** (1952), **Great South African Christians** (1951), **Christian Deviations** (1954), **Christian Worship, Its History and Meaning** (1958), and **Varieties of English Preaching, 1900-1960.**

More recent works: **Sacred Art in a Secular Century** (1978), written collaboratively with his son, Hugh Davies; **Holy Days and Holidays: the Medieval Pilgrimage to Compostela** (1982), co-authored by Marie-Hélène Davies, his second wife; **Studies of the Church in History** (1983), essays honoring a fellow church historian and friend Dr. Robert S. Paul on the occasion of his 65th birthday celebration was edited by Horton Davies. This last work (**Studies of the Church in History**) fittingly encapsulates his life's interest as a historian of Christianity.

Christine D. Wade

SELECTED BIBLIOGRAPHY

I. BOOKS

Christian Worship; its making and meaning. Wallington, England; Religious Education Press, 1946, 107.

The Worship of the English Puritans. Westminster, London: Dacre Press, 1948. 304.

Great South African Christians. (A republication of articles from The Outspan, Bloemfontein, South Africa.) Cape Town, London, New York: Oxford University Press, 1951. 190.

The English Free Churches. London and New York: Oxford University Press, 1952. 208.

Christian Deviations; essays in defence of the Christian Faith. London: SCM Press, 1954 (twice), rep. 1955, 1956, 1957. New York: The Philosophical Library, 1954. 126.

South African Missions, 1800–1950, an anthology. Compiled by Horton Davies and R. H. W. Shepherd. London and New York: Nelson, 1954. 232.

Christian Worship; its history and meaning. Revised edition. New York: Abingdon Press, 1957. 128. incl. bibliography. Wallington, England: Religious Education Press, 1957. 122.

A mirror of the ministry in modern novels. New York: Oxford University Press, 1959. 211. incl. bibliography and index.

Worship and Theology in England. Vol. 3. **From Watts and Wesley to Maurice, 1690–1850.** Princeton University Press and London: Oxford University Press, 1961. Xiv, 355. 8 plates, 19 illust., incl. bibliography and index.

Christian Deviations; the challenge of the sects. (rev. and enl.) London: SCM Press, 1961 (also trans. into Chinese, French and Spanish). 176.

The challenge of the Sects. Philadelphia: Westminster Press, 1962. 176.

Worship and Theology in England. Vol. 4. **From Newman to Martineau, 1850–1900.** Princeton University Press and London: Oxford University Press, 1962. Xiv, 390, 8 plates, 16 illustr., incl. bibliography and index.

The English Free Churches. 2nd edition. London and New York: Oxford University Press, 1963. Viii, 208. Bibliography, 201-204.

Varieties of English Preaching, 1900-1960. London: SCM Press and Englewood Cliffs, N.J.: Prentice Hall, 1963. Viii, 208, illustr.

Christian Deviations; the challenge of the new spiritual movements. 2nd revised edition. London: SCM Press, 1965, 1967. Philadelphia: Westminster Press, 1965. 144.

Worship and Theology in England. Vol. 5. **The ecumenical century, 1900-1965.** Princeton University Press and London: Oxford University Press, 1965. Xix, 496, 16 plates, 32 illust., incl. bibliography and index.

Great South African Christians. Reprint. Westport, Conn.: Greenwood Press, 1970. Vii, 190.

A mirror of the ministry in modern novels. Reprint. Freeport, New York: Books for Libraries Press, 1970. Xi, 221.

Worship and Theology in England. Vol. 1. **From Cranmer to Hooker, 1534-1603.** Princeton University Press and London: Oxford University Press, 1970. Xii, 482, 11 plates, 11 illustr., incl. bibliography and index.

Christian Deviations; the challenge of the new spiritual movements. Third revised edition. London: SCM Press, 1972 and Philadelphia: Westminster Press, 1973. Viii, 133.

Worship and Theology in England. Vol. 2. **From Andrewes to Baxter and Fox, 1603-1690.** Princeton University Press, 1975. Xiii, 592, 16 plates, 16 illustr., incl. bibliography and index.

Prayers and other resources for public worship, compiled by Horton Davies and Morris Slifer. Nashville: Abingdon Press, 1976. 96.

Sacred Art in a secular century, by Horton and Hugh Davies. Collegeville, Minn.: The Liturgical Press, 1978. Vii. 106, 74 plates, incl. bibliography.

Holy Days and holidays. The medieval pilgrimage to Compostela, by Horton and Marie-Hélène Davies. Lewisburg: Bucknell University Press, London and Toronto: Associated University Presses, 1982. 255, bibliography, 229-243.

Studies of the Church in History, Essays honoring Robert S. Paul on his 65th birthday, edited by Horton Davies. Allison Park, Penn.: Pickwick Publications, 1983. X, 276, with illustr. and bibliography.

Awaiting publication:

'Catching the conscience': Essays correlating modern fiction with the Christian faith.

The witty preachers: The English metaphysical pulpit, 1588-1645.

II. SHORTER WRITINGS AND CONTRIBUTIONS

"Church History in the service of the ministry." in **The Congregational ministry in the modern world,** ed. by H. Cunliffe-Jones, London: Independent Press Ltd., 1955. 65-97.

"The Puritan-Pietist tradition in spirituality." in **Protestants and Catholics on the spiritual life.** Edited by Michael Marx, O.S.B., Collegeville, Minn.: The Liturgical Press, 1965. 34-41.

Biographical contributións to **The Encyclopedia Americana.** Danbury, Conn.: Americana Corporation.

Introduction to **The Lord's Day Service,** produced by the United Church of Christ Commission on Worship, 196.

"Free Churches." in **The New Encyclopedia Britannica.** 15th edition. Chicago, c. 1977. **Macropaedia,** vol. 7, 710-712.

"Ten characteristics of English metaphysical preaching." in **Studies of the Church in History. Essays honoring Robert S. Paul on his 65th birthday.** Allison Park, Penn.: Pickwick Publications, 1983. 103-148.

III. ARTICLES (excluding a series on living Christian leaders in South Africa, published in The Outspan Bloemfontein, South Africa)

"The God of Nature and the God of Grace." (A Harvest Festival sermon) The Christian World Pulpit, London, 751, No. 3: 101-102, Sept. 23, 1943.

"The Great Assize." (A sermon). The Christian World Pulpit, 759, No. 3: 161-162, Nov. 18, 1943.

"April in Berlin." The Christian World, London, May 1946.

"Towards an ecumenical theology and a united church." (inaugural lecture delivered at Rhodes University) Rhodes University College, Grahamstown, South Africa, 3-16, 1948.

"Ministers of tomorrow, their duties and training." Hibbert Journal London, 48: 226-230, April 1950.

"How far is South Africa a Christian democracy?" The South African Weekly, Johannesburg, 1-8, November 17, 1950.

"Race-tensions in South Africa: formative factors and suggested solutions." Hibbert Journal, 49: 118-127, January 1951.

"The University and the Church." The South African Weekly, Johannesburg, 1-8, March 30, 1951.

"Doctors, artists and missions." The Christian Recorder, Standerton, Transvaal, July 20, 1951.

"Peace on earth to men of goodwill." The Christian Recorder, 2-3, December 21, 1951.

"Salute to the memory of Dr. John Philip, 1775-1851." The Congregational Quarterly, London, 30: 57-64, January 1952.

"Fear and faith in South Africa." Christianity and Crisis, New York, 12, No. 2: 10-13, February 18, 1952.

"Alan Paton: literary artist and Anglican." Hibbert Journal, 50: 262-268, April 1952.

"Religion in America to-day." The Christian World, London, August and September 1952.

"Four men in a boat." The Christian Recorder, October 23, 1953.

" 'The Pope's men' under fire." The Christian Recorder, November 13, 1953.

"Oxford and Cambridge Universities versus the rest." The Christian Recorder, November 27, 1953.

"A post mortem on the Mau Mau." The Christian Recorder, December 25, 1953.

"Schweitzer, Africa's G.O.C.M." The Christian Recorder, January 8, 1954.

"Controversial bishop had advanced views." The Christian Recorder, January 22, 1954.

"Coventry Cathedral. A twentieth-century shrine to the glory of God." The Christian Recorder, February 5, 1954.

"The disappearing clergy." The Christian Recorder, February 19, 1954.

"Novels as mirrors of the ministry." The British Weekly, London, February or March 1954.

"The Church and the working classes." <u>The Christian Century</u>, Chicago, March 5, 1954.

"Appealing to the workman." <u>The Christian Recorder</u>, March 19, 1954.

"Reaching the working classes." <u>The Christian Recorder</u>, April 2, 1954.

"Why are you a Christian?" <u>The Christian Recorder</u>, April 16, 1954.

"A Free Church cathedral in London." <u>The Christian Recorder</u>, April 30, 1954.

"Dr. Billy Graham, Streamlined evangelist." <u>The Christian Recorder</u>, May 14, 1954.

"On taking comic strips seriously." <u>The Christian Recorder</u>, May 28, 1954.

"London's new ecclesiastical look." <u>The Christian Recorder</u>. June 11, 1954.

"Horton Davies replies." <u>The Christian Recorder</u>, June 18, 1954.

"The gift of humour." <u>The Christian Recorder</u>, June 25, 1954.

"South Africa and ourselves." <u>The Congregational Quarterly</u>, London, 32: 241-246, July 1954.

"Humanity and the hydrogen-bomb." <u>The Christian Recorder</u>, July 23, 1954.

"The Netherlands revisited." <u>The British Weekly</u>, 2f., August 5, 1954.

"The Netherlands revisited." <u>The Christian Recorder</u>, August 6 & 20, September 3, 10 & 17, 1954.

"Liturgical reform in nineteenth century congregationalism." <u>Congregational Historical Society. Transactions</u>, London, 17: 73-82, August 1954.

"That they may all be one." <u>The Christian Recorder</u>, October 1, 1954.

"A Black man's burden." <u>The Christian Recorder</u>, October 15, 1954.

"Gap in the Iron Curtain." <u>The Christian Recorder</u>, October 29, 1954.

"Holidays and holy days." <u>The Christian Recorder</u>, November 12, 1954.

"The future of religious journalism in South Africa." <u>The Christian Recorder</u>, November 26, 1954.

"Revolutionary clergyman." <u>The Christian Recorder</u>, December 10, 1954.

"Specialized ministerial workers aid clergy." <u>The Christian Recorder</u>, December 11, 1954.

"Christmas in three countries." The Christian Recorder, December 24, 1954.

"Dead Stones or living people?" The Christian Recorder, January 7, 1955.

"The first Christian artists." The Christian Recorder, January 21, 1955.

"Going somewhere with their eyes open." The British Weekly, London, January 27, 1955.

"Weather prayers." The Christian Recorder, February 4, 1955.

"To Bethlehem via Moscow." The British Weekly, February 17, 1955.

"The ordeal of a chaplain." The Christian Recorder, February 18, 1955.

"Back to the soil and the soul." The Christian Recorder, March 4, 1955.

"Saints out of slime." The British Weekly, March 10, 1955.

"The needs of elderly people." The Christian Recorder, March 18, 1955.

"Harringay retrospect." The Christian Recorder, April 1, 1955.

"Saint and civil servant." The British Weekly, April 7, 1955.

"Saints from slime. John Wesley's preaching." The Christian Recorder, April 15, 1955.

"Lost horizon." The Christian Recorder, April 29, 1955.

"Seeing God at second-hand." The British Weekly, May 12, 1955.

"The Kirk and the Kremlin." The Christian Recorder, May 13, 1955.

"Dissent as the mid-wife of modern education." The British Weekly, May 19, 1955.

"Politics and religion." The Christian Recorder, June 10, 1955.

"The new Nigeria." The Christian Recorder, June 24, 1955.

"Revaluations." The British Weekly, July 7, 1955.

"Three martyrs of the Reformed faith." The Christian Recorder, July 8, 1955.

"The African Augustine." The British Weekly, July 14, 1955.

"Religious migrations." The Christian Recorder, July 22, 1955.

"Undergraduate Christianity." The Christian Recorder, August 5, 1955.

"Clerical Collars for all or none." The Christian Recorder, August 19, 1955.

"For the love of God." The Christian Recorder, September 2, 1955.

"The Master and money." The Christian Recorder, September 16, 1955.

"Alpine view." The Christian Recorder, September 30, 1955.

"Thermonuclear." The British Weekly, October 6, 1955.

"Missionary minds." The Christian Recorder, October 14 & 28, 1955.

"Protestantism still protesting." The British Weekly, December 8, 1955.

"If Christmas hadn't happened." The Christian Recorder, December 16, 1955.

"An impatient man takes the risk of offence." The British Weekly, January 5, 1956.

"The drift from the ministry." The Christian Recorder, January 20, 1956.

"Latimer--the laughing preacher." The Christian Recorder, February 3,1956.

"A-huh?" The British Weekly, February 16, 1956.

"American peek, squint or glimpse?" The British Weekly, February 23, 1956.

"New Harvest Festivals for old." The Christian Recorder, February 24, 1956.

"My cousin the Coelacanth." The British Weekly, March 16, 1956.

"Wistful anxieties of would-be Christians." The British Weekly, March 23, 1956.

"A Christian or a commerical calendar." The British Weekly, April 19, 1956.

"A philosophy in a sentence." The British Weekly, June 7, 1956.

"Theological Fisticuffs." The British Weekly, June 14, 1956.

"Centrifugal Christian sects." Religion in Life, Nashville, Tenn. 25: 323-335, Summer 1956.

"Steel and the spirit." The British Weekly, July 5, 1956.

"The parish church." The British Weekly, August 2, 1956.

"Africa's place in the Gospel." The Christian Recorder, September 7, 1956.

"A cautionary story." The British Weekly, September 20, 1956.

"American behaviour." The British Weekly, October 18, 1956.

"Heartbreak House." The British Weekly, November 29, 1956.

"Dissent and the origins of liberalism." The British Weekly, October 11, 1956.

"Going to school in America." The British Weekly, January 24, 1957.

"Emmigrants. Textbook for the use of." The British Weekly, March 28, 1957.

"The worship of the first American Congregationalists." Bulletin of the Congregational Library, Boston, Mass., 9: 5-14, January 1958.

"A new kind of ministry?" The British Weekly, 1-6, July 18, 1958.

"God made the country." The British Weekly, 1-4, September 19, 1958.

"The Christian use of the novel." The British Weekly, February 6, 1959.

"Christianity and the colour-crisis: the urgency of the problem." The Christian Recorder, 1-4, March 27, 1959.

"The contemporary liturgical movement; non-Episcopal Protestantism in England." Encounter, Indianapolis, 20: 257-268, Spring 1959.

"The South African situation: room for improvement." The Christian Recorder, 1-5, May 15, 1959.

"Protestantism reconsidered." The Christian Recorder, 1-4, August 28, 1959.

"The Gospel and the visual arts." The Christian Recorder, February 12, 1960.

"Dean Inge: the outspoken oracle." Religion in Life, 31, No. 2: 244-253 Spring 1962.

"C. S. Lewis and B. L. Manning: lay champions of Christianity." Religion in Life, 31: 598-609, Autumn 1962.

"Expository Preaching: Charles Haddon Spurgeon." Foundations, American Baptist Historical Society, Rochester, N.Y., 6:14-25, January 1963.

"The expression of the social Gospel in worship." Studia Liturgica, Amsterdam, 2: 174-192, September 1963.

"Art of adoration: the modern liturgical movement in Europe." Moravian Theological Seminary Bulletin, Bethlehem, Penn., 1-13, 1963.

"Implications of the European liturgical movement for the U.S.A." Moravian Theological Seminary Bulletin, Bethlehem, Penn., 14-24, 1963.

"Rediscovering the art of corporate Christian worship." The Christian Recorder, 1-4, February 28, 1964.

"Breaking down the walls in worship." United Church Herald, New York., 7-9, June 1, 1964.

"The continental liturgical movement in the Roman Catholic Church." Canadian Journal of Theology, 10: 148-165, July 1964.

"The integrity of worship: the marriage of word and sacrament, worship and service." Theology in Life, New Brighton, Minn., 7: 219-229, Autumn 1964.

"Orthodox, Anglican and Free Church contributions to the liturgical movement." Canadian Journal of Theology, 10: 223-236, October 1964.

"Pentacostalism: threat or promise?" Expository Times, Aberdeen, Scotland, 76: 197-199, March 1965.

"Thinking and acting towards unity." Theology Today, Princeton, N.J., 22: 12-15, April 1965.

"Reshaping the worship of the United Church of Christ." Worship, Collegeville, Minn., 41: 542-551, November 1967.

"Catching the conscience: Graham Greene's Plays." Religion in Life, 36: 605-614, Winter 1967.

"Ecumenism: a Protestant view." La Salle, Philadelphia, Penn., 2-4, Winter 1967.

"The God of Light and the dark deities: a revaluation of D. H. Lawrence." Religion in Life, 38: 229-241, Summer 1969.

"Elizabethan Puritan preaching." Worship, 44: 93-108 and 154-170, February-March 1970.

"Gerald Manley Hopkins: the self-caged skylark." Religion in Life, 39: 446-456, Autumn 1970.

"Prière liturgique et prière spontanée dans le débat entre anglicans et puritains." Maison-Dieu, Paris, France, 111: 31-42, 1972.

"Jesus Christ in history and legend." The Illustrated Weekly of India, Bombay, 6-11, December 22, 1974.

"Worship at Taize: a Protestant monastic community." Worship 49: 23-35, January 1975.

"On this (Plymouth) rock . . . " Reform, London, 8-10, July 1976.

"The draft proposed Book of Common Prayer: a Free churchman's evaluation." Anglican Theological Review, Evanston, Illinois, 58: 369-376, July 1976.

"Jacob's Ladder: a study of experiment and tradition in modern Christian worship." Encounter, Indianapolis, 39: 367-383, Autumn 1978.

"The God of storm and stillness: the fiction of Flannery O'Connor and Frederick Buechner." (with Marie-Hélène Davies) Religion in Life, 188-196, Summer 1979.

"Frederick Buechner and the strange work of grace." Theology Today, 36: 186-194, July 1979.

"The Berakah award and response: A Protestant vindication of Liturgies." Worship, 53: 371-378, July 1979.

"Reflections on teaching Liturgics in the United States: resources and problems." Liturgical Review, Edinburgh, 2-14, May 1980.

"Anagogical signals in Flannery O'Connor's fiction." Thought, New York, 55: 428-438, December 1980.

"Hoping against hope." (A sermon) The Princeton Seminary Bulletin, Princeton, N.J., 3, No. 2: 182-185, 1981.

"Christianity in the United States and the United Kingdom: a Protestant ecumenist's comparison." The American Benedictine Review, 48-61, March 1983.

"The value of modern fiction for preachers." Journal for preachers, Decatur, GA., 7, No. 2, Lent 1984.

IV. REVIEWS: Reviews have been contributed to the following journals in alphabetical order:

The British Weekly (London)

The Christian Recorder (Standerton, South Africa)

Church History (Chicago, Illinois)

The Congregational Quarterly (London)

The New York Times Sunday Book Review (New York)

The Princeton Theological Bulletin (Princeton, New Jersey)

Religion in Life (Nashville, Tennessee)

The South African Weekly (Johannesburg, South Africa)

Theology Today (Princeton, New Jersey)

The Union Seminary Quarterly (New York)

Worship (Collegeville, Minnesota)

V. STUDIES ON HORTON DAVIES

Massey H. Shepherd, Jr., "Horton Davies's **Worship and Theology in England.**" _The Journal of Religion_, 58, No. 2: 182-193, April 1978.

James F. White, "Writing the History of English Worship. The achievement of Horton Davies." _Church History_, 47, 434-440, December 1978.

Rupert J. Ray: An analysis of the versions of **Christian Deviations** (Still untitled) M.A. Thesis, department of Religious Studies, Indiana University, Bloomington, Indiana. In preparation.

Marie-Hélène Davies

CONGRATULATORY LIST

Diogenes Allen, Princeton, New Jersey

Randall H. Balmer, Princeton, New Jersey
Frederick H. Borsch, Princeton, New Jersey
Lawrence Bothwell, Maine, New York
V. J. Bredenkamp, Pietermaritzburg, South Africa
Robert H. Bullock, Jr., Allen, Texas

George Cleaves, Ealing, London, United Kingdom
Joe Coalter, Denver, Colorado
John Crocker, Jr., Princeton, New Jersey

Dorian Davies, Woking, Surrey, England
Marie-Hélène Davies, Princeton, New Jersey
Marlais Davies, Southampton, Hants, England
Philip Davies, Roxbury, Massachusetts
G. Scott Davis, New York, New York
John W. De Gruchy, Rondebosch, South Africa
Malcolm L. Diamond, Princeton, New Jersey

Gerard Farrell, Princeton, New Jersey

John G. Gager, Princeton, New Jersey
Jack H. Goodwin, Alexandria, Virginia
R. C. Gordon-McCutchan, Santa Barbara, California

Jean W. Hadidian, Allison Park, Pennsylvania
Leon Hammond/Ms. Ellen Brady, Summit, New Jersey
Howard J. Happ, Reseda, California
Helen Hardacre, Princeton, New Jersey
Martha Himmelfarb, Princeton, New Jersey
David L. Holmes, Williamsburg, Virginia

Charles H. Lippy, Clemson, South Carolina
Mason I. Lowance, Amherst, Massachusetts
Eugene Y. Lowe, Jr., Princeton, New Jersey

David B. McIlhiney, Exeter, New Hampshire
Lawrence McIntosh, Parkville, Australia
John Merrill, Princeton, New Jersey
Daniel L. Migliore, Princeton, New Jersey
Roger B. Miles, Washington, D.C.
David P. Moessner, New Haven, Connecticut

Elaine Pagels, Princeton, New Jersey
James M. Phillips, Ventnor, New Jersey
Speer Library, Princeton Theological Seminary, Princeton, New Jersey

Albert J. Raboteau, Princeton, New Jersey
Paul Ramsey, Princeton, New Jersey
Thomas P. Roche, Jr., Princeton, New Jersey
Margaret Routley, Skillman, New Jersey

Rodney J. Sawatsky, Waterloo, Ontario, Canada
Leigh E. Schmidt and Linda Tyler-Schmidt, Princeton, New Jersey
Stephen Schulhofer and Laurie Wohl, Haverford, Pennsylvania
David H. Smith, Bloomington, Indiana
Alan Sponberg, Princeton, New Jersey
A. Orley Swartzentruber, Princeton, New Jersey

Mrs. George F. Thomas, Princeton, New Jersey
Mr. & Mrs. Basil Turton, Whitney, Oxon, England

Mark Valeri, Princeton, New Jersey

Christine Wade, Irvington, New York
David A. Weir, Princeton, New Jersey
Chava Weissler, Princeton, New Jersey
B. R. White, Oxford, England
Douglas and Linn Wood, Princeton, New Jersey

www.ingramcontent.com/pod-product-compliance
Lightning Source LLC
Chambersburg PA
CBHW060332100426
42812CB00003B/960

* 9 7 8 1 4 9 8 2 2 8 1 6 9 *